America's Girl

Tim Dahlberg

with Mary Ederle Ward and

Brenda Greene

America's Girl

The Incredible Story of
How Swimmer Gertrude Ederle
Changed the Nation

St. Martin's Press New York

Title-page photograph: Gertrude Ederle basks in the adulation of some
of the 2 million people who welcomed her home with the biggest
ticker-tape parade given an athlete in New York City.
(*Gertrude Ederle personal collection*)

AMERICA'S GIRL. Copyright © 2009 by Tim Dahlberg with Mary Ederle Ward and Brenda
Greene. All rights reserved. Printed in the United States of America. For information,
address St. Martin's Press, 175 Fifth Avenue, New York, N.Y. 10010.

www.stmartins.com

Book design by Kathryn Parise

LIBRARY OF CONGRESS CATALOGING-IN-PUBLICATION DATA

Dahlberg, Tim.
    America's girl : the incredible story of how swimmer Gertrude Ederle changed
the nation / Tim Dahlberg with Mary Ederle Ward and Brenda Greene. — 1st ed.
        p. cm.
    ISBN-13: 978-0-312-38265-0
    ISBN-10: 0-312-38265-0
    1. Ederle, Gertrude, 1906–2003.   2. Swimmers—United States—Biography.
3. Women swimmers—United States—Biography.   I. Ward, Mary Ederle.
II. Greene, Brenda M., 1950–   III. Title.
    GV838.E34D34 2009
    797.2'1092—dc22
    [B]

                                                              2008046034

First Edition: August 2009

10   9   8   7   6   5   4   3   2   1

In memory of my aunts Helen, Margaret, Trudy,
and my father, Henry, with love and gratitude

—Mary Ederle Ward

Contents

Acknowledgments

The authors would like to acknowledge the following for their contributions to the book:

Robert Ederle, who supplied Gertrude Ederle's diary, personal memoir, and many of the pictures used in the book, and who gave constant support and encouragement for it.

Bob Duenkel, executive director and curator of the International Swimming Hall of Fame in Fort Lauderdale, Florida, for the tape recording of his conversation with Gertrude Ederle and his continued support of the book project.

George Schneider, who gave invaluable knowledge of the Ederle family history.

Richard and Stephen Ederle for their continued encouragement, and Mary Ederle Ward's husband, Martin, and children, Eileen, Brendan, and Erin, for helping take care of Aunt Trudy in her later years and sharing the excitement over a book about her life.

Leroy Sweeney of Ace Reprographics in Paterson, New Jersey, for his copying of Gertrude Ederle's archives.

The Hawthorne, New Jersey, library staff for locating out-of-print books and assisting in research.

I

"Bring on Your Old Channel"

August 1925, Cape Gris-Nez, France

The grease was the worst. Inside the engine room of the tug *La Morinie* bobbing up and down just off the coast of France, Gertrude Ederle was having it slathered on anyway, one layer at a time. She would need all the protection she could get, even though it was mid-August and the always-chilly English Channel was as warm as it had been in two years.

The sharks were another thing. There wasn't much protection against them, just the hope that the commotion of a tug carrying an odd assortment of journalists, musicians, trainers, friends, and the simply curious would keep them at bay as Ederle swam alongside. Two nights earlier, fishermen had caught two six-footers seven miles off the French coast, giving the young swimmer one more thing to worry about as she excitedly got ready for the adventure of her life. Ederle's camp tried to keep the news about the sharks from her, but it was hard to keep a secret when the offending sharks were hung up in front of the central post office in the nearby town of Boulogne.

Trying to swim the Channel was difficult enough without troubling thoughts to weigh on a young girl's mind. It was only twenty-one miles from the rocky outcropping of Cape Gris-Nez to the English shore, but veterans knew the swim was at least half again that because of the tide from the Atlantic Ocean, which continually moved in and back out.

From the French side, the white cliffs of Dover looked tantalizingly close on a clear day, but the punishing waves, tricky currents, frigid waters, and assorted marine life combined to beat back almost everyone who dared challenge this stretch of water. Scores had tried over the years, but only a handful had succeeded, and all had been men.

The Channel was an uneasy beast to master. If the cold wasn't enough, the waves, which seemed to rise from nowhere, could stop any would-be conqueror. Every day it was a battle zone of sorts, with the North Sea forcing itself through the Strait of Dover into the narrow opening, only to be pushed back by currents from the Atlantic. Add to that the biting jellyfish, Portuguese men-of-war, sunken ships, and even the occasional shark waiting in the water, none of them particularly happy about sharing their environment with a foreigner, and the swim was treacherous indeed.

The body of water had stretched the imagination of those who had stood on its shores for centuries. Julius Caesar had prepared his long-beaked ships to cross it half a century before the beginning of the Christian era, and William the Conqueror had tried it with a great fleet of flat-bottomed boats eleven centuries later. Napoléon had eyed it longingly, certain that it held the key to his domination of Europe, and assembled a fleet of specially prepared ships at Boulogne for an invasion that never occurred.

"Let me be master of the Channel for six hours and we are masters of the world," Napoléon said to his staff as they contemplated their great army encamped on the heights above town. Napoléon wouldn't succeed, and a group of desperate British airmen more than a century later made sure Adolf Hitler wouldn't, either. The great Channel refused to be taken easily by anyone, whether in great ships or in a simple swimsuit. The thought of a woman doing it seemed preposterous to many, especially when it came to a teenager who couldn't understand the difficulties she would face.

Ederle, a sturdy New Yorker with a pocketful of Olympic medals and a shy but endearing smile, wasn't the first of the fairer sex to try the Channel. There had been several attempts, and as the summer of 1925 wore on, Argentina's Lillian Harrison was there to try for a fourth time. France's Jeanne Sion would also make an attempt, as would London typist Mercedes Gleitze.

None had Ederle's pedigree. And none had her grit.

"I'm not sure I'll make it, but I'll try my best," Ederle said before getting on the Cunard liner *Berengaria* and crossing the Atlantic. "If I don't make it the first time, I may try again."

Oddsmakers thought little about the chances of this daughter of German immigrants, a girl who had learned to swim while tied to a rope in the river off the family summer home in New Jersey. Lloyd's of London opened betting at 20–1 against her reaching land in England, though a rush of money wired from the United States brought that down to 7–1 by the time she entered the water.

The bookies knew what they were doing. Though a few men had managed to make it across, there were a dozen who had failed for every one who had succeeded. Even when the the swimmers were slathered in grease to ward off the cold, the swim was such a marathon that the elements usually won. If they didn't, the masses of jellyfish picked off the rest with bites that were both painful and poisonous.

The summer of 1925 was a big one on the Channel. England was at peace and rebuilding from the Great War, the Roaring Twenties were adding to a new prosperity in the United States, and swimmers were arriving from around the world to test the most dangerous—and famous—swim of the times. Adding to the intrigue was a curious phenomenon that had developed over the previous few years, as brash women made their way to France to try and strike a blow for their gender and show everyone that the weaker sex wasn't so weak after all.

If any woman had a chance, it was the nineteen-year-old with a shy yet engaging smile and broad shoulders whom everyone called Trudy.

She was a swimming wunderkind, this daughter of a portly German butcher and his equally stout wife, who had emigrated to the United States years earlier. Trudy spent her summers at the beach, loved to swim in the ocean, and had been smashing world records since the age of fifteen.

America was captivated by this tomboy, who had muscles but professed her love for housework and family. Newspapers followed her every move as she set records at one meet, only to break them at the next. Trudy wasn't only good; she was good copy. Modest and unassuming, she was the antithesis to the flappers of the day, a clean-living young woman whose smiling face became a fixture of the tabloids and broadsheets that engaged in fierce daily battles for circulation in New York City.

The *Evening World* summed up the spirit of the times in a lengthy feature on Ederle that extolled her as "just a normal home and fun loving American." To prove its point, she was shown doing housework and talking about how cooking was one of her favorite things to do. In one picture, Trudy was manning a skillet, and the caption read "Kitchen work is good training."

The paper then broke into verse about her:

> *She loves sports and fun.*
> *She loves home and family.*
> *She's everything the converse of the flighty flapper.*
> *She's an American and a New Yorker.*

Another columnist was more taken with how the women swimmers seemed in perfect physical condition and radiated health. These weren't the floozies who partied at illicit speakeasies and wore dresses that crept up to shocking heights. They were all-American girls, so modest that, more often than not, they would don heavy sweaters over their swimming suits whenever a photographer was near.

"It is insignificant of these young athletes that their conversations, which mirror their minds, are as sound, as wholesome as their bodies," Jane Dixon wrote. "They display none of the characteristics of exotic young ladies of flapperdom whose chief offensive weapon in the eternal feminine game of being attractive is a lipstick and a pot of rouge." Dixon rhapsodized that if swimming could build this kind of girl, it was the duty of the country to get girls to swim or do other sports, "so that America may continue to be supreme on land and sea."

Indeed, for the first time, women were beginning to make their mark in sports that previously had been the exclusive province of men. Females were playing tennis (though they played in long skirts), and girls were playing on basketball and even hockey teams. Women had just gotten the vote five years earlier, and they were taking advantage of liberating times to push their daughters across frontiers they had never had a chance to cross.

The swimmers captured the most attention. Ederle was the young sensation, but she had plenty of company among both sexes. A muscular young man named Johnny Weissmuller was the star of the 1924 Olympics, winning three gold medals, while the American men and women won all but three swimming and diving events and swept the medals in six of them.

Among the women swimmers, Ederle stood out, partly because she was so young, but mainly because she was so good. She had been smashing world records much of the decade, and had won three medals herself at the Paris Olympics the year before. Newspapers were so taken with her that they were breathless in their comparisons to the great athletes of the time. Babe Ruth and Jack Dempsey had nothing on Trudy, one reported, because she had a chest expansion of eight inches, while Dempsey had only three and a half and Ruth only three and a quarter. Even heavyweight Tom Sharkey, who bragged about his chest, could only expand it six inches.

"Nature has equipped Miss Ederle for prodigious feats in the water," columnist Frank F. O'Neill wrote. "She has great strength and her muscles and nerve tissues are well coated with a protecting layer of cold resisting fat, although she is perfectly molded."

Trudy's exploits were known around the nation, which embraced her with the kind of exuberance with which it was embracing the decade. Calvin Coolidge was president, and his wife, Grace, was so impressed with the young swimmers in the summer of 1925 that she hired a swimming coach to teach her the eight-beat American crawl, which Trudy and other members of the Women's Swimming Association used in the water. For weeks, the First Lady practiced it off the coast of Swampscott, Massachusetts, where the summer White House was located.

Ederle was still a teen, though she wasn't as young as the newspapers reported. They thought she was eighteen, but she was actually a year older and had already traveled the world, winning medals and setting records. The discrepancy in age was likely a function of the WSA, which liked its swimmers to be as young as possible so that more donations could be raised, and Trudy played along with this throughout her career.

As the summer of 1925 approached, Trudy still held a number of world records, though a stumble in the Olympics a year earlier had taken some of her aura of invincibility away. The next Olympics were three years away, an eternity for a young woman, but she seemed content to spend another season traveling with her WSA teammates to meets and exhibitions around the country.

Fellow Olympian Helen Wainwright had another idea. She had heard about the flurry of challenges to attempt swimming the Channel and knew that an American swimmer, Mille Gade Corson, had nearly made it across two years earlier. She also knew that the country was ready to celebrate the success of any woman who might pull off such a spectacular feat.

Wainwright asked the WSA to sponsor her on the swim, and Charlotte Epstein, the club's founder, readily agreed, despite a prohibitive price tag of about nine thousand dollars. The young club was dominating women's swimming in the United States, but Epstein knew that a lot more glory could be had if one of its members became the first woman to swim the Channel. A chaperone for Wainwright was picked, and arrangements were made for her to leave in June for France and a try at the angry Channel.

Ederle's older sister, Margaret, a swimmer herself, heard about the plans at a meet at the City Athletic Club and urged her younger sister to apply to the WSA board of directors to make a try herself, since she had already beaten Wainwright in open-water swims. The two of them could go overseas together, help each other train, and maybe even spur each other on to greater things, Margaret suggested.

"Margaret, what, are you crazy? I never swam long distances like that," Trudy replied.

The idea began to grow, mostly because Meg never stopped pushing her sister to try. Finally, Trudy stepped forward and asked to go herself, and Epstein agreed to dig into the club's savings for more money to fund both women. But in late spring, Wainwright slipped while getting on a trolley car and strained a thigh muscle, and suddenly Ederle was facing the swim of a lifetime by herself.

Ederle was shocked when she found out Wainwright wasn't going. But she had already been swimming in the Shrewsbury River in Highlands, New Jersey, to accustom herself to the icy waters she would face in the Channel, and she had gotten used to the idea that this would be a grand adventure, despite the risk.

So when the press rushed up to her and asked if she would still go overseas, she had her answer ready. Wainwright's withdrawal may have taken some of the glamour out of the trip, but Ederle was nothing but determined once she made up her mind.

"I said I would go, and I'm going," Ederle quickly replied.

From across the ocean, the Channel was calling. And Trudy was hearing it loud and clear.

The morning of August 18 dawned clear, and the waters on the rocky French shore were as calm as those of an Italian lake. Ederle slept well before beating the sun up at 4:00 A.M. for a breakfast of well-done apple fritters and hot tea. It seemed a good day to make history, and she was more than ready to go. She had been testing the waters of the Channel for weeks now, sidelined only by a bout of stomach flu, and as her hours in the chilly waters mounted, she had grown increasingly confident of her chances.

Yet all had not gone well in camp. To prepare her for the swim, the WSA had hired a portly man named Jabez Wolffe to be her trainer.

Wolffe seemed an odd choice, having set a record in futility for swimming the Channel by failing in twenty-two attempts himself, but he knew both the currents and the whims of the tempestuous Channel better than anyone and was thought to be well worth the fifty dollars a week his expertise would cost.

Though Wolffe may have been the unluckiest Channel aspirant, he had a lot of ideas about what would work and what wouldn't work in the water, mostly because he had spent so much time in it. He had tried almost everything to get across, including having a man play the bagpipes to keep his stroke in rhythm, and it had almost paid off. In 1911, he missed making it across by mere yards, and only by a mile on three other occasions.

Trudy liked Wolffe upon meeting him, but it was not long before friction surfaced between the two. She was a natural swimmer imbued with God-given speed and the cockiness of youth, while he seemed to her like a fat old man who talked too much about things she never worried herself about. For his part, Wolffe was particularly upset over Ederle's refusal to submit to proper massaging, which the trainer said was necessary to harden her muscles for the swim.

Ederle would train four hours a day, walking for two hours and swimming for two more. The rest of the time, she liked either to read or hang around the assortment of swimmers who had come for their own Channel attempts, often with her prized ukulele in her hands.

Her ukulele playing irritated Wolffe, who thought that his swimmer was too lighthearted in approaching what to him seemed such a serious task. She would strum the instrument in front of Wolffe, who sometimes asked for certain songs, but more often than not he would mutter about Ederle wasting her time. As the days went on, Ederle grew tired of Wolffe's constant carping at her about the dangers and difficulties of the Channel, which had defeated him so many times before.

"I need all the encouragement that can be given me," she said. "After all, I'm no Jack Dempsey and I don't get half a million dollars for my efforts. So if I dance in the evening or pick a ukulele for pleasure, I don't think it should be reported as a scandal in the training camp. You swim the Channel for the fun and the glory of it. So why should it be regarded as a solemn effort?"

Wolffe thought it should be, and he was so upset with his young charge that he nearly took a boat home to England two days before the attempt. Friends prevailed on him to stay, and Wolffe grudgingly did, motivated by the chance that he could bask in the reflected glory of the first woman to tame the mighty Channel.

Wolffe knew that Trudy had a rare talent, and if he didn't understand it when she first arrived from the States, watching her swim day after day in training convinced him. On the eve of the swim, he was a believer in the brash American girl, though he would have felt better had Ederle actually listened to some of his advice.

"Miss Ederle doubtless is the finest exponent of swimming of any man or woman who has ever tried the Channel," Wolffe said. "She can swim the Channel, and I would have felt confident of her success had she followed my training instructions. She may be one of those athletic marvels who don't require any special training for tremendous tasks. If she succeeds she will prove herself not only the greatest living swimmer, but the greatest swimmer of all time."

The Channel, Wolffe well knew, was unforgiving. It could beat down the most physically fit and force even the most mentally tough to quit. On a calm day, it was tough enough, forcing swimmers to deal with the cold, the tides, the sand shelves, and the sharks and jellyfish. But there was seldom a calm day on the sliver of water between England and France.

Wolffe seldom stopped telling Trudy about how tough the Channel was, that she might have to swim up to fifty miles to conquer it, and that many horrors awaited anyone who tried. He also thought she had the wrong stroke for making it across, feeling the Channel favored a slow and deliberate swimmer, not one built for speed like the strongly built American. He wanted to change her swimming style to the breaststroke to slow her down, something Trudy wasn't about to do, since her American crawl stroke was as necessary to her swimming as breathing was to living.

While Trudy may have been just nineteen, she was the greatest female amateur swimming champion in the world, something that gave her more than a little bargaining power with her trainer. Trudy argued successfully, with help from chaperone Elsie Viets from the WSA and others, that she would swim the stroke she knew best, but she couldn't help but notice that Wolffe's attitude changed and he was never quite as happy with his young charge as before.

The week before her attempt, Ederle swam about nine miles, off the French coast, in three hours, which many thought remarkable because it was known as a difficult stretch of water. She was getting herself into shape the only way she knew how, swimming the Channel like she swam the currents of the Shrewsbury outside her family's summer home in New Jersey. Trudy had ideas of her own about how to prepare for the historic swim, and they didn't always mesh with those of Wolffe.

"I don't go in for skipping, jumping, or any special training stunts in my training and I don't do any special dieting," she said.

She also didn't think much about getting a rubdown. To Wolffe, daily massages were the only way to toughen and harden her muscles, but Trudy wanted no part of it. Neither did Viets, a stern woman who wasn't going to let this barrel of a man touch any part of the young girl's body, if she had anything to say about it.

Before moving her training camp to France, Ederle spent a few weeks in England getting ready, taking daily dips in the Channel off the coast of Brighton to get used to the water. Large crowds gathered on the pier to watch her practice, and the buzz about this confident girl with the smooth and powerful stroke began to grow on both sides of the Channel.

England was beginning to find out what America already knew: Ederle was different, and as modest as she was good. That was the trait Americans expected of their athletes, especially if they were female, in an era where the best in most sports were amateurs and only a few boxers and baseball players made any serious money.

"I am just an ordinary swimmer and have no particular stroke," Trudy told one reporter.

But she was much more than that. Newspapers marveled at her broad shoulders and easy athleticism. Before leaving for England, she was pictured exercising in Central Park, flexing her muscles and playing leapfrog with another swimmer, and playfully boxing with her sister Margaret.

By the time she left for England, there weren't many in the United States who didn't know about Trudy and her historic attempt. Newspapers turned out to take pictures of her going up the ramp of the liner wearing a rounded hat with a flower in it, her mother standing next to her to say good-bye. The trip over would be filled with long days at sea, but Trudy was used to it. She was an experienced traveler by now, having crossed the ocean the year before to compete in the Paris Olympics, and she planned daily workouts in the ship's pool to stay in shape.

Two days before leaving, Ederle tested herself in her home waters by swimming twenty-one miles from the Battery in New York to Sandy Hook, New Jersey, following a route that had been used by male swimmers in several races. She began while the city was mostly asleep, her father driving her down to the Battery at 4:00 A.M. She was clothed in just her bathing suit and a raincoat for cover.

Ederle wasn't sure what to expect, so she did the swim without notifying the press, though she was followed by a tug carrying her father and members of the WSA. She misjudged the current and battled the last of the flood tide in the Buttermilk Channel, swimming in one spot for nearly two hours. Trudy was in pain from her swimsuit cutting deeply into her skin, and the salt water made the open wounds even worse.

Ederle swam on, though, through the morning darkness and then through heavy fog. She considered quitting, but couldn't stand the thought of letting her sister down. Finally, the fog lifted and she got her second wind, though she couldn't see because the salt water was burning her eyes. She followed a rowboat in, sprinting the final one hundred yards as those on the tug cheered her on.

When her time was added up, Ederle had covered the distance in seven hours and eleven minutes, breaking the men's record by eight minutes. That was such a stunning performance that the *New York World*'s Heywood Broun said some of the theories of male supremacy would now have to be reevaluated. "The urge among men to surrender subway seats must be a little less now that a girl has swum from the Battery to Sandy Hook," Broun wrote.

Broun wasn't the only one impressed. The European sporting world was agape at the idea that this American girl might do what no woman had ever done. French and British swimming experts agreed that Ederle's speed gave her the best chance of any woman who had tried, and even skeptics were beginning to become believers once they watched her effortlessly swim against the tide in her Channel warm-ups.

Ederle was not the first to try. Women had been attempting to swim the Channel since 1900, when a Viennese postal worker by the name of Madame Isacescue started from Calais and made it fourteen miles in nine hours before giving up. Swimming sensation Annette Kellerman tried in 1905 and then twice more in 1906, but with no success. There was a long period when no one made the attempt, until Jeanne Sion of France swam for fourteen hours in 1922 and showed that there might be a possibility a woman could cross the Channel.

The next year, with an English newspaper's offer of five thousand dollars, Sion swam for sixteen hours before quitting. The same summer, Mille Gade Corson, a mother of two from New York, came within two miles of Cape Gris-Nez after fifteen and a half hours, but a storm finally caused her to quit.

The Channel was turning into an equal-opportunity spoiler. Man or woman, if the water or tides didn't get them, there was always a good chance of running into jellyfish, seaweed, and the occasional plank of wood. It didn't help that it was one of the busiest shipping lanes in the world, and swimmers always had to be on the lookout for one of the six hundred tankers and two hundred ferries that plied its waters daily.

The original plan was to make the attempt July 20, but a stomach ailment slowed Trudy down and pushed the swim back. Though the later days of summer were considered best for swimming the Channel, time was of the essence because Ederle was not the only woman there that summer trying to make history.

Channel swimming, Sparrow Robertson noted in his "Sporting Gossip" column in the *New York Herald Tribune,* was "almost becoming epidemic," and the normally sleepy coastal town of Cape Gris-Nez was booked solid with swimmers, trainers, coaches, journalists, and tug-boat operators.

Sion, the old lady of Channel swimming at the age of forty-eight, had the first shot at it, entering the Channel just a week before Ederle set off. Sion looked for much of her swim like she was going to make it across, getting to within a mile and a quarter of shore, but she faltered in the cold and wind and the ebb tide off the coast near Dover and had to be pulled from the water.

Next up was the Argentine, Lillian Harrison, who slipped into the sea from Cape Gris-Nez, only to encounter a hailstorm an hour out. Harrison had been making good time, swimming four miles in a little over two hours, and after seven hours she was only eight miles from Dover. No other swimmer, man or woman, had ever gotten out so fast, but Harrison had gone too fast. She was worn-out and called out to the Egyptian swimmer, Ishak Helmy, who was pacing her, "Catch me, Helmy."

Helmy grabbed Harrison, who fainted into his arms. It was her fourth attempt at the dreaded Channel, and it would be her last. Aboard the tug, she murmured, "I will never try it again."

Now that the morning she had been waiting for had finally arrived, Ederle hurried to get ready. In her excitement, she had put her skirt on inside out, a fact noticed by Viets, who asked her young charge if she wanted to go back to her room to get it right. But Trudy had other things on her mind, and making a fashion statement wasn't one of them.

"I wouldn't like to change it now," she told her chaperone. "I feel it will bring me good luck."

Trudy was confident, if not brash. She was a natural open-water swimmer anyway, and she hadn't found anything out about the Channel in the time she had been in England and France to make her believe it was anything worse than the waters off Manhattan. She would attack it like Harrison had, using her speed to get an early jump in the calm waters, and then try to hang on if the going got tough all the way over to the English side.

The morning of the swim, though, brought a touch of nerves as Trudy seemed to finally realize what was ahead of her.

"How I wish tomorrow was today," she told friends at the breakfast table.

The swim was, by nature, a lonely one, but Ederle would not be alone. The *Morinie* would chug alongside her, carrying a colorful collection of about one hundred journalists, officials, celebrities of the day, fellow swimmers, and curious onlookers. There was even a four-piece jazz band to give her comfort as she stroked her way across the Channel.

Her attempt generated so much publicity that, for the first time, there was a Marconi wireless set on the tug, and an operator dressed in suit and tie was on duty to send hourly dispatches to newspapers and wire services in England as she made her away across.

Ederle would start off from the rocks off the coast of Cape Gris-Nez by herself, but several fellow Channel hopefuls were on the tug, ready to swim alongside her for stretches. The unofficial rules of the Channel swim allowed that, though if anyone actually touched Ederle, she would be immediately disqualified. Touching was the one rule everyone understood.

Among the swimmers were Sion and Harrison, along with the dashing Ishak Helmy, "the Egyptian Colossus," who was a Channel hopeful himself and quite a presence that summer off the coast of France. Helmy, the son of a famous Egyptian general, enjoyed himself greatly and played the role of confidant and water companion to the women who came in the summer of 1925 to make their attempts.

Helmy fulfilled that role well as Ederle trained, though she was wise to keep an eye on a man whose father had four wives and twenty-one children and who often espoused the virtues of "polygamy for aristocrats." Helmy's ideas were a bit wild even for the time, but his good nature and affable personality helped keep things loose during training, and Ederle quickly bonded with him.

"Some persons are inevitably cast in the role of a big brother," one columnist wrote. "That seems to be Helmy's mission in life and he discharges his obligations admirably."

Indeed he did. Helmy was pictured in one photo dancing on the beach with Sion as Ederle strummed her ukulele on an adjacent rock. But the big and suave Egyptian had some plans of his own for the Channel, and was as bitten with the idea of making it across as any.

Helmy would try to swim the Channel the next month himself for the first time, but he didn't make it across. He tried five more times, including once from England to France to try to shake up his luck, before finally making it in the summer of 1928, thus setting off a Channel swimming craze among his fellow Egyptians.

Ederle was happy with both herself and her preparations, and she was beginning to get along with Wolffe. If she had any misgivings over the number of people who would follow her across and the frenzy her attempt had created, it didn't show. She slept well the night before, cheerfully downed her breakfast, and looked forward for the adventure of an already adventurous life.

Now, rising from the breakfast table in the early-morning darkness, Trudy declared it was time to go for a swim.

"I'm all ready for it," she said. "Bring on your old Channel."

In the engine room of the *Morinie,* Ederle slathered herself down with a triple layer of grease. She started with a quarter-inch of lanolin, followed it with a light coat of Vaseline, and finished it off with another quarter-inch of a preparation Wolffe had concocted from the heaviest grease he could find.

Over the years, the makeup of the protective coating had changed. The earliest contenders had used pure lard, while later swimmers used a dark mixture that almost had the appearance of a soft leather casing over the skin. But recently, most swimmers had favored a mixture of lard and lanolin, which stuck on the body so well that it required a scrub with gasoline and hot water to remove it at the finish.

Ederle was not used to swimming all greased up, and she had trained for an entire month in the Channel without using it. But it was a must if she was to spend hours in the chilly water.

"I hate that sticky stuff," she said.

Ederle had to worry about her eyes, as well. Like most swimmers, she used goggles glued to her face with tar or some similar substance in the often futile bid to keep the seawater from blinding her eyes.

The final decision was what to wear. The men who swam the Channel mostly did it naked, but that wouldn't do for a woman. The twenties may have been roaring, but there were limits. Trudy decided on a one-piece suit with a modesty panel and an American flag on the front, ready to make a statement for both her gender and her country.

And what a statement it would be. It had been exactly half a century since the first man, an English sailor named Capt. Matthew Webb, made it from England to France. It wasn't until thirty-six years later than another man, Tom Burgess, made it across, and it wasn't until the 1920s that Channel swimming became the rage.

Two years before Ederle made her swim, a wealthy Argentine named Enrique Tiraboschi set the record for the fastest time across, making it in sixteen hours and thirty-three minutes, to break Webb's mark by five hours and twelve minutes. Tiraboschi was the first to cross the Channel from the Continent to England, but even he failed twice before finally succeeding on August 12, 1923. He had spent 250,000 francs on his attempts, and when he finally made it, he collapsed on the shore.

"The secret of fast swimming, as well as endurance," Tiraboschi said, "lies in keeping the mind occupied with something else."

The Argentine did that by hiring a jazz band to accompany him on the tug that followed him across. A husky South American beat the drum as Tiraboschi swam along, and he found inspiration in the music.

"I wanted twice to quit when I struck the cold currents," Tiraboschi said. "But the trombone blared out encouragingly in the midst of the foggy darkness, so I kept going."

The tug *Morinie* was filled with so many people, their arms filled with so many things, that it looked more like an ocean cruise than a sporting event. The water was calm as Ederle came aboard to cheers. She greased up and then went out on deck, a pink rubber cap on her head.

"Why the bright color?" a newspaperman asked.

"So they can see me coming farther off from Dover," she replied.

The mood on the tug was gay. Ederle sat on the deck, laughing with her friends and singing "Hail! Hail! The Gang's All Here!" as they headed from the tug's base in Boulogne toward the farthest west rock outcropping of northern France. The smile never left her face as she stepped into a rowboat, which was towed to the rocks by a speedboat hired by the United Press to carry its reporters and photographers. An American flag was raised on the tug as Trudy climbed out of the rowboat onto a large rock.

Wolffe wanted her to wait, but by now Trudy was done listening to him. She quickly jumped into the water, her historic attempt finally under way.

"I was eager to be away. I'd have started at midnight if they would have let me," she said later. "Finally I was allowed to dive off. What a feeling! I was on my way. I did not use the breaststroke, as many of my predecessors had done, and for this reason I guess those accompanying me thought I was swimming too fast."

Indeed they did.

Wolffe's worst fears came true when Ederle covered three miles in the first hour. From the tug, he yelled at her, "Not so fast, not so fast."

Ederle did seem terribly fast because, unlike others before her, she was using a strong overhand style called the American crawl, which had been perfected by her coach at the WSA, while most others had used the breaststroke. She went out at twenty-seven strokes a minute, then had to be talked into dropping down to twenty-five strokes to conserve her energy.

On the tug, Burgess, the second man to swim the Channel and a breaststroker himself, watched in amazement. He told those around him that he had never seen anyone swim so fast so early into the swim. From the water, though, Trudy saw things differently.

"I was swimming as slowly as I possibly could with the stroke I was employing," she said.

Ederle was buoyant as she swam west from the French coast with the tugboat just in front of her and to the side. Early in the swim, she was handed a bottle of beef broth, but it slipped from her hands because of the grease and she laughingly dived after it before merrily lifting it up in a toast to those on board.

On the deck of the *Morinie*, the musicians got their instruments out and played "Yes! We Have No Bananas" and other tunes of the time to keep Trudy going. The tug was crowded, but spirits were high as the water remained manageable and Ederle swam strongly through the chilly waters.

The plan was for Ederle to enter the water at the point of Cape Gris-Nez four hours and twenty minutes before high tide, instead of the traditional four hours to get the full advantage of the strong current. Wolffe figured it would carry Ederle as far to the southwest as possible before the tide turned and swept toward Calais and into the North Sea.

The cold was bad, but the strong tides were even worse. They ran at between four and five miles an hour and strong winds made them even faster, but swimmers tried to catch a period of slack tides, known as "neap tides," when the currents would slow. Those usually happened between July and September, and that was the window of opportunity that drew men and women to the Channel in the summer of 1925.

Swimmers also had to deal with the possibility of sharks and the hated jellyfish, which forced many to abandon their swims after being stung. Unfortunately, while a long stretch of warm weather was necessary to bring the Channel temperatures up to bearable levels, it also drew swarms of jellyfish into the Channel.

None of that mattered much to the American girl, who largely kept out of the conferences among her trainers and counselors to formulate strategy. She was going to take whatever the Channel gave her, and she was going to win.

"Just look after all those details," she told Viets. "My job is to swim the Channel."

Back home, the weeks leading up to the swim merely helped to pique the country's interest. Newspapers followed the attempt with breathless articles and pictures sent over from England, tracking Trudy's every move. The *Seattle Daily Times* ran an entire page, with pictures of Ederle going through a final workout and also preparing an appetizing meal for her party.

The *New York Times* hired a Capt. Alec Rutherford, whom it identified as a "Famous British Expert on the Cross Channel Swim," to analyze the swim and report from the tugboat as Ederle made her way across.

In assessing her odds, Rutherford kept a stiff upper lip.

"Everyone who has seen this cheerful American girl during her training period here is confident that she will make a remarkable effort," he wrote. "She has made an excellent impression on everyone, both by her attractive personality and by her swimming technique. Her beautifully proportioned and athletic figure, her power and her complete mastery of the eight-beat crawl, and given all her 'will to win,' have convinced the British experts here that with reasonable luck as to tides and weather, and an absence of accidents, she has an excellent chance of securing the honor of being the first woman to conquer the Channel."

Rutherford, like Wolffe, worried that she might go out too fast. Ederle had reduced her speed from twenty-seven to twenty-five strokes a minute, but Wolfe wanted her at twenty-three or even twenty-two. Too fast a start, they feared, and she would run out of gas somewhere in the middle of the Channel.

"This makes for endurance, and while there is a corresponding loss in pace, the swimmer must always have a reserve in hand should a spurt be necessary in order to catch a tide or get past a troublesome current," Rutherford opined.

That was the common thinking of the time, though Rutherford wasn't always as expert as the *Times* thought. In his final piece before the attempt, he told how Ederle was going to begin her quest in the dark, at 10:00 P.M., and said that Harrison would race her across the Channel.

Instead, Ederle began at 7:08 in the morning, and Harrison was nice and cozy inside the tug.

Still, Rutherford was nimble enough to get on the tug, where he and other reporters began wiring bulletins as the swim progressed. The International News Service reported that as of 10:30 A.M., Ederle was five miles northwest of Cape Gris-Nez and going at a "perfect even pace, with all indications that she would complete her crossing of the Channel." The early tide was helping carry Ederle westward and she was making good progress. From the water, Ederle watched as a plane roared overhead, headed for Paris.

Trudy's fellow swimmers were on deck in their suits, ready to keep her company when needed. She swam alone early on, but about four miles into the swim, she shouted, "Send someone in with me. I am getting lonesome." Vera Tanner, a member of the British Olympic team the year before, jumped in and swam alongside the American.

The water remained relatively calm, though Wolffe cast a wary eye on the English sky. He had enough experience in the water to know the signs of a storm approaching. He also knew Trudy had hours left in the water, even in the best of conditions, and that her quick start meant little toward her ultimate success.

The band, meanwhile, played on. When the musicians took a break, the gramophone was cranked up to keep Trudy amused. So far, the English Channel didn't seem so daunting after all. A little more than two hours into the swim, the liner *Cap Polonio*, bound from Buenos Aires to Bremen, passed, raising large waves in the water. Ederle waved to the passengers on deck, then resumed a lively conversation with Harrison, who was now keeping her company in the water.

"Cut that talking out, girls!" Wolffe yelled from his rowboat, which was being towed behind the tug, alongside the swimmers.

The United Press was on the scene in its special speedboat to wire the latest reports. The news service filed hourly updates, and a full story about 1:30 P.M., when it judged Ederle was halfway across. The news was mostly good, but bad weather was on the horizon, it said, a troubling thought for those rooting for the American girl.

The demand for immediate news of her swim was so intense that the Marconi wireless set installed on the tug to relay reports was constantly in use. Other papers sent launches out to the Channel to send dispatches from those onboard, while movie men were grinding away from the start to the finish. Photographers jostled one another for position, leaning over the edge of the tug to get the best shot of Trudy in the water.

Ederle swam relentlessly toward the English coast, keeping up her brisk pace. In just three hours, she had gone eight miles, a performance thought impossible until then. But it wasn't long before the wind that Wolffe feared came from the southwest and the sea became choppy. The Channel was just beginning to warm up to its reputation as a seething, foaming, daunting body of water.

The swim had started out as a race against time. Now it was becoming a battle against the elements.

Henry Ederle was worried, though he did his best not to show it. He stood on the front porch of the family's summer home, smoking a cigar and paying little attention to the commotion going on around him.

Much of the town of Highlands seemed to be in the Ederles' yard on Steamboat Lane that morning, many wearing swimsuits on their way to the beach. Every few minutes, the phone rang—either Uncle John calling from the Ederle Brothers Meat Market at 110 Amsterdam Avenue in New York or Charlotte Epstein calling with news. Sisters Helen, Margaret, and Emma took turns with brother George, sprinting across the sand to bring back the latest communications.

"Leave it to Trudy!" the family yelled after each announcement.

Henry Ederle stared into the Atlantic, deep in thought, almost as if he were peering across the ocean to see Trudy make her swim.

"I'll bet a butcher shop she makes it," he said.

Henry Ederle had come across the Atlantic thirty years earlier from the town of Bissingen, outside of Stuttgart, part of a huge wave of German migration to the United States at the time. The family patriarch was sixteen at the time, one of twenty-two children of a cattle herder who owned large amounts of farm property, and had learned a trade as a bologna maker before heading to a new land of opportunity. Once there, the stout farm boy grew even broader, carrying quarters of beef on his shoulders to support his growing family, which would eventually include six children.

Pop Ederle was a success in his new country, joining his brother to open the butcher shop in 1904, and later investing with him in apartment buildings and other real estate in the New York area. The family was thriving, sufficiently well-off to have its own summer place at Highlands and be well respected in the German-American community.

Trudy had been worried on the trip over about her father, who was unable to make it to the pier to see her off. Henry Ederle had lost some thirty pounds after undergoing a stomach operation and was suffering from complications of the surgery, but Trudy got a telegram just before the ship docked in England. It said he was doing fine, which relieved her worries.

Like her husband, Gertrude Ederle was a stout immigrant, though from East Prussia, and it was easy to see where Trudy got her strong constitution. These were robust people with German work ethics that they instilled in their active children.

Trudy's older sister, Margaret, was a champion swimmer herself, having won the Metropolitan 440-yard race four years earlier, before giving up her sport for a business career. Margaret knew early on that while she might be one of the best swimmers in the city, she would never be the best swimmer in her household.

Margaret also knew her sister and worried that she would not listen to her trainer and would try to swim the Channel too fast.

"She just hates to go slow," Margaret said.

Ma Ederle was worried about other things. She could almost feel the cold, the chill her daughter must be feeling.

"That water's so icy cold," she said. "It bites to the bone."

Like Ederle, the four-piece jazz band started out strong. But soon the wind was blowing hard and the water became increasingly rough. On the tug, people began getting seasick as it bobbed up and down amid the swelling waves. It wasn't long before the band began to falter, its members turning queasy and heading to the rail for relief.

The trombonist went first, quickly followed by the cornet player and then the guy with the clarinet. The man with the concertina played on alone, until he also could no longer keep his breakfast down. Someone cranked up the gramophone to replace them as they hung over the side of the *Morinie,* and another chorus of "Yes! We Have No Bananas" could be heard from those not yet fully nauseated.

In the water, Ederle swam along, fortified with drinks of hot chocolate and what Wolffe told her was beef bouillon. Swimmers took turns accompanying her, and Wolffe handed her encouragement and refreshment from a small rowboat along side the tug.

Ederle continued to swim strongly, but by now the rough seas were causing her some problems, too. The cresting waves were smashing into her, and she was gulping seawater, despite her best efforts not to. She had gone out fast, but had now slowed down as the tides and waves began to take their toll.

She was also puzzled at the instructions Wolffe was giving her. He kept telling her to go slower. She switched to the breaststroke occasionally to try to do so, but it was like trying to reign in a Thoroughbred horse. Even more irritating to her was that Wolffe, in his rowboat, was forcing her away from the shelter of the tug and making her swim a zigzag route. He also made her stop every half hour to eat chocolate and have some of his beef tea.

Trudy would later talk about her distrust of the beef broth and Wolffe's insistence that she drink it. It gave her a warm, burning sensation, which made her think it might be wine or liquor. Wolffe would tell her it was just juices of genuine beef, but this butcher's daughter knew what beef and its broth tasted like, and it tasted nothing like this.

A few reporters who had not become seasick had taken over the band's instruments by now, hoping to cheer Ederle up. They played, albeit badly, as the tug chugged alongside the American girl with the bright pink cap on her head. Four motorboats crowded with people hoping to cheer Trudy on came out from the English side to join the festivities as Ederle crept closer to the coast. But the water was becoming increasingly rough and her stroke was becoming increasingly irregular.

Sion and Helmy had been swimming alongside, but Sion had been bitten by jellyfish and retired to the rowboat. Ederle's stroke seemed to be faltering and her hands were shaking as Wolffe offered her more beef broth, this time with sugar cubes in it. She drank it and rested a few minutes, then resumed swimming.

The seas were turbulent, but Trudy was still making progress. She wasn't aware that the mood on the boat had grown pessimistic, and she was buoyed by the messages of support from her mother that were arriving on the Marconi wireless.

That's not to say she was without problems. A large piece of driftwood almost hit her on the head, but Wolffe managed to spear it away with a long boat hook, and she had a headache. Still, as the cameramen were grinding away on their shots, she was making progress, and the English side was getting closer.

At one point, someone in the boat shouted, "Look, there's Dover just ahead of you." Just then, a big wave hit Trudy square in the face and gave her a mouthful of water that she held in so as not to swallow it. She coughed it up, and Wolffe, thinking she was in trouble just six-and-a-half miles off the English coast, yelled over to Helmy, "Grab her!"

Helmy did just that, and he and Sion helped get Ederle into the rowboat, where Sion put her arm around the American girl and gave her a kiss. Wolffe rowed them to the tug and Trudy was pulled aboard, where she was wrapped in blankets and put in a deck chair.

Ederle was furious at being pulled out. She refused to let anyone on the tug touch her, and she wouldn't talk to them. She couldn't understand why, at the first sign of trouble, Wolffe had ordered Helmy to take her out. For the first time in her young life, she felt like a failure.

The tug turned about and headed back to Boulogne. Trudy ate a chocolate bar, then quickly fell asleep. She had been in the water eight hours and forty-six minutes and had made it two-thirds of the way across the Channel, better time than anyone who had ever attempted the swim had managed.

"It was the roughest going I have ever known," she told reporters, not letting on her displeasure. "I was going well until the storm came."

At their summer home in Highlands, the Ederles were so confident Trudy would make it that many in the family went for a swim. Margaret demonstrated to onlookers the strokes she thought her sister was using at that very moment, and the family prepared to celebrate. Then came unexpected news: Trudy had collapsed.

"Well, I'll tell you this," Henry Ederle said. "There's no swimming record that Gertrude can't bust. She set out to cross that Channel and I'm here to tell you she's going to. What's more, she is not coming back home until she does, and that's that."

That Ederle had made it as far as she had under the conditions was enough to amaze most. A young Ed Sullivan, who would later go on to bigger things as host of a television show, was one of them, writing in his "Sports Whirl" column that Trudy had done all anyone could have done.

"No swimmer, man or woman, could have lived in that tempest," Sullivan wrote. "The youngster gave all that she had physically and when the giant Egyptian swimmer Helmy reached her side she was choking and almost unconscious from the cruel treatment of the waves."

Paul Gallico went even further in his assessment in the *New York Daily News.*

"The reason that I admire Miss Gertrude Ederle's courage so much is that she battled the most terrifying opponents that can be met on this earth and didn't quit to them. She collapsed. But scare her? Not a bit. Who were they? Cold, storms, tides, currents. Brrrr! Dirty cowards, every one of them."

According to Sullivan, bettors had a lot riding on Ederle's attempt. He said Wall Street handled $25,000 in commissions, while Lloyd's of London dealt with twice that amount.

There was talk of Ederle making a second attempt, something her father surely wanted, and she stayed abroad for weeks, planning to do just that. But she wanted nothing more to do with Wolffe, so Viets hired Burgess to guide her in the second attempt. He put her immediately back in training for the next period of promising tides and currents, due at the end of August. But the Channel became even more chilly and stormy, and it wasn't long before she and Viets headed home on the liner *Mauretania,* defeated but still unbowed.

Ederle wasn't the only star on that ship crossing the Atlantic. The actress Rosamond Pinchot was onboard, returning home after playing the nun in Morris Gest's *Miracle* on a European tour that summer. Actor

George Arliss was also a passenger, along with Countess Szechenyi, the former Gladys Vanderbilt. The press didn't care much about anyone but Ederle. They were waiting to question her the minute the ship docked in New York Harbor.

Her first attempt to swim the Channel was over. It wouldn't be long before the recriminations would begin.

2

Humbled but Not Beaten

The trip back home was a somber one, with Ederle spending hours slouched in her deck chair, thinking about what had gone wrong. She was anxious to put the entire summer behind her and begin planning for another swim, but her thoughts seldom strayed from the moment Wolffe ordered her pulled from the Channel. She told Viets that she was determined to try again and would either swim the Channel this time or it would be "actual collapse, or nothing." Just how she was going to make that happen was unclear, but one thing that was certain was that Wolffe would have no part of it.

Ederle knew the odds had been against her, and she also knew there was a lot of money bet against her chances in both London and New York. She couldn't help think that perhaps Wolffe had ordered her from the water because he might have bet on her not to make it across. There was also the thought that since Wolffe had failed twenty-two times himself, he couldn't stand the sight of a teenager—and a girl at that—doing what he had found impossible.

Ederle remembered thinking it was odd at the time she was pulled onto the boat that Wolffe slipped the rescue towel over her tightly. Her initial reaction was that he was trying to knock the breath out of her, but later she would think he was posing with her to try to make the collapse appear realistic for the photographers and movie cameramen who were on the tug, recording her every move.

Whatever the case, she brooded about it on the long voyage home, and couldn't help considering herself a failure for not making it across as she most confidently had thought she would.

The *Mauretania* arrived in New York on September 18, a beautiful fall morning in the city, and the tranquillity of the early hours as the ship steamed into the harbor quickly vanished as a stampede of excited reporters and photographers thundered down the ship's deck to ask a barrage of rapid-fire questions.

Viets didn't want her answering anything, and she tried to hold Ederle incommunicado on the ship, telling reporters that the Women's Swimming Association didn't want her to make any statements "until after certain matters had been cleared up."

Reporters, though, were having none of it. They loudly complained to Charlotte Epstein, who had come aboard to welcome the club's most famous swimmer, and she allowed Trudy to answer the questions.

"Could you have gone on?" one reporter asked.

"Yes I could have."

"What caused you to stop?"

"Because Helmy touched me and that was disqualification," Trudy replied.

"What made him do that?"

"Ask Wolffe."

Wolffe was just as determined to spin things his way, telling the Associated Press in London that he had given no instructions to remove her from the water. But the facts seemed to be on Trudy's side, and Viets, who had been aboard the *Morinie*, watching the entire time, backed her young charge up.

She issued a statement saying Trudy had followed Wolffe's instructions to the letter and that motion pictures taken from the tug clearly showed that Trudy had not collapsed. Moreover, she said, she had the written testimony of onlookers—including Helmy himself—that Wolffe had ordered her out of the water.

"I distinctly heard Wolffe cry out, 'Grab her, Helmy!' " Viets said.

Viets wasn't done, partly since she had never liked the portly trainer from the moment she was supposed to hand control of Trudy over to him. She complained that Wolffe did everything in training to try to break Trudy's morale, never allowed her to practice with other swimmers, and kept her in shallow water during training, despite her request to get out where it was deep. Viets said Wolffe scared Trudy by telling her there were sharks in the Channel, "though he must have known the fish seen were porpoises," and told everyone he saw that Trudy had no chance of making it.

Trudy had other supporters. Rutherford, the Channel-swimming expert of the *Times* and the North American Newspaper Alliance, issued a statement from London on Ederle's behalf, in which he discounted criticism of a lack of cooperation between Ederle and Wolffe.

"The lack was not on the part of Miss Ederle," Rutherford said. "It seemed to me that Wolffe on every possible occasion jammed down her throat the difficulties she would meet, the struggles she would have, the possible illnesses she would experience. He appeared to take an antagonistic attitude toward all connected with Miss Ederle."

Ederle showed she knew a little bit about defending herself, too. She may have been shy in public, but she wasn't shy about letting America know what she thought were the real reasons behind her failure. A few days after her arrival, she went into the new studios of WOR on Broadway, determined to tell a curious city the real reasons why she had not made it across. She laid the blame at the feet of Wolffe, saying she would have made it farther—and possibly all the way across—if not for the trainer. She also said for the first time publicly that she was going to try to swim the Channel again the following summer, this time with Burgess as her trainer and coach.

"My motto is, if at first you don't succeed, try, try again," she told New Yorkers. "And I want the public to know that I am going to attempt to swim the English Channel again next July."

A picture in the *Daily News* the next day showed Ederle simulating her crawl stroke while dressed in a one-piece suit in front of a WOR microphone. In another, she was in a striped dress, talking into the same microphone. The city was abuzz about the young swimmer, even if she hadn't finished what she had started. Ederle soon got a taste of what being a celebrity was like when she was the guest of honor at a reception sponsored by the WSA at the Hippodrome, where she saw her name in the lights over a theater marquee for the first time in her life. Ederle was only the third nonperformer—war hero General John Pershing and the Prince of Wales were the others—honored by the billing at the famous show house.

Annette Kellerman, the Australian swimmer who won fame in the water and on stage in vaudeville in her daring one-piece suit, was the master of ceremonies and also gave a diving exhibition in a glass tank. That ordinarily would have been plenty to please the men in the audience, but on this night, Trudy was the star attraction.

Over the stage was a banner that read GOOD SPORTSMANSHIP IS GREATER THAN VICTORY, the official motto of the WSA. It didn't take long for one speaker to draw applause by saying that while Trudy "had been warned of sharks in the Channel, no one had cautioned her against a Wolffe."

Ederle was uncomfortable enough to begin with, having had to wear a dress when she would have much preferred sportswear. She wasn't prepared to sit in the center box as the star attraction, and she was so overwhelmed by the tribute to her that she refused to go onstage to receive a diamond bracelet the WSA was giving her for her effort. It was all Trudy could do to mouth "Thank you" when WSA president Margaret Johnson entered her box to give it to her.

Ederle considered herself a failure, even if the rest of the country did not. Most Americans were happy that she had tried her best and made it as far as she had, rationalizing the defeat in the way of the optimistic times. One newspaper predicted that it would spark a great boom among the feminine sex, with thousands of girls trying to become champion swimmers like Trudy. No previous Channel attempt—indeed, no previous female sporting endeavor—had been reported in the way that Trudy's had. New York's newspapers had a lot invested in the young swimmer, and now they were filled with reports about her having shown admirable pluck and character, only to have been overcome by the stormy seas.

No one was prouder of Ederle—or more eager to share in her success—than the German-Americans of New York City, who embraced her as one of their own and celebrated her as being emblematic of fine German heritage. Ederle was an important symbol for the large German-American community, which had had its loyalties questioned just a few years earlier, during the war, and was still trying to find both its footing and voice once again. Members of the powerful German-American National Alliance had made the mistake of engaging in blatant pro-Kaiser propaganda in the years leading up to the war, and though Germans were the largest and most influential of the immigrant groups, many people still viewed them with suspicion long after the war was over.

It had been only three years since the United States welcomed a new German ambassador after five years without one, and the same person who had led the delegation greeting the new ambassador was now heading the cheerleading for Ederle. Charles A. Oberwager, a former newspaperman turned lawyer, had defended future German chancellor Franz von Papen in 1915, when he was accused of being a German spy plotting to blow up munitions plants. Oberwager was now a city magistrate and the powerful head of the United German Societies of New York, an umbrella group for hundreds of German-American social clubs. It was in this capacity that he wasted no time in feting the daughter of German immigrants on her valiant swim.

On November 2, Oberwager presided over the annual celebration of German Day, and some 4,500 people turned out in commemoration of the landing of the first German pilgrims in America in 1583. The event was held at the Mecca Temple on West Fifty-fifth Street, and Ederle was the center of attention in an auditorium filled from top to bottom and so crowded that people stood in the aisles. On a stage decorated with the flags of both the United States and Germany, the Richard Wagner Symphony Orchestra opened with the "The Star-Spangled Banner," then followed it with "Deutschland Uber Alles," which brought the audience to its feet to sing along. There was a gymnastic exhibition, and a choral society of about one hundred sang German numbers before Ederle was brought onstage and presented a large bouquet of red roses.

The teenager, who had never gotten past the tenth grade in school and had no concept of worldly affairs, smiled shyly and listened as Oberwager gave the keynote speech in German, in which he declared that Germans had and always would have faith in the institutions of the United States. Showing no repentance, or perhaps just figuring he was speaking to a friendly audience, Oberwager then went on to say that the war had been part of a world plot to deprive Germany of its colonies and that the Kaiser Wilhelm had been a promoter of peace who couldn't hold back the tide.

"Since the war great tasks devolve upon Americans of German descent here to urge the various governments to disclose all secret information, thereby proving that Germany was not responsible for the beginning of the war," he said.

It would not be the last time Ederle would be taken advantage of by Oberwager.

Trudy had a lot on her mind at the time, but none of it had to do with German nationalism or the reasons behind the war. She and her sister Meg had been trying to lay plans for how she was going to swim the Channel the following year, and they had come to the conclusion that she had to do it on her own, without the help of the WSA. Two days later, she revealed in a blockbuster announcement that she and fellow Olympic gold medalist Aileen Riggin were quitting amateur swimming to become pros. The news stunned everyone at the WSA, including Epstein, who had hinted to Trudy that her second attempt would be funded like the first one but had never actually come out and committed the money to it.

The WSA had put up nine thousand dollars—an immense sum at the time for an amateur program—for the first swim, and Trudy wasn't about to get on her knees and beg for it again, especially after she had failed the first time. Rumors floated that Ederle was unhappy with the club for not backing her up more in her dispute with Wolffe, but the real reason she turned pro was simply financial.

"Perhaps their defection will cause our team to suffer a setback," a dismayed Epstein said, "but it should only be temporary as we have plenty of fine younger material on hand."

What Epstein and the WSA didn't know was that Ederle and Riggin had already negotiated deals with the new Deauville Casino in Miami Beach to serve as swimming instructors and performers, with the understanding that the casino would advance money for the second attempt at crossing the Channel. They would head to Florida and begin their first paying jobs on January 1.

Before that, Ederle sat down at the family kitchen table on Amsterdam Avenue and drafted a letter to Burgess. She would be returning to France as her own boss this time, and she wanted the trainer and champion of the Channel himself to know that if she hired him for the effort, she wanted his undivided attention and did not expect it to be shared with any other swimmers, male or female.

Burgess wrote back on November 29, 1925, telling Ederle he had heard she turned professional and was going to make this swim on her own without help from the WSA. He warned her that it would be tough going in the Channel, and to expect to make at least three attempts once she got to France.

In the letter, Burgess wrote that she would face even more difficulty the second time, particularly since Wolffe said she would never swim as well as she did the year before. Burgess told Trudy it was up to her to show him he was wrong.

The new year that began for Ederle in the warm Florida sun would turn into one filled with the triumph and heartbreak of sport. If the 1920s were indeed the Golden Age of Sports, as *Daily News* writer Paul Gallico would later make the case, 1926 was the most golden year of them all.

Jack Dempsey and Gene Tunney would fight in the biggest heavyweight fight ever, Bobby Jones would win his first British Open title and his second U.S. Open, and Babe Ruth would mark a comeback year by hitting home runs at a prodigious rate in the house he built in the Bronx. College football gave the nation a big game seemingly every week, none bigger than what may have been the best Army-Navy game ever, a 21–21 tie at Soldier Field between the two best teams in the nation.

Horse racing drew millions to the tracks to spend some of the economic riches of the times, Ty Cobb was both managing and playing for the Tigers, and St. Louis would win its first World Series behind wonder batter Rogers Hornsby. The Galloping Ghost himself, Red Grange, was finishing a barnstorming tour for the Chicago Bears that would herald a new era in professional sports for the fledgling National Football League.

While America was flexing its athletic muscles, the rest of the world was discovering the wonder of sports, too. The heavyweight title stayed in America, but other major titles were won around the world, while a German set the half-mile record in track and field and a Swede smashed the two-mile mark. Germany was still recovering from the war, but it was becoming powerful in sports like swimming, track, and billiards.

For the first time, female athletes were being celebrated almost as much as male ones. A new era in women's sports had dawned with a new generation of women, and they were now playing everything from golf to basketball. Readers couldn't get enough of the exploits of the top swimmers, tennis players, and golfers, even though most of them were amateurs swaddled in layers of clothing and playing for little more than silver cups.

The swimmers held big promise, and the approaching summer would bring them both public fame and disappointment. But on the tennis circuit, a frenzy surrounded the first—and only—meeting of American tennis player Helen Wills with Suzanne Lenglen, the Frenchwoman who had already won six times at Wimbledon and five times in the French Championships and hadn't lost a match in five years.

Wills, known as "Little Miss Poker Face" for her unemotional style on the court, had some pedigree of her own. She won a gold and silver medal in the 1924 Olympics and, at the age of twenty, was already a three-time defending U.S. Open champion and the unquestioned queen of the game in her home country, where she played attired in skirt, hose, and hat. Wills would go on to win eight Wimbledon singles titles of her own, losing only once on the grass in England.

It would be another half century before Billie Jean King would play Bobby Riggs, but the papers were so taken by Wills that they were already speculating what might happen if a woman played a man.

"In the case of Miss Wills, there probably are not more than six men who could consistently defeat her on the courts," one columnist opined.

With the United States in the midst of Prohibition, the match took on the qualities of good versus evil, with the virtuous American woman taking up a noble cause against a French opponent who was known not only for her dramatic overtones but for liking to take a nip or two during a match.

The match took place in Cannes, France, on February 16 in the finals of the Carlton tennis tournament. The pairing caused such a frenzy that workers spent the night putting up temporary bleachers, and people hired others to stand in line when the ticket window opened at 8:00 A.M. to get seats. Others leaned out of nearby windows or stood on rooftops to see the two greatest players of their time go after each other.

A week earlier, British bookies had made it 5–1 that Lenglen would beat Wills should they meet, but after watching the California woman in the semifinals, they lowered the betting to 2–1. Wills impressed them by coming back from being down 4–1 in the first set to win her semifinal with aggressive play, while Lenglen complained her way through a semifinal win of her own, which proved totally uninteresting to the gathered crowd.

The final had a World Series feel to it, with women nearly fainting when some four thousand people rushed for their seats as the gates opened, while thousands more stood outside just to listen. A hundred photographers crowded around the court while police struggled to keep order and fans chattered between themselves and cheered every shot. The noise greatly irritated Lenglen, who took it upon herself several times to order the crowd to keep quiet.

Wills played strongly from the start, grabbing the lead in the first set before dropping it 6–3, then opened the second set by winning four of the first five games. Lenglen struggled to regain the momentum and her poise, stopping several times between games to take frequent sips of champagne on the sidelines. She began to cough after losing the fourth game of the set, dramatically placed a hand over her heart, and went to the sidelines, where she took a long drink of cognac. Properly fortified, she won the next three games and ended up taking the set and the match, by a score of 8–6.

While the French celebrated, the loss stunned a country that, spurred by its success at the 1924 Olympics, was beginning to gain a strut and belief that Americans were the best in everything. Indeed, most American writers told of Wills putting up a strong fight against a nervous opponent and losing only because of the crowd and the linesman. They predicted that Lenglen would have little chance if she came to the United States to play Wills in the U.S. Open. (Lenglen, whose last singles loss came in 1921 at the Open, would turn pro later that year and never play in the tournament again.)

On one side of the pond at least, there was a need to set things straight in the world order, and America looked to its female swimmers to do just that. It was, after all, the year of the woman, with 2 women governors in office, along with 3 congresswomen and 150 members of state legislatures. The numbers may have been small, but they were remarkable, considering women had only won the right to vote six years earlier and that they were still frowned upon for smoking or wearing a bathing suit on the beach.

The suffrage movement had been founded on more basic ideals, with little thought given to sports. But it had ushered in both new thoughts and a new breed of women. They were freed of the shackles of old, when women had been deemed too fragile for sport or, if they did participate, were expected to develop muscles like men. These were women like the pioneer swimmers of the WSA, who helped change attitudes around the country toward the role of women in sports.

It was easy to see why the Deauville Casino and Hotel was so eager to sign Ederle and Riggin for the winter. Ederle was by far the best swimmer of her time, while Riggin was both an accomplished swimmer and a fancy diver, and having the two of them around the hotel pool every day would draw much-needed crowds to this out-of-the-way resort. The move to Florida also made sense for Ederle, who could train in the hotel pool and the warm waters off the Florida coast through the winter for her next attempt at the Channel.

The Deauville was a palatial hotel and casino built by Joseph Eisener, who recognized the need for some star power for his new resort. The Florida real estate boom was at its peak, but there was nothing like champion swimmers and bathing suit photos to get New Yorkers tired of sleet and snow to hop on the train and head south.

The Deauville had what was billed as the largest swimming pool in Florida, 165 feet long and 100 feet wide, located behind the hotel rooms by the ocean. It was there that Ederle would put on swimming exhibitions and Riggin would wow vacationers with her expert dives. The two American stars were now pros at a time when being an amateur was considered a virtue and there was something unseemly about women taking money for sports. Ederle, who tended not to think deeply about such things, didn't seem to mind much, but Riggin hated the fact that she had to put on shows to make a living.

Ederle and Riggin would hang out by the pool all day, greeting people and giving small swimming and diving exhibitions. A full band in dress uniform played every day for the amusement of vacationers, and on some nights the swimmers would have dinner in the large and elegant dining room. Riggin spent many of her evenings out on dates, sometimes on double dates with breaststroker Eleanor Coleman, but Ederle had little interest in joining them.

The casino got its money's worth out of the swimmers, who posed for pictures that were often seen in the New York tabloids. The rage at the time was to wear beach pajamas over swimsuits, and Ederle was shown in one picture on the beach with Riggin and Coleman, all of them wearing what looked like Chinese smoking robes. Ederle was enjoying herself, but she was itching to do some real swimming outside the pool, so she jumped at the chance to enter the first Miami marathon in February, a race from the Hialeah bridge to the Royal Palm Yacht Basin on the Miami

River. It drew a field of twenty-one, and the rich of Miami came out in lavishly decorated yachts filled with bathing beauties to accompany the swimmers.

Ederle showed them she was just as good as a pro as she was as an amateur in her first race where there was more than just a trophy at stake. She swam the eight miles in two hours and three minutes, seven minutes ahead of the next-best finisher, and did it with an ease that amazed *Miami Herald* sportswriter Stanley Zaring.

Zaring wrote that Ederle won the women's trophy, though he failed to mention in his report that she also beat the men. Impressed, though, he said she "seemed to slide through the water with little or no effort. She faced the waves with the same determination that characterized her courageous battle with the elements in the Channel."

Ederle wasn't quite used to the whole pro thing yet, and it cost her. She was so pleased with the win that she forgot not only to pick up her trophy but the five hundred dollars in cash that went to the winner. After a friend reminded her, she finally went back to get the money, but by now it was long gone.

"I learned quickly to correct this fault after a few months of professionalism," Ederle said.

The five hundred bucks wasn't her only worry. Though she was enjoying the benefits of being outside in the sun, which helped keep her tanned and fit, she was hearing rumors that the casino wasn't doing well, and she began worrying whether it would come up with the promised money for her swim. The Florida real estate bubble was on the verge of bursting, and the Deauville in Miami Beach was too far for people even in Miami to go to, especially during Prohibition, when they couldn't get a drink. (The Deauville was badly damaged later that year in a hurricane, which spelled the end of the Florida boom of the 1920s.) If the casino was having trouble—and one look around the lightly populated grounds was enough to indicate that was the case—how could it come up with the money for her swim?

The thought wasn't far from her mind when, by chance, one afternoon she met one of the most prominent personalities of the elite of

New York society that gathered at the club. Dudley Field Malone was an international divorce attorney who knew how to handle a spurned wife but knew nothing about swimming. He did know an opportunity when he saw one, though, and he saw one in the teenager who had grabbed the country's attention only a few months earlier.

Malone got his chance to exercise that opportunity when Ederle asked him to advise her on how to protect her contract with the club. Malone suggested that she permit him to secure a release from the contract and that he would personally guarantee the five thousand dollars in expenses for the swim. Trudy took the offer to her father, who told her he would pay the entire amount instead. She argued that it was an uncertain gamble, but Henry Ederle insisted he had lost a great deal more in his now-thriving butcher shop over the years and had no qualms about taking a chance on his own daughter. In the end, it was decided that the two men would split the cost, and Dudley drew up an unusual contract, in which Trudy became an "infant" by law to her "Uncle Dudley" for the purposes of the swim.

The pairing with Malone was certainly a curious one, this teenager who had no clue about business or contracts suddenly becoming partners with a dapper lawyer of Irish descent who had a taste for fashion and made his living separating rich divorcées from their money. Malone also moved in top political circles, and he had made a reputation the year before as one of the lawyers who defended John T. Scopes in the famous "Monkey Trial."

Malone, who teamed with Clarence Darrow during the epic showdown, gave what was widely considered the greatest speech of the trial in defense of academic freedom, including the soon-to-be-famous quote: "I have never learned anything from any man who agreed with me." Malone wasn't the featured attorney in the trial, but he was seen often on newsreels and his speech was featured prominently in newspapers that carried his words into homes across the nation.

Malone had also been a campaigner in the women's suffrage movement, and he was the only male leader in the final drive for passage of the national suffrage amendment in 1920. More important to the parched in

New York was that he was active in campaigning against Prohibition, beginning a year after its enactment to its eventual repeal. Malone was wearing none of those hats in Florida, however, where he had come to enjoy the new casino and the sun, only to find even more enjoyment watching the performances of the young swimming stars. Malone knew who Ederle was, of course, and had heard her blame Wolffe on WOR radio after her failed attempt to swim across the Channel. He also knew that he had a potential star on his hands, someone who could bring him far more return than the few thousand dollars he was willing to risk on her swim.

With the money now in hand, Ederle called Meg in New York and asked her to help make arrangements for a trip overseas, which this time would also include her sister and her father. Ederle then sent another letter to Burgess in England, asking him to make arrangements for her return there in the summer.

Malone, meanwhile, went looking for some place to lay off his action. He hadn't become rich by betting on long shots, and there didn't seem a whole lot of upside to him laying out thousands of dollars in the hope Trudy would accomplish the seemingly impossible. Unfortunately, not a lot of other business types thought so, either, and as Trudy's sailing date got nearer, Malone was getting increasingly desperate to find another backer. He finally found the perfect partner in the New York *Daily News* and the *Chicago Tribune,* both of which agreed to put up $5,000, plus another $2,500 if Trudy made it across. In exchange, Malone granted the news syndicate exclusive stories and photos of everything Trudy did from the time she set sail for France until she stepped foot in the water to make her second attempt to cross the Channel.

Trudy had yet to sail and Malone had already doubled his money on her swim.

Malone had good reason to be careful. The odds were still against anyone swimming the Channel, but they were even longer against a woman. Opinion was split among newspapermen, with many dismissing the possibility that Ederle or any other woman had either the strength or endurance to make it across. Others grudgingly admitted she had a chance, though for reasons that were sometimes hard to comprehend.

Among those was Sullivan, who wrote in his "Sports Whirl" column that Ederle just might make it because she lacked imagination and "a swimmer who was highly imaginative would never attempt the Channel swim a second time after a disastrous experience."

Following that logic, Sullivan compared Ederle to the popular boxer Paul Berlenbach, a friend of Ederle's who, like her, came from German stock. Sullivan said both the swimmer and the boxer had courage and endurance but that both lacked the imagination to scale great heights. "The lack of imagination and courage are so closely allied that it is hard to tell where one starts and the other ends," he wrote.

If Trudy was reading, she wasn't listening. She was brimming with a confidence that Sullivan could only imagine as she signed her contract with the *Daily News–Chicago Tribune* syndicate and got on the *Berengaria* to head overseas. She had reason to be confident, too, after shattering her own world record in the 150 meters three days before she set sail. She was not only wiser after her swim from the previous year but in peak swimming shape and more dominant in the water than ever.

This time, things were going to be different. She was not going to allow anyone to pull her out of the Channel, and she was determined to make that clear to everyone around her. She might fail, but if she did, she was going to do it on her own terms.

The Channel was going to be crowded in the summer of 1926, with swimmers from around the world drawn by the attention paid to Ederle's near miss the year before. A veritable League of Nations would gather on both sides, with its members hoping to bring glory to both themselves and their respective countries by navigating the small but tricky stretch of water between England and France.

The most startling difference this summer was the number of women who couldn't wait to get overseas to make the attempt and make history at the same time. The thinking seemed to be that if Ederle had become such a national sensation merely by trying, imagine what would happen if a woman actually joined the exclusive club of those who had made it across. The biggest threat seemed to come from Corson, a Danish native, who, like Ederle, had already attempted the swim once and knew what to expect. Three years earlier, she had tried to swim from France to England, only to be forced to quit just two miles off the coast when a treacherous tide forced her back after more than fifteen hours in the water. But Corson was more than just experienced. She was an excellent swimmer who, much like Trudy, was filled with determination and inspired by a goal. She was also the mother of two, a fact she never ceased to mention and one that brought her a lot of attention in the tabloids.

Corson was a woman with big dreams, which had been put on hold after her first attempt, when she had her second child and was forced to concentrate on motherhood instead of swimming. She was the wife of the deputy superintendent on the USS *Illinois*, part of the New York State Naval Militia based at the foot of West Ninety-sixth Street in the Hudson River, and worked part-time as a swimming instructor for the men on the ship.

Corson was well-known in Denmark before she ever came to the United States, running her own swimming school at the age of sixteen and being decorated three times by King Christian for saving lives in the water. She emigrated to the United States in 1919, where she was awarded the Carnegie medal for heroism after saving another life. But she had her eye set on starring as a swimmer, not as a rescuer.

"I came to America to do some big swims," she told the *New York Times*. "It was funny, very funny, to come to this big country where nobody knew me; at home all people know who I am, a big swimmer in a country where there are many. For the women of Denmark are not like American women; they are big, heavy built and very strong."

Corson's first big splash in America was a swim around the island of Manhattan, one she undertook after standing near the Hudson River one day, looking at the water, and asking a passerby how far he thought it went. She didn't even know at the time that water encircled the island, and she had no idea it was forty-two miles around it. Corson went down to the *Illinois* the next day to ask the ship's commander for help in mapping the river and finding out more about it. He referred her to Lt. Clemington Corson, who went to great lengths both to teach her the river and to win her affections at the same time.

She would make the swim in just fifteen hours and fifty-seven seconds, and later that year she did a trudgeon crawl from Albany to New York City, a span of 153 miles, which she made in sixty-three hours and thirty-five minutes, stopping only at night to sleep. Accompanying her in a rowboat was Lieutenant Corson, who would later succeed in his pursuit and marry this woman he so fancied. Despite the marriage and two children, she was committed to her swimming and was not content to live her life sitting at home as a housewife and mother.

While most swimmers trained merely by taking dips in the water or long walks through the woods, Corson hired a personal trainer to get her ready for her second Channel attempt. Louis Liebgold, a champion heel-and-toe walker and physical-training director on the USS *Illinois*, put together a detailed exercise plan that included plenty of heel-and-toe walking to strengthen her legs. It helped that his pupil not only was a sturdy five-foot-five, 168-pound athlete but that she didn't smoke or drink and preferred vegetables to anything else on the dinner table.

It was through Liebgold that Corson came upon a sponsor for a summer overseas, an expense that was out of reach for the wife of a naval officer with a meager income. Liebgold had been training lightweight champion Benny Leonard at the country estate of L. Walter Lissberger, chairman of the board of the Malcom Tire Company, and he introduced Corson to Lissberger and told him of her plan to swim the Channel. Lissberger was so taken with Corson that he agreed to give her three thousand dollars for the trip. But he wasn't done there. In addition to investing in her swim, Lissberger invested in her chances of making it across by putting five thousand dollars down at 20–1 odds with Lloyd's of London. If Corson proved successful, the tire magnate would be not only the proud sponsor of a Channel crosser but another one hundred thousand dollars richer himself.

Corson wasn't the only other contender heading overseas with a résumé. A Baltimore swimmer by the name of Lillian Cannon was so eager to become the first woman to swim the Channel that she became the first to sail to France, arriving in mid-May to train with Burgess, who—unknown to Ederle—had agreed to take both her and Ederle as his charges for the summer.

Like Ederle, Cannon came from a family of swimmers and was the youngest of three sisters who competed in various meets on the East Coast. She had limited experience when it came to long distances, but the summer before she had swum from Tolchester to Bay Shore in Chesapeake Bay to test her endurance and ability to endure cold water. She made it in eleven hours and announced right after she got out of the water that she would be swimming the English Channel the following year.

The twenty-three-year-old blonde from Chesapeake Bay was also a pro, having lost her amateur standing in 1922 on a bit of a technicality when she became the only woman lifeguard at Bay Shore, a beach near Baltimore. This actually proved helpful for Cannon, who came from a family with limited means, because it freed her both to make and accept money for her skills in the water.

Like Ederle, Cannon had some newspaper backing of her own. The NEA Service, an agency that distributed feature articles to newspapers around the country, agreed to fund Cannon in exchange for her writing byline stories for the agency and for exclusive access to anything she did overseas. The arrangement was particularly good for the agency because its member newspapers could all trumpet the fact that they were backing Cannon, conveniently failing to mention that they were doing so as a cooperative and not through any individual effort on their own.

Thus, while Ederle was sponsored by the New York *Daily News* and the *Chicago Tribune*, Cannon was backed by newspapers like the *Sheboygan* [Wisconsin] *Press* and the *Baltimore Post*. Readers in those places assumed it was the hometown newspaper that was sponsoring the swimming, and they cheered on every bit of news that came from France about their new favorite swimmer.

Like Ederle, Cannon went south for the winter to get ready for the Channel, spending several months at Daytona Beach and swimming long distances in the ocean to prepare herself. She was accompanied most of the time by her two dogs, Chesacroft Drake and Chesacroft Mary Montauk, who seemed to like the water just as much as she did, and who would board the liner *Volendam* with her to head for France. There were reports that the two large dogs, who had grown up diving for waterfowl on the Chesapeake Bay, would swim the Channel with her doggy-style.

"If I fail," Cannon told friends, "at least my dogs might win."

Cannon wasn't alone among the possible contenders. Lillian Harrison was also expected to be back for another try at the Channel, despite her protestations from the year before, as was Jeanne Sion, who was now almost fifty. Mercedes Gleitze, the London typist who twice the previous year made it just a few miles into the Channel, was also said to be preparing another attempt. Gleitze would later become famous for wearing a new type of waterproof watch by Rolex on one of her swims, but for now she was trying to become famous simply by becoming the first woman to make it across. The fact that she was British, as well as being female and a very capable long-distance swimmer, would make the British press pay even more attention to the Channel endeavors this season.

And finally there was Clarabelle Barrett, whose very appearance on the English side of the Channel caused quite a stir that summer. At six-three and weighing more than two hundred pounds, she was an imposing specimen who attracted stares and curious onlookers wherever she went. But she could swim in the open water, having learned from her father while growing up in New Rochelle, New York, on Long Island Sound.

Barrett, who had won several WSA meets as a youngster and was widely regarded as a top swimming talent, taught swimming at the newly opened Bronx High School. Newspapers saw little to gain by featuring this giant of a woman on their pages, and she got little publicity for her efforts. While Ederle and Cannon were being backed by newspaper syndicates and Corson had a tire magnate financing her swim, Barrett would go overseas with hat in hand. If it hadn't been for twenty friends contributing one hundred dollars apiece, she and her friend Grace Leister would not even have had enough money for the third-class passage to England. As it was, they barely had enough left over for a small room in Dover, so Barrett would have to try the swim from the more difficult English side because they couldn't afford the more expensive French accommodations at Cape Gris-Nez.

The thirty-two-year-old Barrett and her ever-present companion were two lonely women in a faraway land when they arrived in England on July 9 with a few suitcases and a letter of introduction to British Olympic coach Walter Brickett, who watched Barrett swim at Brighton and agreed to take a week off from work to train her. Brickett agreed to work on the cheap, but the mission would still be run on a shoestring. The woman didn't realize how much the swim would cost and there was no way they could afford $350 for a tug, so they ended up renting a small boat captained by a Dover man for $75 for Barrett's swim.

Across the Channel, conditions were quite different as Trudy frolicked. She had few worries, a professional trainer, and an escort in Helmy. She enjoyed outings to Paris, her family and friends were around, everything was paid for, and there were blissful weeks filled with walks and picnics. She was the youngest of the hopefuls, but she had all the advantages that money could buy, and all the experience of someone who had tried it once before.

But like most female athletes of her time, she always had one problem: She had to find something to wear.

3

Suited for a Swim

The summer of 1921 got off to a hot start in the tiny New Jersey beachfront town of Somers Point, where a social experiment of a most unlikely sort unfolded during the first week of June. At the center of it was the town's mayor, a seventy-two-year-old who was trying to have some fun with his bigger neighbor in Atlantic City and maybe put his town on the map at the same time.

After censors on the boardwalk opened the bathing season by demanding that women wear both skirts and hosiery as part of their bathing attire, Somers Point mayor Robert Crissye extended an open invitation to any woman who wanted to bathe on his city's beaches bare-legged and in a one-piece suit. Australian swimmer and vaudeville performer Annette Kellerman had popularized the daring look, which scandalized many.

The mayor didn't have to ask twice. More than one hundred women, tired of trying to swim in long woolen leggings and suits with skirts that bogged them down in the water, showed up that weekend in the provocative suits that were appearing in more and more stores but were rarely seen outside the home. With no bathhouses at the beach, many changed in cars with the curtains drawn or at the Bay View Hotel.

It wasn't long before pasty body parts were on display across Great Egg Harbor Bay, with forms of various shapes everywhere the casual eye could see. Traffic stopped on the main highway leading into the city, there weren't many men at church services, and gawkers came by the thousands to see in person what they had only been able to dream about seeing before. A thicket of trees lining the beach and the bridge between Somers Point and Ocean City was soon turned into an impromptu grandstand for the parade of beauty.

The Women's Republican League expressed outrage and immediately scheduled a meeting to figure out how to uphold local mores. Mary North Chenoweth, president of the league and the wife of a high school teacher, declared, "We will permit nothing here that they do not allow in Atlantic City. Somers Point wants nothing immodest."

The next day, William Tanguy, a retired Philadelphia manufacturer who owned a large estate near the bathing district, said he would be willing to be appointed the official censor for the beach and would expect no pay.

"Although I'm 70 years old, I'm still able to see right well without the aid of glasses," he told the *New York Times*. "I understand the city has no funds available to pay for the services of a censor for the beach. I'll take the job for nothing."

Tanguy indicated he had his own idea about what would be permissible to wear, saying, "I'm not in favor of restricting the girls too much in their swimming togs."

The year before had been a big one for women, who had won not only the right to vote—courtesy of the Nineteenth Amendment—but the right to smoke on most beaches, though the question of how much they should cover up while sunning themselves or going on a swim continued to draw controversy. Local authorities in beach towns met in the spring months to discuss what to allow, and most erred on the side of caution and opted for full leggings and skirts for women.

The controversy was not new; in fact, it had been raging for years as women sought a way they could go to the beach and actually swim instead of just wade into the water. The issue was a seasonal one and had been put on the back burner while the suffrage movement put its energy into more pressing concerns. But it wasn't going to go away, particularly as women began exploring their talents in various athletics and swimming became a sport they could participate in.

A prominent Chicago doctor had tested the mores of the time a few years earlier only to be arrested when she refused to wear a skirt with her bathing suit while swimming on a city beach. Rosalie M. Ladova, an expert swimmer, was accustomed to wearing a heavy two-piece suit with full bloomers, but this time she laid her skirt on the water's edge and swam into the lake, followed by a lifeguard, who told her to put the skirt on or she would be hauled in.

"Men have absolutely no right to go around with their limbs bare and compel women to wear cumbersome suits," she said. "The system is wrong. Men and women should bathe separately but women should not be persecuted when they dress as comfortably as men do."

Ladova planned to make her arrest a test case of the law covering indecent exposure, which was widely interpreted at the time to draw the line at anything that even hinted at the possibility of skin or body form underneath. But she was swimming upstream against an America that still had puritanical ideas about women and their place in society.

It would be seven more years before the doctor and those of her gender were even given the right to vote, and while titillating to some, the idea of women walking around in public not covered by all sorts of billowing material was as shocking to most as the sight of a flapper girl in her short skirt.

Credit an Australian with both shocking America's mores and helping to change them. Annette Kellerman began swimming because of rickets she contracted as a baby, and she would go on to become one of the top swimmers of her time, but it was what she wore as much as what she did in the water that made her both famous and infamous around the world.

Kellerman had two things that men of the time admired: She could swim like a fish, and she had a body that was not only easy to look at but one she was not afraid to show. That by itself didn't cause all that much of a stir in classless and anything goes Sydney, but when Kellerman took her act on the road, she found out that people in other parts of the world weren't quite so open-minded.

Kellerman grew up wanting to be a ballerina, but as her talent in the water became more apparent, so did her career path. While women in the United States were still desperately trying to stay afloat in preposterous garments that limited them from doing much else, she swam ten miles on the Yarra River at the age of seventeen, gaining wide attention for making what was billed as the longest swim ever by a woman. With Australia in the midst of a depression and her musician parents unable to sustain their once-comfortable lifestyle, Kellerman began supporting the family by performing dives and exhibition swims around the country. The Melbourne Exhibition Hall paid her ten pounds a week to display her talents in its aquarium, and it was there that Kellerman mastered the double-armed trudgeon, a version of the Australian crawl, which made her so much faster than the men, who were still relying on the breaststroke to propel them.

More importantly for her future career, though, was that she, like many Australian swimmers of the time, abandoned the wool stockings and revealed her bare thighs in her shorter one-piece suit.

Kellerman did well in her exhibitions, but the money was limited in Australia, so her father decided to take her to England, where, he hoped, she would find success in vaudeville. To establish her credentials, he devised a plan in June 1904 for her to swim the Thames River from Putney to Blackwall, a distance of twenty-six miles. The gimmick worked when Kellerman came through against great odds, a feat that landed her on the front pages of most London newspapers the next morning.

Knowing a good thing when they saw it, editors at the *Daily Mirror,* England's first newspaper to have pictures instead of illustrations, offered her eight guineas a week to swim along the coast six days a week. The editors knew, of course, that pictures of Kellerman in her risqué one-piece suit would sell newspapers, and indeed she was featured daily in the *Mirror*'s pages as "the Australian Mermaid."

Though her father complained to the editors that the daily swims would be far too rigorous, they assured him by saying, "This will be the greatest campaign ever launched about a young girl." And it was, with the swims proving such a sensation that crowds who lined the beach to see her had to be cordoned off by police.

When her two-month contract expired, the newspaper came up with another audacious idea to showcase both Kellerman's ample talents and her eighteen-year-old body. She would try to break the men's record of swimming twenty-four miles from Dover to Margate on the English Channel, something most thought impossible for a woman.

With Jabez Wolffe training her, she not only broke the record but caused such a stir that huge crowds lined the beach and cliffs at Margate to anxiously await her arrival.

By now, Kellerman was in great demand at every swimming club in London, and one of the places she was asked to perform was the Bath Club, a resplendent pool with a domed glass ceiling, frequented by only the best of British high society. When the Duke and Duchess of Connaught were scheduled to watch one of the exhibitions, though, an official at the Bath Club paid Kellerman a visit at home and requested she not appear in front of royalty in a bathing suit that showed her bare legs.

Kellerman argued that stockings were now passé in Australia, but the official wouldn't budge, so she compromised and bought a pair of stockings to cover up. When she tried the outfit on for her father, though, there was still a gap between the suit and stockings that showed a few inches of skin. So she went back to the store and bought the longest pair of stockings she could find, then sewed them on to the bottom edge of the suit.

The result was nothing short of sensational.

Kellerman appeared in a black suit, which clung so tightly to her that it showed every curve of her quite curvaceous body, giving the royal crowd something to get excited about while at the same time giving them no reason to be offended over the showing of any skin. She had stumbled on an idea that would not only further her career but benefit any woman struggling with the idea of what to wear in the water.

Kellerman would later add to her stature by finishing third against men in a race up the Seine River in Paris, but though she was now the toast of Europe, she still wasn't making a lot of money. That would change when the *Daily Mirror* agreed to sponsor her in the 1905 Webb Memorial Channel Race, thought up by newspaper executives to celebrate both her feminine attributes and the thirtieth anniversary of Webb's first swim across the Channel. No one had been able to swim the Channel since Webb, who died in 1883 in an ill-fated attempt to swim Niagara Falls, but the newspaper trumpeted its lineup as having the best chance to get across. If they did, they would be bucking long odds and the failures of many swimmers who, beginning about the turn of the century, decided it was their time to match Webb's feat.

There were only five contestants, including two who would figure in Ederle's Channel exploits two decades later. Burgess and Wolffe joined Kellerman, Montague Holbien, and Horace Mew in the swim from Dover across the Channel. Kellerman's deal with the paper called for her to be paid a significant lump sum for the first three hours plus an additional amount, depending on how many hours she lasted in the Channel. No one expected her to last long, but the newspaper editors didn't really care because they knew it would be long enough to get photographs of her now famous body in the next day's editions.

The buildup to the swim was intense, and the swimmers seemed intent during their training on making it across. The *Daily Mirror* chronicled all the efforts, including a chance meeting one day in the sea between Burgess and Kellerman, who shook hands and wished each other luck while treading water. Burgess, who six years later would become the second man to cross the Channel successfully, told the newspaper that Kellerman seemed to make her way through the water with little effort using her double-armed stroke and was the most disciplined swimmer he had ever seen.

For the men, what to wear posed no problems. They would be allowed to swim nude, as was the custom for Channel swimmers, covered only in a layer of grease, should they choose. Though Kellerman had crossed one barrier with her one-piece suit, the Brits had their limits, and she had to wear her suit, which, she would later say, badly chaffed her arms. That was the least of her problems, though, for she ran into a westerly tide and became seasick several hours into the race while battling the waves. She was eventually taken from the water after about six hours, nauseous and exhausted by the entire ordeal.

Not making it to France was nothing to be ashamed of, because none of the men made it, either. Kellerman would later try to swim the Channel two more times—reportedly naked on her final attempt, when she was in the water for ten hours and had the French coastline in sight before collapsing—but would never be able to master this stretch of water.

Having titillated England for much of a year, Kellerman set her sights on bigger things. In 1907, she was invited to the United States to appear at the White City Amusement Park in Chicago, where she performed in the diving pool and put on fifty-five shows per week. Her stay there was so successful that she was asked to sign with the largest amusement park in the world, Wonderland, which was built for one million dollars and took up twenty-five acres at the tip of Revere Beach, just north of Boston.

It was there that she changed the course of women's swimwear in America.

Kellerman hadn't been in an ocean since arriving in the States, so her manager encouraged her to go to Revere Beach for a swim to limber up and get a feel for the water. But the minute she set foot on the beach in her one-piece suit, her legs bare, other modest bathers shrieked and she was quickly surrounded by a large crowd. A policeman demanded to know what she was doing in a suit that was smaller than any he had ever seen.

"You don't expect me to go for a three-mile swim in a bathing costume like those over there," she replied.

The policeman apparently did, and Kellerman was promptly arrested and made to appear in court on a charge of public indecency. Once there, Kellerman, who saw herself as both an entertainer and a health crusader, took full advantage of her platform. She told the judge that swimming had cured her of a crippling disability and that someday every hospital in the United States would have its own pool, impressing him so much that he decided against fining her or putting her in jail. However, he sternly told her, from now on she had to wear a robe on the beach when she wasn't in the water.

Kellerman's court appearance was great fodder for the newspapers, and the publicity was perfect for her show at Wonderland, which now advertised her with the tag line "When the robe came off, the police moved in." America was still prudish, but she got so much favorable publicity from the scandal that she was allowed to design the first "modern bathing suit"—a unitard that resembled a tight-fitting skirt that came down to just above the knees over the existing bathing suit, an early form of the modesty panel that would be used in swimsuits well into the 1960s.

Paul Gallico, the sportswriter, remembered it as a slightly bulky affair, even though it was sleeveless and didn't have a separate skirt. "Nevertheless," he wrote, "it made the question of how ladies were put together no longer a matter of vague speculation."

And put together, Kellerman was. She was deemed the perfect woman when Harvard professor Dudley Sargent compared her vital statistics to those of the Venus de Milo, and there was no man who saw her who was going to argue the professor's point. Kellerman would go on to a long career on Broadway, drawing shocked women and ecstatic men to watch her—as smooth and glistening as a seal performing in a glass tank on the stage of the old Colonial Theatre, and later at the Hippodrome, demonstrating her vast and ample talents. She was the highest-paid women athlete in vaudeville, making $1,250 a week touring and giving exhibitions. She is considered not only the inventor of the modern suit but the mother of synchronized swimming.

Though the "Annette Kellerman" suit was available, it took a generation before it was embraced by most American woman. That was partly because of the vigilance of local authorities who didn't want the immorality of naked legs on their beaches, and partly because the idea of women competing in athletic endeavors, such as running and swimming, was still the subject of much debate.

Skirts and bloomers still predominated until the end of the war years, though progress was being made. Sleeves were getting shorter on the "pouter pigeon" chest–shaped costume that predominated from 1910 until 1919. Still, the battle was waged around the country every summer, with both men and women who were determined to bathe in as little as possible finding themselves up against local officials equally determined to enforce the morality of the times. More often than not, the epicenter was at the beach, and things usually got hotter as the days got longer.

Authorities in Queens began a campaign against immodest suits in 1915, worried that bathers were taking advantage of lax supervision, even though it was reported by the *New York Times* that it "grieved them to do so." Five men were arrested in Rockaway for wearing bathing costumes that didn't overlap at the waist, and half-a-dozen women were sent scampering to the bathhouses to cover up with skirts no higher than three inches above the knee.

On July 25 of that year, with 330,000 people crowded into Coney Island on a sweltering Sunday, two men were arrested for walking around in improper bathing suits, and police went around with measuring tapes to make sure skirts were of the proper length. Meanwhile, there were reports that the boardwalk in Atlantic City was blocked by crowds watching a score of men who appeared in bathing suits while carrying dainty multicolored parasols to mock the enforcement campaign.

In a desperate effort to uphold the modesty of his beach, Queens sheriff Samuel Mitchell would swear in a score of women for duty in the Rockaways that summer. They were named the "Sheriffettes," and their duty was to watch out for both gambling and bathing suits that might offer a glimpse of skin if looked at from just the right angle.

Gallico would look back on it later and say that the country was filled with "heavy-handed hypocritical, censorious prudes" who couldn't understand that while much of the appeal of wearing less was visual, a lot was practical, too.

"We had but recently emerged from the age of the long-stockinged, full-skirted, bosom-swaddling bathing costume, the most ridiculous collection of woolen garments ever to conceal the female form divine," he said. "Men looked silly enough in their long drawers and half-sleeved candy-striped jersey tops, but it was the women, dressed, apparently, more for going down into a mine than entering the sea, who really took the cake."

The tide of the battle appeared to shift in 1921, the same year that the residents of Somers Point were inundated by bathers in suits that didn't show all but showed plenty more than anyone had ever seen before. By then, even local authorities were realizing the absurdity of rules on some beaches, such as the ones in Long Beach, New York, where the chief of police said not only would everyone have to wear two-piece suits but that any bald men who stared at women would get into trouble.

Across the country the same summer, fights over bathing suits turned into a riot at a crowded beach near Santa Monica, California, on the Fourth of July. Sheriff's officers had to come in to quell the disturbance, but it was becoming clear that things had changed and the new suits would not go away. A short time later, two weeks of warnings failed to stop arrests at Rockaway, when eighteen women and three men were taken into custody for not covering up. Six women and one man were pulled from a taxi and ordered to the police station, where they loudly protested their arrests and a large crowd gathered to cheer them on.

The defining blow, though, was cast on the boardwalk, not the beach. In Atlantic City, they held the Inter-City Beauty Pageant, and some 150,000 gawkers jammed the boardwalk to see more than one thousand women in swimming apparel, most of them in one-piece suits.

Atlantic City was eager to make the pageant a success and spur tourism, so for two days the censor's ban on bare knees and skintight suits was suspended, and thousands of spectators gasped as they applauded the women. Kellerman was one of the hosts of the event, handing out trophies and samples of her swimwear, while Miss Washington, D.C., Margaret Gorman, won both the swimsuit contest and what would later become the first Miss America crown and its five-thousand-dollar prize.

In the midst of the bathing-suit revolution, the Women's Swimming Association was formed in New York City in 1917 by a scattering of young secretaries and career girls who made use of a small pool on the Lower East Side. Charlotte Epstein, a court stenographer, was the director, L. de B. Handley the coach, and their goal was to develop female swimmers and promote swimming as a sport, something that couldn't be done under the constraints and weights of the apparel women were supposed to swim in.

Both Epstein and Handley knew that if women were going to swim in the Olympics or make a name for themselves in races, they couldn't do it in the billowing skirts and sleeves that brought forward movement to a halt when waterlogged. Annoyed in 1919 that the Amateur Athletic Union—which just two years before had yielded to Epstein's demands and endorsed women's swimming as a sport—was still dictating costumes that showed no skin, Epstein staged a publicity stunt to force the AAU's hand. She got several tabloids to send photographers and reporters to a practice swim at Manhattan Beach, where she removed the stockings from the club's top swimmers, Ethelda Bleibtrey and Charlotte Boyle, causing them to be promptly arrested for public indecency.

While the girls weren't prosecuted, the spectacle did just what Epstein had intended it to do—bring attention to the problems of competing in bathing suits with stockings. After the newspapers splashed the story all over their front pages, the AAU relented and allowed swimmers to remove their stockings for competition as long as they quickly put on a robe once they got out of the water.

The publicity helped the WSA recruit more than three hundred swimmers in one month to join the one hundred who already swam at the club—a group that included Ederle and the top women swimmers of the time. The new swimmers would compete with the established stars for the rights to represent their country in the 1924 Olympics in Paris, where women would have five swimming events to compete in.

The New York tabloids, which knew a good photo opportunity when they saw one, wasted no time in giving the girl swimmers plenty of attention. But the rules were strict, and whenever there were photographers or even reporters at a meet, the swimmers would always have to put on capes quickly or get another suit to put over their silk racing suits the minute they got out of the water. In the case of the WSA, it would always be a black suit.

The women weren't always successful in this endeavor to cover up, because the photographers were almost as nimble as the swimmers, and a good photograph meant a lot. Newspapers discovered that where reproductions of nightclub cuties in leotards or tights might get them barred from the U.S. mail, photographs of women lined up at the end of the pool in wet, clinging one-piece garments were legitimate, even though far more revealing. Likewise, a big part of the great Florida real estate boom in the early 1920s was built on photos of girl swimmers in the ads.

The tabloid wars made it de rigueur that a woman was featured somewhere in a swimming suit in almost every issue of every paper. So while they not only won and set records, the WSA swimmers also became beauty queens and celebrities equal almost in stature with those doing silent movies in Hollywood. Riggin, Bleibtrey, Martha Norelius, Helen Wainwright, and two sensational blondes, Georgia Coleman and Dorothy Poynton, became household names—at least among the men in those households—while Esther Williams and Eleanor Holm were also known for their beauty in a suit.

Ederle had more than her share of pictures in the tabloids, doing everything from demonstrating how she cooked at home to showing how she looked in a bathing suit. As she began rising in prominence, the papers wasted no excuse in trying to get her in a bathing suit for a picture. Short and sturdy, she wasn't pinup material, but she did have wholesome good looks that seemed to appeal to both the serious readers and the voyeurs.

Times were changing quickly. In just a few short years, Epstein got the AAU not only to accept women's swimming as a sport but to allow swimmers to wear suits they could compete in. Suddenly, swimming wasn't just something a woman did at the beach in the summer or when she fell into the water while sailing to keep from drowning. American girls were not only swimming; they were beginning to set records at almost every big meet, and Americans admired their spunk and their perseverance. More than anything, though, American men admired the women swimmers because they could see things they had never been able to before.

American women would compete in swimming in the 1920 Olympics for the first time, and they would do it mostly in the black silk racing suits of the WSA. The plan had been to wear the official uniform handed out by U.S. Olympic officials, but the female swimmers quickly vetoed that after finding out that it was made out of mercerized cotton, which was nearly see-through, and clung tightly to the body when wet. The suits also didn't have the modesty skirts used on the WSA suits, and the times hadn't changed so much that the swimmers were going to risk exposing themselves even more.

Bleibtrey won both the individual golds, while also anchoring the U.S. relay team to a third gold. The best female swimmers in the world were Americans, and the best American swimmers were members of the WSA.

Men were still watching closely, but now they were watching for other reasons, too. While ogling the swimmers' bodies, they discovered something else: These girls were good.

4

Swifter, Higher, Stronger

The mood was confident, bordering on cocky, among the young athletes on the SS *America* as it sailed from Hoboken, New Jersey, with its precious cargo, headed toward France. And why not, because the United States had never fielded an Olympic team as big and formidable as this, and it had never had a generation of athletes quite like this.

More than three hundred of them sailed for Paris, carrying the hopes of their country across the Atlantic to a continent that just a few years earlier had been enveloped in the Great War and was still trying to heal the scars that it had caused. The 1924 games weren't the first Olympics since the war (the games had been held in Belgium four years earlier), but they were the first with this new generation of young athletes, who had both the time and the opportunity to train for their sports.

The U.S. team was loaded with talent, from teenage tennis star Helen Wills to swimming ace Johnny Weissmuller, and, along with Great Britain and Finland, was favored to contend for the overall medal total. For the first time, there would be a significant number of women competing, though they were limited mostly to swimming, diving, fencing, and tennis.

One look around the deck was all it took to know this was no ordinary cruise to Europe. Crowded onto almost every open spot was an apparatus of some sort, and everywhere there was some form of sport breaking out. Boxers traded blows in a makeshift ring, wrestlers grappled on mats, and track and field athletes ran around the edge of the main deck to keep in shape as the ship slowly made its way to France.

The swimmers weren't left out, though this took a bit of ingenuity on the part of U.S. Olympic officials, who had a small canvas pool built on a platform on deck, where two swimmers at a time could practice their strokes. The swimmers did it by putting on what looked like large dog collars with a rope attached to them around their waists; the other end of the rope was anchored securely to logs in opposite corners of the pool. Swimmers joked that they felt like elephants in a bathtub, but the contraption did what it was meant to do by keeping them in one spot while they worked on their strokes to stay in shape. Handley, who coached much of what would become the women's team at the WSA pool in New York, was the women's coach and would stand on the side and tell swimmers how much distance they had left to cover and urge them to sprint in the final meters, even though they were going nowhere fast.

Each swimmer got two practice times a day on the ship, and Ederle's were at 11:00 A.M. and 4:00 P.M. She had only five minutes each time, and this was more to loosen her swimming muscles than to provide any real training. Handley wasn't about to tinker with the strokes of his team at this point, and the only instruction he gave his young charges was to do whatever they thought would work best to help them win.

The swimmers had it better than the divers, who had a low springboard to practice on, but no water deep enough to dive in other than the ocean, which, for obvious reasons, was off-limits. They were attached to ropes held by a man on each side so they could practice somersaults both forward and backward, but instead of diving into the small canvas pool, they would test the spring of the board by jumping in feetfirst.

Though the SS *America* wasn't a luxury steamer by any means, the method of travel was a relief for Riggin and Wainwright, both swimming and diving double threats who were part of the 1920 team, which had spent thirteen days getting overseas on the badly misnamed *Princess Matoika*. That ship had been anything but a steamer fitting royalty as it plied the Atlantic on its usual mission of resupplying the 350,000 troops in the Allied Expeditionary Force still in Europe after the war. On the return trips, it had carried the bodies of soldiers still being unearthed after the war.

Riggin would later talk about her mixed emotions after coming home victorious from the Antwerp games, where she won a gold medal and Wainwright captured the silver in springboard diving. As the victorious team boarded the ship, they watched, fighting back tears, as hundreds of caskets of American servicemen were loaded onboard.

In 1924, though, the terrible toll of the war was the last thing on the mind of this group of excited and frisky athletes, who bonded as a team on the trip over with potato races on deck and sing-alongs that went into the night. To keep order, Olympic head coach Lawson Robertson gave strict orders to the athletes that they were still "candidates" for the team and that their participation depended on them behaving themselves while onboard. Prohibition was now in its fourth year, alcohol was strictly forbidden on the ship, and the Olympians were expected to be in bed by 10:45 P.M. and up the next morning at 7:30.

The restrictions didn't much bother Ederle, who trained daily with teammates who had some remarkable credentials of their own, like Sybil Bauer and Mariechen Wehselau, the Hawaiian swimmer who held the world's record in the one-hundred-meter freestyle. Trudy tended to shy away from the group gatherings and could usually be found not in the middle of a group of athletes telling stories or singing, but sitting in a deck chair or in the ship's library, deep into one of her beloved mysteries.

There was no escaping the fact that the pressure was on Ederle, who was regarded as the world's best female amateur swimmer and almost a lock to win the three races she was entered in. She was as much a prohibitive favorite as was Weissmuller, who would swim in three events and also try for a fourth medal in water polo.

The Associated Press had a reporter on the trip and he sent a story to hundreds of newspapers back home via wireless that the team was looking for spectacular performances by Ederle and Weissmuller, both of whom, he reported, were in excellent condition. Handley went even further, saying he expected Ederle to shatter several world marks when she finally got to France.

Handley had a lot of reason to be optimistic. The new swimming suits, coupled with better training methods, meant records were falling at almost every meet, and between them, Weissmuller and Ederle had set nine of the eleven new marks recorded in 1923. Trudy herself had set twenty-two new freestyle swimming records in her young career, breaking her own records several times, and there was every reason to think that with the strong competition pushing her in Paris, she would not only win gold medals but lower the times in the new pool that had been specially constructed for the games.

"The heavier the odds, the greater rises Trudy's determination to win," Handley wrote in his pre-Olympic preview.

Ederle wasn't the only favorite on ship. U.S. athletes had a lot to live up to after the success of the 1920 games in Antwerp, where they had won forty-one gold medals, easily besting the number taken home by second-place Sweden, which had won seventeen. Swimmers had won eleven of fifteen possible golds, including three by Bleibtrey, who had won every race she'd entered. One of those wins was in the three-hundred-meter freestyle, a race run because Olympic officials felt at the time that women weren't strong enough to last in the four-hundred-meter freestyle the men were racing.

Bleibtrey had turned pro in 1922, leaving a gap that the 10 women swimmers on the 1924 team were more than eager to fill. These 10 were among only 136 women who would share the Olympic stage with 2,956 men, but they would make up for their small number by bringing home more than their share of medals for the favored team.

Among them were a pair of swimmers from the Illinois Athletic Club, trained by "Big Bill" Bachrach, who also trained Weissmuller and was serving as the men's Olympic swimming coach. Ethel Lackie was given a good chance to win a medal, as was Sybil Bauer, a twenty-year-old student at Northwestern.

Bauer had already made swimming history two years earlier, when she was the first woman to break a world's record held by a man. Bauer beat Stubby Kruger's 440-yard backstroke record of six minutes and twenty-eight seconds by four seconds, though the meet in Bermuda was not sanctioned and the record was never officially recognized.

Almost as important for most of the women aboard the SS *America* was that it seemed a perfect opportunity to do what women of the 1920s were supposed to do—size up and snare a good man to marry. But Epstein was keeping a close eye on her charges, who had the unfortunate luck to be the only members of the Olympic team who would be shepherded by chaperones from the time they left New York until they returned home. Romance was discouraged, and the young women were urged to keep their thoughts on swimming, something that was not always easy on a boat where able-bodied and handsome men outnumbered women nine to one.

Epstein, forty at the time, was thought of as an old lady by the young teens she was supervising, but they obeyed her every command nevertheless. An aggressive, behind-the-scenes administrator who knew how to bring talented people together, she was never one to back away from a fight—like the one she won in 1919 when she told her swimmers to take their stockings off, despite the risk of arrest.

It was also "Eppie" who played the crucial role in giving Wainwright and Riggin the chance to compete in the 1920 Olympics. The AAU had balked at taking the two fourteen-year-olds because of their age, but Epstein argued successfully with Olympic officials that they were plenty old enough not only to compete but to win.

"They didn't want to take children to the Olympics," Riggin said later. "They asked who would take care of us. But our club manager, Charlotte Epstein, went down there and said, 'What are you doing to these kids who worked so hard?' And we wound up going."

Epstein was also a strong fund-raiser, and the money she collected was needed, because she made sure her young swimmers always stayed in the best places and dined at the finest restaurants. Her swimmers followed her faithfully because they knew she always had their best interests at heart while wading through waters never charted before as the manager of a team of women athletes.

While the women were closely watched, some of the men were, too—but for different reasons. Weissmuller was the undisputed star of the men's team, and the unbeaten and gregarious swimmer was always willing to put on a show for the girls. While Ederle and Weissmuller were exact opposites in personality, both were cool and efficient record-setting machines in the pool, and there was little doubt onboard the ship that both were going to star in Paris.

Weissmuller had come off of the streets of Chicago with little except a magnificent body before being molded by Bachrach into a champion swimmer, but it was his personality as much as his talent and looks that drew both women and men to him. That showed on the second-to-last night of the nine-day voyage, when the athletes put on a talent show that was dominated by Hawaiian swimmers, who brought guitars and ukuleles to match their beautiful voices.

Not to be outdone, Weissmuller capped off the evening by jumping on a table and then hitching himself to a chandelier. As he swung in the air, he scratched his side and half-yodeled and half-yelped—Weissmuller hadn't had any voice lessons yet—so the athletes onboard remembered this high-pitched performance as a precursor to his Tarzan cry.

Though Weissmuller was easily the greatest male swimmer of his time, his coach would later tell Ederle that he didn't think Weissmuller could have swum the English Channel because he didn't have the mental concentration to spend that much time in tough waters.

It was a happy group that got off the ship in Cherbourg, France, lustily singing "Goodbye Broadway, Hello France" while a band from the nearby SS *Pittsburgh* played alongside. Crowds formed to get a peek at the famous American athletes and Frantz Reichel, the general secretary of the French Olympic Committee, declared, "This is the finest party of athletes I've ever seen in my life."

Not everyone was as excited to receive the Americans, though most of the French still had fond memories of the doughboys who had helped win the war. A man on a bike made the unfortunate mistake of shouting slurs at the team as they headed inland on the train, only to get it back tenfold and more by the testosterone-laden group of mostly male athletes. Weissmuller got so worked up by it all that he jumped off the train when it rumbled into the next station and pummeled the surprised cyclist until he was left bloodied in the tracks with his bicycle.

Weissmuller was brought before Olympic officials—and could have been disqualified immediately from the games—but his coach rallied behind him, as did the other athletes, and the Olympic Committee avoided the brouhaha that a disqualification would have caused. Weissmuller was allowed to swim in his upcoming events, but he was reprimanded and told that he had better behave—or else.

Weissmuller was known to his fellow athletes as happy-go-lucky and easygoing, so they were just as surprised as the officials by his outburst. But there may have been more behind his patriotic fervor than was known. In reality, Weissmuller was an immigrant himself, having been born in Freidorf (now part of Romania) in 1904, and he had been so worried about qualifying for the team because of his lack of citizenship that he'd fudged his papers by altering his younger brother's birth certificate, stating he'd been born in Pennsylvania in 1905.

Weissmuller was hardly alone in a nation of immigrants, though he would carry his secret all through his life. Although a bill was signed into law in 1924 that severely limited immigration, especially when it came to ethnic groups deemed undesirable, nearly one-third of Americans in the 1920s were either immigrants or first-generation offspring, including many of the athletes on board the SS *America.* Among those were swimmer Martha Norelius, who was born in Sweden, and Ederle, who was the daughter of German immigrants.

The trip toward Paris proceeded without further incident, though the American team would not be staying in the city itself, where some army barracks had been converted into the first real Olympic Village for athletes. Instead, they would stay at an estate in Rocquencourt, near Versailles, where Napoléon had fought his last battle a century before.

The women settled into two carriage houses on the estate, happy to be there and eager to get on with the business at hand.

The Olympics were about to begin, and the Americans couldn't have been more ready.

The tomboy who lived in a walk-up next to the butcher shop on Amsterdam Avenue wasn't much of a dreamer. She was a reluctant competitor at best, more worried about how she fit in than how she would do in a race. But she loved sports, including baseball and basketball, and liked to roller-skate through her West Side neighborhood in Manhattan. Most of all, she loved the water.

Gertrude Ederle found it early, and she found it often. As a three-year-old, she would race around the corner from her father's butcher shop to the local blacksmith and jump into the horse's trough before a relative, always following close behind, could pull her out. That fun ceased one day when a horse came up and raised his hoof at her in the trough, a near catastrophe that frightened her parents so much that they put an end to her wandering about.

Trudy, the third of six children, was born October 23, 1905. She gravitated to sports not only because she was naturally athletic but because she figured out early on that this was an easy way to make friends. It didn't matter that she beat those friends in almost everything they competed in; she was just happy to have them around.

Henry and Gertrude Ederle first discovered their daughter had a problem, which would plague her throughout her life, when one of her early teachers told them she wasn't hearing the lessons in class. Though her mother took her to several ear specialists, it was to no avail. Her hearing had been damaged by measles, and there wasn't a lot the medical experts at the time could do for her.

The handicap made her shy and self-conscious, and she kept to herself much of the time. But it brought her closer to her older sister, Meg, who would later play a big role in her swimming career and become her inspiration for trying to swim the English Channel. From the time she was a small child, Trudy idolized Meg and wanted to do anything that would please her.

Meg was with her in the spring of 1914 when Henry Ederle loaded the family on a steamer bound for Europe to visit his mother back home in Germany. The trip was a great success, except that Trudy, Meg, and sister Helen went on an adventure one day and walked the shaky plank that ran out to the town's dam. All three ended up in the water, bringing panicked folks running from the village, yelling that the American children were about to drown.

Despite the near disasters in the horse trough and in Germany, Trudy remained fascinated by water. That fascination grew the next year when her father bought a summer bungalow at Highlands, New Jersey, where the Shrewsbury River ran swiftly just off the porch. Trudy begged her father to put a rope around her waist and lower her over the edge into the river, and it was there that she did her first stroke, the dog paddle.

She immediately wanted more. She wanted to go fast. Trudy had seen the men from town swimming with an overarm stroke in the river; noticing how quickly they got through the water, she wanted to do that herself. She went off to practice, and in a few weeks' time she had learned to stay afloat and was challenging them in the water with a wild stroke that was ineffective and that the other swimmers found very humorous.

Summers from then on were spent in the river, with Trudy donning her bathing suit shortly after breakfast and not taking it off again until nightfall. But it wasn't until a few years later at the annual carnival that marked the end of summer in Highlands that a chance encounter would turn her summer fun into a more serious activity. After easily beating the other neighborhood children in a race, she drew the attention of a man whose daughter was a member of the WSA. The man suggested that she join the WSA, if for nothing more than to have a place to swim during the winter. Meg thought it was a good idea, and it wasn't long before the two, joined by their sister Helen, went over to the club and signed up with Eppie, paying the three dollars a year in dues.

Handley promptly asked her to swim the length of the pool alone to get an idea of what she could do in the water. Trudy was terrified, but she struck out with her wild arm-over-arm stroke—not even stopping to breathe—before finally making it to the end of the pool. Though she didn't hear well, she did manage to hear the club's diving instructor re-mark on her style to the coach.

"She'll never make a swimmer. She swims too wild," the woman told Handley.

It was a comment Trudy would never forget, one that would be with her the rest of her life. So angry at what she heard, she vowed right then and there to herself that she would become an expert swimmer if it was the last thing she ever did.

She had come to the right place for that. The WSA was already the center of competitive women's swimming, a sport that was becoming increasingly popular with the evolution of a bathing suit that made it easier to get through the water. The club's tiny indoor pool was more often as steamy as a sauna, there was no diving board, and the pool itself was shallow and no more than thirty feet long. But the dues were priced right and Handley, who had played water polo on the 1904 Olympic team, was volunteering his most capable services as a coach to the women swimmers. Handley hadn't been a speed swimmer, but he was a student of swimming and was particularly interested in coming up with a new stroke that would better the Australian crawl that everyone was doing at the time.

Handley, a gentleman's gentleman, would come to the pool dressed in a suit and tie, then invariably shed his jacket in the heat and humid-ity of the small room. His swimmers respected him because he treated everyone equally, whether they were championship contenders or raw swimmers with little technique like Trudy and her sisters.

Handley thought that the Australian crawl, in which swimmers did three kicks and then turned on their side to take a breath and do a scissors kick, could be improved. He practiced with swimmers doing various beats before settling on the six-beat crawl, which consisted of three kicks to each arm stroke. He then modified the arm stroke a bit and, in a move that changed swimming, had swimmers simply turn their necks and grab a gulp of air instead of turning on their side to breathe.

The finished product—and its eight-beat variation, which Ederle would use—became the American crawl, and Handley was its proud father.

The stroke would take his swimmers to world records and Olympic games and make him a recognized authority on the art of swimming over the next four decades. But Handley was also a believer in the true spirit of amateur sports and never took a penny for his efforts, nor did he think that any of his swimmers should take money for theirs. It didn't matter much at the time, because there was no real money for the sport anyway, and no real commercial appeal to anything the women might do other than pose for pictures in their one-piece suits.

Trudy was more than just diligent in practicing the new stroke. Determined to master it, she spent winters in the pool and summers in the Shrewsbury River doing just that. In February 1919, she swam her first race in the Sixtieth Street municipal pool, making the hundred yards in one minute and twenty-two seconds. By the next year, she had improved so much that she was sent to Detroit to compete in the Junior National Relay. Her teammates on the trip were Riggin, Wainwright, and Helen Meany, all of whom would go on to make names for themselves in the pool.

In Detroit, they faced the star team from the Detroit Athletic Club, but it was no contest. The WSA swimmers not only won the relay by more than a lap but also beat the adult girls and set a world's record in doing so. The time caused a sensation at the Detroit pool, with people standing and applauding the achievement of the New Yorkers, even though they had come to cheer on the home team.

The elder Ederles were busy trying to run a business and were hardly stage parents; in fact, they had little clue that their daughter was becoming so good, and they rarely went by the pool to see her swim. They were, however, quite strict, which meant Trudy had to apologize on several occasions for being late to practice because she had been doing the dishes at home. Fun and games were one thing, but chores were another, and Trudy had more than her share of cleaning, ironing, cooking, and dishwashing to do before she ever thought about practicing her new stroke.

In the summer of 1922, the Ederles were going back to Germany again to see relatives. But Trudy and her sisters would not make this trip, partly because Meg was planning to swim in the inaugural Joseph P. Day long-distance swim, which would test the best women swimmers of the time over a three-and-a-half-mile course from Manhattan Beach to Brighton Beach. Although Trudy didn't know it, her big sister wanted her to swim in the race, too.

Trudy was sixteen by now and had won several races, but she attracted little attention among the all-star cast of swimmers in the WSA. And she had yet to swim more than the 220-yard race competitively, even though she would swim for long distances in the Shrewsbury nearly every summer day. She was reluctant as ever to try anything new, but one day Meg insisted that she join her in the Day swim, much to Trudy's consternation.

It turned out that Trudy was trapped, and all because of a haircut. She wanted to have her hair bobbed that year and appealed to her father just before he left with her mother and younger brother on their trip to allow her to have it done. Pop Ederle was tying his shoes, ready to head out the door, and agreed without looking up. But there was a catch: He told her she must enter every major race that Meg entered that summer so she would keep occupied while they were gone in Europe. Trudy agreed, forgetting for a moment that one of those races was a three-and-a-half-mile swim that she felt totally unprepared for.

That would change, though, as she and Meg swam daily in the Shrewsbury, with Meg upping the distance a little more each time. Meg was a good swimmer herself, but she realized early on that her younger sister had a raw talent and would eventually surpass not only her but the rest of the swimmers, too. Meg filled out the entry form for Trudy and sent it in along with hers for a race that would change Trudy's life.

Wainwright was the American all-around champion and was considered the favorite, though British champion Hilda James had also been invited to compete, and Riggin and Doris O'Mara were also in the race. Newspapers described the competitors as the greatest women's swimming field ever assembled in one place. In all, fifty-two women struggled to line up with the rowboats that would accompany each of them on a cold rainy day in August 1922. Trudy was among them, though in the changing room beforehand she confided to Epstein that she just hoped to finish, even if it took her a week.

At the sound of a cannon shot, the women dived into the water, and the attention of the sporting press soon focused on Wainwright, James, and Riggin. At the half-mile point, when it appeared Wainwright had a slight lead over James, somebody in the press boat shouted out, "Out front! Who is that out front?"

A highly excitable WSA official gave him the answer. "My God! That's Ederle!"

Trudy was, in fact, ahead, and she never gave up the lead, even though the quick pace dictated that she would soon tire. Instead, her stroke seemed to get stronger as rain fell and she plowed through the rough waters. Spectators thought she couldn't last another 440 yards at the speed she was going, and Wainwright fought hard to overtake her, but Trudy was as determined to finish first as she was to learn the American crawl, and there was no stopping her as she swam on the home stretch into Brighton Bay.

Trudy's time of 1:01:34 ⅗ not only set a mark that stood for decades but obliterated the record set for both three-and-a-half miles and three miles. She did it by more than four minutes, beating Wainwright by forty-five seconds, while James and Riggin rounded out the top four. Meg ended up twenty-sixth, seventeen minutes back.

For the first time, Trudy had to talk to the press, a task that wasn't easy for someone who struggled in public and who was still so young. About all she managed to say was, "I did my best," though she didn't add what she really thought, which was that she had done it for her sister Meg.

The stunning win would prove to be a coming-out party of sorts for Trudy, who faced resentment from some of the other swimmers, who saw that she had been listed as a substitute in race entries and felt she had just gotten lucky. But if they weren't believers then, they were by the end of summer, when she would smash the women's 220 record set by Bleibtrey by twelve seconds, win a big race in the Brighton Beach pool, and then set a new world's record in the 440, breaking the old mark by seventeen seconds and beating both Wainwright and James in the process.

"Gosh, Gert, what have you got on your feet, propellers?" Wainwright asked her as she sat on the float at the end of the race, waiting for the other swimmers to finish.

Ederle collected a gold Amateur Athletic Union medal, a beautiful overnight bag, and a silver cup for beating the old world record by more than fifteen seconds. But she was collecting more than that as the swimming world took note of this wunderkind and began treating her with more respect for her abilities. The next summer, she began a streak of breaking her own records, and Handley himself offered rare praise for her in an article he penned for a New York newspaper. The raw swimmer he first saw flailing her way across the WSA pool was now ensconced as the most dominant athlete in her sport and there seemed nothing that Ederle couldn't do in the water.

"All doubt has been set aside concerning Gertrude Ederle's rights to title of 'All Around Champion Swimmer'—she is recognized as the greatest swimmer ever developed!" he wrote.

With success came expectations. Trudy could no longer sneak up on the field like she had in the Joseph P. Day swim, and now it was the other swimmers who had her in their crosshairs in every meet she entered. With success also came a lot more attention, and the demand for Trudy was great as she led a boom in the popularity of women's swimming across the nation. For Trudy, the first casualty was school. She quit after her sophomore year, leaving the books behind to pursue what was still very much an amateur career in swimming. Though she wasn't being paid any money, her traveling expenses were provided by the WSA, and Trudy spent much of 1923 setting records in pools across the country and even beyond.

The WSA sent her to Hawaii to take on the greatest sprint swimmers of the islands to find out just how good she was. She competed in the one-hundred- , two-hundred- , and four-hundred-yard races, which would help decide which swimmers might be on the next year's Olympic team, and not only won each event but broke the existing records doing it. She won the four-hundred-yard race by forty-five yards, and the Hawaiians honored her by giving her native garlands as she got on the ship to leave the islands.

But it was the tours with other WSA stars that took up much of her time. They crossed the country with their chaperones, staying in fine hotels and traveling first-class on trains, giving exhibitions everywhere they went. And the troop of swimmers went everywhere, traveling around the country and going to Canada, Honolulu, and Bermuda. They also went to Europe and impressed so many people that President Coolidge and the Prince of Wales called them "ambassadors of sports and good will."

Her hearing was still a problem, though, and she was shy around strangers. To avoid conversation, Ederle would take along mystery books, take a seat in the corner of the train compartment, and become lost to the world. Still, she bonded with teammates like Riggin and Wainwright and would often join them on the observation platform, where she and Wainwright would strum ukuleles and sing to the other passengers.

The newspapers couldn't get enough of the swimmers, and the girls posed for pictures everywhere, though they would cover up in sweaters or dresses when photographers came around looking for shots of them in formfitting bathing suits. When they were touring in Florida for the winter, few gimmicks went unused as photographers eager to sell pictures promoting the state got the women to demonstrate swimming motions, pretend they were playing leapfrog, or even pose with animals.

Ed Sullivan wrote about meeting Ederle that winter in Miami Beach, where one photographer wanted to pose a young bear cub with the swimmers. No one would handle the cub until Trudy walked out of the group, grasped the cub by the chain, and held on to him until the photographs had been taken, even as the cub scratched her shoulders and arms painfully. "Someone had to hold him," she told Sullivan as they dabbed iodine on her wounds.

The tour ended at the huge Hippodrome Theater in New York, where the women got an early glimpse at a life they would later lead. They were promoting something called Sports Week, and the swimmers joined athletes from golf, tennis, and other sports for a twice-daily show that drew more than five thousand people each performance. They used the huge tank that Kellerman helped design for the Hippodrome and were the hit of the show as they put on swimming and diving exhibitions, which proved so popular that the engagement was extended for two weeks.

It was now 1924, and as spring came, the preparations began in earnest for the Olympics, which would begin in July in Paris. Ederle would go into the games as the record holder in the one-hundred- and four-hundred-meter races, and she easily qualified for both events. She would also be a part of the relay team for the four-hundred-meter race, which was the heavy early favorite for the gold.

As she boarded the SS *America* for the voyage to France, she did so as the undisputed queen of women's swimming. Few doubted she would come home with at least three gold medals, and Ederle herself was as confident and determined as ever.

No one, it seemed, could beat the butcher's daughter.

Bringing home the gold was serious business for an American team eager to expand on the country's recent sporting success. But being in Paris also meant there was time for fun, and the American women enjoyed themselves playing games, such as seeing how many girls (eight) could squeeze into a taxi and finding the best ice cream in the city (there wasn't any).

The decision to stay outside the city in Rocquencourt was made partially because American Olympic officials didn't want their young women exposed to the lures of Paris any more than they had to be, but this proved to be a problem. The Les Tourelles pool, the first pool built expressly for an Olympics, was in the heart of Paris, and getting there and back required uncomfortable rides on the bumpy roads in the hard-riding vehicles of the time. Though the estate at Rocquencourt was magnificent in its grandeur, the women would have to leave in the morning for the hour-plus drive to the pool, get their practice in, and then return to their quarters for lunch. If there were heats later in the day, they would head back to the pool in the afternoon. On most days, the women spent four to five hours on the bus.

Practice time was doled out at only an hour a day for the team in the unchlorinated fifty-meter pool in the center of the city. (The pool had been completed a year earlier and cost four million francs.) That meant an hour for not only men and women swimmers but also for the divers on the team. And that presented a problem because the springboard and diving platform were in the congested middle of the pool.

"You had to watch out when you were diving, or you might land on Johnny Weissmuller's back," Riggin said.

It soon became apparent that the schedule was not working well for the team's best woman swimmer. The Associated Press reported on July 11 that the American team was still expected to be strong but that coaches were concerned about Ederle's poor form. They said she was slowly getting into condition after suffering from serious muscular trouble, partly due to the bone-jarring rides she took daily into the city and back. By this time, U.S. officials had realized their mistake and moved the women into a hotel in the city, but Ederle would never fully recover her form.

Though women had competed in the 1900 Olympics in croquet, and swimming and diving had been added in 1912, this was only the second U.S. team to have female swimmers and divers. Women generally were treated as an afterthought in the games, mostly because Pierre de Coubertin, considered the father of the Olympics and the IOC president in 1924, didn't see much future for female athletes.

Still, women's fencing would make its debut at these games, at which the Olympic motto, *Citius, Altius, Fortius* (Swifter, Higher, Stronger) was introduced, as was the closing-ceremony ritual of raising the flag of the International Olympic Committee, the flag of the host nation, and the flag of the upcoming host nation. With the world's economy recovering from the war, the number of participating nations jumped from twenty-nine to forty-four, and some one thousand journalists came to chronicle the event.

There were only five women's swimming events in the Paris games, and the most anticipated race was the one-hundred-meter freestyle, in which Ederle and Mariechen Wehselau were expected to fight it out for the gold. Trudy got off to a quick start and hit the water first when the gun was fired, but Mariechen pulled ahead and seemed headed for victory before Ethel Lackie of the Illinois Athletic Club came from nowhere to beat both to the finish.

Lackie won with a time of 1:12.4, while Wehselau was four-tenths of a second back and Ederle came in third at 1:14.2. Handley, who was officiating the race, was dumbfounded at the stunning upset, having assumed the honors would go to the WSA.

Ederle admitted to "heartfelt disappointment" after the race, blaming it on her "bad legs," but there would be more disappointment to come. There were only four swimmers entered in the four-hundred-meter freestyle, and Ederle was the favorite again. But in another upset, Martha Norelius broke an Olympic record and won easily with a time of 6:02.2. Wainwright came in just behind her, while Trudy was more than two seconds off the pace and had to settle for her second bronze medal in an American sweep of the top three places.

There would be no denying Ederle a gold in the final event, the four-hundred-meter relay, which everyone believed would surely go to the dominant American team, unless one of them accidentally drowned. None did, and with Ederle handing Euphrasia Donnelly a five-meter lead after going the first one hundred meters, the Americans never looked back.

It was a disappointing Olympics for Ederle, though that was mostly overlooked in the excitement over the success of the rest of the team. With Weissmuller leading the way with a sweep of his events, American swimmers dominated as never before, winning nine of eleven events, the biggest thrashing in any sport since the modern Olympics began in 1896.

Among the winners was Bauer, who took gold in the backstroke and then jokingly suggested that the women should be able to challenge the men in swimming and diving, an idea that horrified Olympic officials quickly quashed. (Bauer would die in January 1927, ninety-two days after falling out of a car during a parade and subsequently being diagnosed with cancer. She was engaged to be married to sportswriter Ed Sullivan at the time of her death, and she received floral arrangements from Ederle, Jack Dempsey, boxing promoter Tex Rickard, and many others.)

Other American athletes were nearly as impressive. The three hundred who sailed on the SS *America* would return home with ninety-nine medals, forty-five of them gold. Included among the top-winning group was a young Benjamin Spock, a member of the rowing team from Yale; Helen Wills, who took home two golds, and William Dehart Hubbard, the first black man to win an individual gold with his long jump of twenty-four feet, five inches.

The team would return home together on the same ship, greeted not only by friends and family but by New Yorkers eager to embrace their success. They were paraded down Fifth Avenue to City Hall, where each athlete got a medal from the mayor, and was cheered by tens of thousands. (The 1924 Olympic plaque in the Canyon of Heroes is about half a block from Trudy's Channel plaque, which is across the street from the U.S. Customs House, near Beaver Street and Broadway.) It was a magical moment for Ederle, though she would later say her failure to win three golds in the games was the biggest disappointment of her career. The next Olympics seemed so far away, and she was now unsure just where her swimming career would lead her or how far she would pursue it.

She had done just about everything she could do in the water, and her only real options were doing them again and breaking her own records in the process, which didn't excite her terribly.

For her, the English Channel was just something a boat took when heading to France. It would be months before the thought of swimming across it even entered her mind.

5

Different Time, Same Old Channel

Ederle's first attempt at the Channel had been thrown together quickly, a spur-of-the-moment effort that seemed to bewilder the young swimmer, who had no grand plan other than swimming from the rocky shore of France to the beaches of Dover. She'd failed, but that very failure was what made her so determined to do it again, only this time on her own terms. Ederle came back in 1926 a year older, much more comfortable with what she had to do, and even more confident that she would do it.

Her new trainer was key, not only because Burgess had successfully swum the Channel himself but because Trudy had bonded with him and grown to trust him during the time they'd spent together while she awaited a second swim, which never came, the summer before. Also, with the WSA not involved in this attempt, she was able to add two crucial members to her entourage who would help her in the otherwise-lonely weeks leading up to the swim.

Her father and Meg joined her on June 2, posing for photographs before boarding the *Berengaria* for Europe. Riggin was there to give her a send-off kiss, and she waved to scores of friends and relatives on hand to see her off. It was yet another grand adventure of her young life, and this one would hold even more promise than the last.

Handley came to the ship with a word of advice for the woman who had helped popularize his American crawl. He urged Ederle to resist any attempt to make her use anything but the stroke that made her such a great swimmer, regardless of the idea ingrained in many that the only way to swim the Channel was to do it in a deliberate manner. He told Ederle that if Burgess or anyone else tried to get her to do the breaststroke or backstroke, she should tune them out. The advice was thoughtful, but Ederle didn't need to hear it again. She had long since decided that she would swim the Channel with her best stroke or not at all.

Ederle's departure was turned into an event by the *Daily News,* which had every intention of getting its money's worth out of her summer overseas. The *News* was New York's biggest tabloid, selling more than a million papers a day at two cents each, and Capt. Joe Patterson, the newspaper's publisher, was determined to keep it that way. Patterson remembered the great success the *Daily Mirror* in England had had two decades earlier sponsoring Kellerman's swims, and he sensed in Ederle the perfect vehicle to keep his papers moving all summer long at newsstands around the city.

The *Daily News* had been launched just seven years earlier as the *Illustrated Daily News,* the only tabloid in the city, and quickly gained in circulation among the more established broadsheet rivals, thanks to the Patterson formula of combining enough sex, mayhem, and violence to gratify the taste of working-class New Yorkers. The newspaper's pages were filled with short stories about crooked politicians, judges on the take, gangsters, showgirls, sports celebrities, and, on a good day, the occasional ax murderer.

Ederle came along at just the right time for the *Daily News,* which by now was facing competition from two new tabloids lured into the mix by the runaway success of the newspaper. William Randolph Hearst had started the *Daily Mirror* two years earlier, and a few months later the *New York Evening Graphic* was born. The three tabloids fought it out daily on New

York streets, vying for the latest in sensational crime news, pictures of pretty young women, and details of lurid sex scandals.

Ed Sullivan was the main sports columnist for the *Evening Graphic,* which newspapermen dubbed the "Evening Pornographic" for its relentless pursuit of sleazy, vulgar journalism. Sullivan wrote "Sports Whirl" and promoted strongman tournaments and dinners attended by the biggest sports figures of the day, including Jack Dempsey, Gene Tunney, Babe Ruth, Red Grange, Gene Sarazen, and even Jimmy Walker, the night life—loving mayor. Sullivan would later take over the Broadway column, but for now his sports column was must reading, and he was about as respected as any journalist who worked for the *Evening Graphic* could be.

Indeed, while the *Daily News* had its own reputation to live down, the *Evening Graphic* was always ready to get in the gutter, whether by tantalizing headlines or pictures of bathing beauties still wet from the pool, their suits clinging tightly to their young bodies.

"Don't tell my mother I'm working on the *Graphic*" went one popular quip of the day. "She thinks I'm a piano player in a whorehouse."

The *Daily News* had big money invested in Ederle and was going to milk the attempt for all it was worth, and Patterson moved quickly to make sure his best people would be on the story. A few weeks before the Ederles were set to sail, he summoned Julia Harpman, who had gained a reputation on the paper as an ace crime reporter, into his office and asked her to be the official chronicler of everything that would take place on the trip. Harpman eagerly agreed to what seemed like an all-expenses-paid European summer vacation, and she took along her husband, Westbrook Pegler, himself a top writer for the *Chicago Tribune.* Art Sorenson, the photo editor of Pacific and Atlantic Photos, completed the newspaper's entourage; his duty was to send back enough photographs to keep Trudy in the paper on a daily basis.

Ederle was getting most of the attention, but one of her competitors was already a step ahead of her as the *Berengaria* sailed. Lillian Cannon and her dogs had left two weeks earlier on the Holland American liner *Volendam,* but not before she took a half-mile swim in the Hudson River with dog Chesacroft Drake, much to the delight of a large crowd comprised mostly of navy sailors, who cheered her on.

While her rivals sailed, Corson would train two more weeks at home under Liebgold, the heel-and-toe walker, before leaving, while Barrett had to wait until the first week of July to sail because she didn't have enough money to stay in England any longer than necessary.

The trip began inauspiciously for the newspaper contingent following Ederle, as Pegler was ill and had to be carried aboard the *Berengaria*. But soon Harpman was chatting with Trudy on the ship's deck and sending back dispatches to the paper, while Sorenson was also getting to know the young athlete and was snapping away, recording her various activities on-board.

Trudy impressed Harpman right away, not only because of her strong will but also because of the unaffected air she had about her. In her first story, Harpman reported that she was as strong as a young oak, sturdily built with wide shoulders and powerful hands. She wrote that Trudy "has a wide-eyed happy face and a queer way of wrinkling her nose and forehead when she is puzzled or perturbed. Her very dark brown hair is short and straight and caught on the right side with an inexpensive barrette. She seems even younger than her few years and amazingly unsophisticated."

Trudy was soon trying her own hand at telling her story. With Harpman as her ghostwriter, she delivered the first of many first-person accounts, which Patterson knew the competition could never match because they weren't paying for her thoughts. The first stories under Ederle's byline found her looking forward to taking on the Channel once again but still bitter about having been pulled out of the water the year before. She said once again that she could have gone on if Wolffe hadn't insisted on pulling her out, and she complained that her former trainer had been so negative about everything that she did that it had affected her swim.

Ederle also indicated there would be some other changes this time around. Most importantly, her sister was going to be there to give her support, as well as her father. The crowd on the tug would also be cut back, and there would be no band to play "Yes! We Have No Bananas," much less to get seasick and vomit overboard.

"Last year there were 70 people on the tug that accompanied me and some of them didn't seem to care very much whether I made it or not," she said.

Harpman certainly cared. She knew that the better Trudy's chances were, the more play her stories would get in the papers in New York and Chicago. Sorenson cared, too, both for the friendly girl he liked from the moment they met and for the chance to spend a few months in Europe taking photographs of one of the most widely anticipated athletic events of the times.

The rest of the entourage had their own duties. Meg was not only there to look after her little sister; she was also responsible for keeping her spirits and confidence up. Henry Ederle, meanwhile, carried with him intense fatherly pride and a wallet flush with cash from his successful butcher shop, money he couldn't wait to put down in London betting shops against oddsmakers who still didn't think it was possible for his daughter to swim the English Channel.

In the summer of 1925, Ederle had been closely chaperoned by the WSA's Viets and had mostly gone along with whatever the adults had planned for her, but this time she was determined to have more of a say. She respected the barrel-chested, mustachioed Burgess as a trainer and would listen to him, but the experience of the previous year had given her some of her own ideas about how to train, what to eat, and what to do when she finally got the chance to make amends for her earlier failure.

"I don't want to be nagged at my training," she wrote. "I want to talk about clothes and shoes and the Charleston and the things in the papers. I can't stand the Channel for breakfast, dinner, and supper. Outside of training hours, I want to forget it.'

Ederle was an experienced traveler, and crossing the ocean on a liner was nothing new to her. Traveling first-class on the luxurious *Berengaria* was a treat normally reserved for the very wealthy and prominent citizens of the time, but Trudy had little use for the extravagant dinners and parties that stretched one into another as the great liner plied its way across the Atlantic. With Prohibition in effect, most passengers counted down the minutes until the ship got twelve miles out at sea and beyond the territorial waters of the United States. Once there, the champagne came out and the gin flowed, but Trudy was content to drink lemon soda and spend her days walking laps around the ship before invariably curling up in a deck chair with one of her favorite mystery books.

This daughter of a German butcher wasn't going to be a drinker.

"I have never in my life drunk alcoholics [*sic*], excepting once as a child when my uncle offered me a penny to drink a glass of beer. I collected, but it was the hardest penny I ever earned because I hated the taste of the stuff," she wrote. "I am not a Prohibitionist, however. I merely am not acquainted with alcoholics and I do not desire to make the acquaintance."

That alone made her different from most Channel swimmers, because the prevailing logic of the day was that brandy or whiskey would help a swimmer ward off the cold. Some had suggested to Trudy that she do the same to keep warm, suggestions she ignored. She also was sure she wasn't going to partake of any more suspicious things like the "beef broth" she was sure had been spiked by Wolffe.

The long days at sea made for much soul-searching. Ederle carried a small red diary that she had gotten for her voyage to France for the Olympics two years earlier, and in it she vowed to herself that she would never, ever, quit, because to her, surrender meant defeat. She also wrote that she would not give in to fear, regardless of what people told her daily about how difficult and dangerous it would be for a woman to swim the Channel.

"Five men have succeeded, why not a woman?" she wrote. "Surely in the athletic club we are near equal in endurance!"

Ederle skipped most of the formal events on the boat, horrified at the idea of having to don a fancy dress to eat dinner. She found her own ways to have fun, hitting golf balls off the upper deck into the ocean and even putting on boxing gloves to engage in some playful sparring with the gym instructor. On deck, she and Meg played leapfrog while Harpman watched and Sorenson took pictures that he would send back on the first ship back home when the *Berengaria* finally docked in France.

Ederle also made an obligatory daily swim in the ship's pool, much to the delight of the passengers, who gathered around to watch, though the pool was so small one good rendition of her famous American crawl carried her halfway across it. Most of her days, though, were spent curled up in a deck chair, where her always-handy books helped provide her shelter from inquiring passengers. Her biggest interest onboard was food, and though she was five-five and a stout 149 pounds already, she hoped to gain ten more pounds before she made her swim. She was delighted at the large amounts of soup, fish, turkey, duck, ice cream, cake, nuts, and fruit brought to her each day by the table steward.

Reporters who had been shut out of any coverage while Trudy was providing Harpman with story after story onboard the ship met the *Berengaria* when it docked at Cherbourg, where she assured them that she was in the "pink of condition" and that this was going to be her last attempt to swim the Channel. She was adamant about that, telling reporters that if she failed, there would be no excuses and that Mother Nature would be declared the true winner. There was a brief hang-up in customs, where the inspector couldn't figure out what the strange ball Trudy had brought along with her was. Overcoming the language barrier, she finally explained the use of the medicine ball as an arm and chest exerciser by flexing her muscles, which greatly amused the government worker.

Cape Gris-Nez was three train rides and a long drive away, but the group decided to go to Paris first for a few days of relaxation before heading toward the coast. The next morning, Trudy ran into Helmy, her Egyptian friend from the summer before, at a restaurant on the Champs-Elysées, and they motored through the Paris boulevards in his car and took in the shops, where green seemed to be the color that summer and skirts with pleated fronts were the latest fashion.

Though Trudy had no interest in fashion and would rather be in a swimsuit than a formal gown, she was concerned about her appearance. Some were telling her that her hair should be cut in the latest Parisian fashion, which was very short, but she said, "I think I would appear far too boyish. I have been noted for my mannish shoulders and carriage and naturally I want to keep my hair over my ears and remain as feminine appearing as possible." Indeed, Trudy did have the shoulders and back of a Jack Dempsey and was a tomboy at heart. She was certainly stocky, but it was that build that helped her go so fast through the water and made her uniquely qualified for the ultimate challenge that lay ahead.

Besides, Trudy didn't need to look like a movie star to get attention. Though the *Daily News* had an exclusive contract to report her deepest thoughts, other reporters and cameramen were just as insistent on getting their scoops. Upon her arrival at the Saint-Lazare train station in Paris, so many of them showed up that a fistfight broke out between rival cameramen jostling for position to get the first photographs of her in Paris. Trudy dutifully posed with the medicine ball, and told reporters that if she was going to buy anything in Paris, it would be sportswear, as she felt uncomfortable in fluffy things or evening dresses.

Six photographers joined Ederle and her entourage for the train ride to Cape Gris-Nez, which by now was a familiar place to the swimmer. This town bordered by sand dunes on the Brittany coast wasn't much—basically two claptrap hotels and a lighthouse, with a few farms in the background. It was chosen not for its modern conveniences, because it had none, but for the strategic location on the edge of a rocky trail that was closest to the English side of the sullen, leaden gray Channel.

A gale-force wind tore through the small huddle of buildings on their arrival, but Trudy was happy to be back again at the Hôtel du Phare (Lighthouse Hotel), which was run by Madame and Monsieur Blondiau, who both greeted her warmly. Trudy was comfortable there, despite the fact that there was no electricity and that any promise of running water was quickly quashed by the sight of cobwebs in the washbasins. Both the basins and a community bathtub were new this year, but it would be another summer before there was any running water hooked up to them. If someone insisted on a bath—which seldom happened—Mrs. Blondiau and the chambermaid would heat water in huge iron vessels on the kitchen range and carry them upstairs to the tub on the second floor.

There was a better hotel just up the road, with running water and electricity, but Ederle had fond memories of the kindness of the Blondiaus on her first trip and insisted on staying there. Helmy, who never worried about money, stayed at the more upscale hotel, as did most of the reporters, who enjoyed expense accounts as they covered the events leading up to the swim.

Writer W. O. McGeehan visited Ederle at her hotel a few weeks later and reported that her "training quarters are rougher than those of any prizefighter I have ever visited. In fact the manager of one of these delicate male athletes would seize his fighter and flee at the first sight of the Hotel of the Lighthouse, with beds that sag in the middle and running water that never runs."

Trudy's first act upon arriving was introducing her party to "Ole Bill" and sitting down to talk to her trainer about their preparations. She told Burgess she was embarrassed by the way the press had played up trivial incidents and casual remarks about Wolffe the year before and said she hoped there would be no friction between them. They also came to agreement that Burgess would not rule the camp autocratically, but would seek Trudy's advice, and that they would mutually discuss the best methods to train. This in itself was a huge change from the previous year, when the teen had meekly followed Wolffe's lead. Now she was a veteran of the swim, much more mature, and determined to follow her own instincts.

Something else Trudy made perfectly clear to Burgess was that she was going to use her American crawl stroke, fulfilling the promise she had made to Handley to prove his theory that it would work on long distances the same as it did in sprints. There would be no orders to do the breaststroke to slow her down, as Wolffe had issued the year before, and for the most part Trudy would be able to set her own pace across the Channel.

Burgess didn't argue, mainly because he had been on the *Morinie* the year before to watch Ederle's swim and believed Wolffe's efforts to slow her down and use a different stroke had hurt her. She was a thoroughbred, not a plow horse, and he wanted her to swim naturally, using whatever method came easiest, believing that her speed might actually help her outrun some of the tides. He cautioned, however, that she should not try so hard to go fast that it cost her strength. Of the five men who had been successful in swimming the Channel, himself in-cluded, he said, all had been slow swimmers.

Though they appeared to be in agreement, all wasn't well between the swimmer and her trainer, and there remained a thorny issue to be re-solved. A few weeks before leaving for France, Trudy had gone to see Cannon off on her voyage, and was surprised when Cannon said she ex-pected Burgess to be her trainer, as well. That contradicted the agree-ment Trudy and Meg had reached corresponding with Burgess, which was that he would train only Trudy and no others unless she gave her ap-proval.

Trudy liked Cannon, even though this swimmer was emerging as her biggest competition as she worked to adapt her breaststroke and overarm strokes to the Channel. But she didn't like her enough to share her trainer on the most important swim of her life, and said she needed Burgess's sole attention if she was going to be successful. On arriving at Cape Gris-Nez, she repeated her position to Burgess, then told Cannon—who was already there, training under the second man to swim the Channel—that she was sure she would find a suitable trainer and wished her well.

Ederle was more than just a little upset, having discovered now that Burgess was planning to train not only Cannon but also Helmy.

"A fine start for my swim when we thought we had everything in readi-ness," she would say later.

And indeed she had believed matters were settled. Burgess had sent her a long, rambling letter in February, offering everything from food to a place to stay to his services, all included in one package price. His salary would be 10,000 francs (about $333 at the exchange rate of the time), and Burgess thought she would need to hire the tug *Alsace* three times, at 2,000 francs for each Channel run. He also wanted to charge 2,000 francs for food for himself, 600 francs for food during training swims, 2,200 francs for a house to stay in, 3,100 francs for boats, and 1,000 francs for "puddings, fruits and cakes."

Burgess promised to go into Boulogne to look for a suitable boat, one big and sturdy enough to make training runs out into the Channel itself, because he wanted Ederle to get used to swimming out into the

Channel, instead of merely following the shore, as she had done the year before. If he couldn't find a boat worthy of making Channel runs, he was going to have one made at a cost of thirteen hundred francs. He also was insistent on putting a new type of Evinrude motor on it so that he could follow her on her training swims without having to row.

Ederle had no need for the housing or the food because she had always planned to return to the Blondiaus and their hotel, where big breakfasts and dinners by candlelight were a bonus. The other matters were negotiable, but one thing that she wasn't going to budge on was sharing her trainer with Cannon. Helmy was another matter, because he was a good friend from the summer before and she liked hanging around with him, but Ederle drew the line at a direct competitor.

The dispute didn't just get the stay in France off to an uncomfortable start; it also reminded Trudy about her problems with Wolffe the year earlier, the types of problems she was determined to avoid in this attempt. She was not only miffed but also embarrassed about the attention other swimmers and their assorted followers were paying to the flare-up between the two American women.

Burgess was wavering, trying to figure out how he could train two women who might make history, while at the same time trying to maximize what looked like a very profitable summer for the Burgess family. For the better part of a long and trying day, the matter remained unsettled, until Harpman stepped in and offered him another ten thousand francs from the *Daily News* expense fund, doubling his salary. That was more than enough to make him happy and forget that he had also promised Cannon that he would be her trainer.

The dustup made for some tense moments between Ederle and Cannon. Cannon was so upset that a few days later, she moved out of the Hôtel du Phare and into the hotel closer to the beach, where most of the press were also staying. Cannon ended up hiring Dover shoemaker Jack Weidman to train her, though that came with some controversy of its own when Weidman told reporters that he had trained Burgess for his Channel swim years earlier, something Burgess categorically denied. The entire incident caused a split between the two camps, so much so that others were forced to pick sides as to which swimmer they were going with. For Helmy, the wealthy son of Egyptian royalty whose perennial attempts at the Channel were a big part of his summers of pleasure, that meant lining up behind his friend from the summer before.

The original plan was for Ederle to make the attempt in mid-July, giving her plenty of time to beef up and train while ensuring that tide and weather conditions would be best. But the weather in June was dreadfully rainy and miserably chilly, and it soon became apparent that the Channel would not warm up enough to make an attempt until at least late July or early August. Burgess got out tidal charts, which showed the best conditions would likely be on July 26, August 10, and August 24, though no one could really be sure.

Ederle didn't swim much the first few days after her arrival because of the wintry weather, but that didn't stop her from training. One day, she, Meg, and Sorenson took a six-mile walk through farmlands, making their way over muddy and rutted roads until they were spotted by a bull that was none too pleased to see Meg's orange linen dress. The bull gave chase and they ran into the brook before spotting the top of the lighthouse on the cape and heading over a sand dune toward it.

They were muddied and wet, and Trudy's white shoes were coated in mud. But as they got to the beach, they saw the wreck of a trawler that had struck a mine during the war. Trudy was so taken with the spot about two miles below Cape Gris-Nez that she thought she might begin her second attempt from there instead of the rocks, which were closer to England but more forbidding.

A few days later, Pop Ederle and Burgess stood on the shore, watching as Trudy made her first real training swim, a forty-five-minute frolic with Meg in the frigid early-season waters. Afterward, they all had chocolate pancakes fried in liquor back at the hotel.

The cold was brutal, with the water temperature just forty-one degrees. Trudy and Meg made a game of timing themselves to discover how long it would take to thaw out after dressing, putting on coats, and being wrapped in woolen blankets while drinking hot tea. There were no hot baths or showers to be had, and it usually took an hour or so before they could begin to feel their fingertips.

On June 28, Harpman reported that Ederle made the longest swim of any so far in training, remaining in the water for three hours off the icy coast. She swam seven and a half miles, from Cape Gris-Nez to Wimereux, bucking a strong tide and a squall in the final two miles. If getting used to discomfort was vital for a Channel swimmer, this was a good session, because the skin at the edge of Trudy's bathing suit was chafed raw where the silk rubbed against her shoulders, which had gotten sunburned while she lay on the beach that morning during a brief and rare warm spell.

Trudy hadn't used grease on her body this day and she swam in pain, while Burgess and others huddled and shivered under heavy sweaters and robes in an accompanying boat. She discarded her goggles along the way because they weren't keeping the salt water out of her eyes—a continuing problem for Trudy in all her swims—and her eyes were as red as her shoulders by the time she got out.

Ederle wasn't happy with the swim, especially because it was her first long stretch in the water and she felt she'd failed the test. At the hotel, she was given a massage by Mrs. Burgess, ate fish soup and roast pork, and finished off the dreary day with a custard pie.

"I suppose you all are as disgusted with me as I am with myself," she said. "I had intended staying in the water four hours and I stayed only three and a half."

Ederle wasn't the only one hurting. Burgess caught a bad cold from the elements and was laid up for a few weeks. About all Trudy could do was keep training lightly, while trying to keep her mind off the many troubles that would likely await her during the Channel swim. Sharks continued to worry her, including the horrid-looking tope, which were European sharks that were fairly harmless but very ugly. She wrote in the *Daily News* that Helmy had met a school of porpoises on a swim the year before and was still haunted by it. She was also concerned with jellyfish.

"The most terrifying feeling I can imagine is to be touched by some unfamiliar object in the water," she wrote. "Often you cannot stop to see what this may be that slides against your back or your leg. You experience a creepy, awful sensation that sends shivers down your spine."

That wasn't the only thing bothering her. Louis Corthes, the overlord of Channel tugs in nearby Boulogne, would visit often at lunch, most often with a few buddies, and they would invariably begin talking about how scary the Channel really was. Only five men had made it across, they would constantly remind Trudy, all of whom had collapsed on the beach, and one had remained unconscious for two hours. Another fought off a shark, while others were stung so badly by jellyfish that they screamed out loud and gave up. Horrors abounded, including the driftwood from wrecked ships, which was a constant danger, for it could be swept up in a wave and bang an offending swimmer over the head.

Trudy would eventually either bury herself in one of her prized books or leave the room rather than hear the horror stories. It was enough to have to face the prospect of swimming the angry Channel, but it was even worse to be reminded daily of just how bad it was going to be.

Every day brought a new challenge as she tried to get ready for the swim and at the same time keep her mind off what it was going to be like. Trudy would wander off by herself for long walks to think about what she was going to have to do, often with Sorenson, the photographer, who was proving the most successful at keeping her mind occupied so that she would not think too much about the upcoming Channel test.

The rest of her time was spent with Harpman and Meg, who had gotten married the year before and, unbeknownst to Trudy, was a few months pregnant with her first child. After a few weeks together, Harpman felt just like family to Trudy, and the feeling was mutual for the hard-driven newswoman. Years later, after Harpman had died, Pegler wrote Ederle and told her that his wife had loved her like the daughter she'd never had.

Part of Harpman's assignment was to shield Ederle from other reporters, lest they get some insight into the swim that the *Daily News* didn't have. The paper was, after all, paying for the scoops, and it wouldn't look good if Patterson were to see stories in other papers that matched or beat those in his tabloid. She wasn't all that successful, however, as writers either already on European vacations or summoned by editors to make their way to France to cover this astonishing story started stopping by the cozy yet decrepit Hôtel du Phare. There were writers around constantly—sitting in the parlor, listening to the toy Victrola that was always going, and hanging around outside to catch a few moments with the girl swimmer.

One of them was McGeehan, the sports editor of the *New York Tribune*, who was taken back not only by Ederle's choice of accommodations but also by her diet, which he described as that "of a stenographer mixed with pickles."

McGeehan filed his story upon his return to Berlin from France, telling of a hotel with spiderwebs and spiders and walls covered in a terrible blue-black-and-red wallpaper, which was mildewed and marked by giant bleach spots. The only lights inside were courtesy of candles, the sheets were always clammy and were changed only every five weeks, and table napkins were changed just once a week. For self-protection, he reported, Ederle had bought wooden napkin rings in Boulogne and carved everyone's names into them.

Worse yet was the nearly complete isolation. There was no phone at the inn, and only two in the village itself. The operator was in the next town and went to bed at seven each night, after which Cape Gris-Nez was effectively cut off from the world, something trainers had to take into consideration if they were going to order an early morning tug.

McGeehan's first impression was that Trudy was dull because she was hard of hearing and "like all swimmers is a mouth breather." But he wrote that she actually displayed a great sense of humor, and that when he left, she was at the door of the hotel with her phonograph, playing a jazz tune.

Ederle, of course, wasn't the only swimmer in town. There had never been so much excitement on the fringe of the northern coast of France as there was this summer, with swimmers from around the world making their way to the shore for practice sessions. The townspeople proved friendly, and seemed excited by the commotion. But they were not all that keen on a woman swimming the Channel, knowing that if it happened, the reputation of the Channel would take a beating and there would not be so many francs available to be spent on future attempts.

Many of the swimmers would stay at the hotel and eat dinner with Trudy, who would give them their personalized napkin rings to take home with them as badges of the "Channel Coo-Coo Club," the name she gave her gang. She was the honorary president, and gracious enough to include even nonswimmers like Harpman and Sorenson in her group.

"For we're all coo-coo or we wouldn't be here to swim the Channel," she said.

To keep from going completely crazy during the long weeks before they could actually make a run, the swimmers would often gather on the solidly packed sands at low tide for a little fun. Trudy would play her famous ukulele and they would dance on the beach, while Pegler would practice his golf game. On Sundays, reporters would join in a pressmen versus Channel swimmers game of baseball on a field laid out in the sand.

Swimmers came and went, but one constant was the giant Helmy, the Egyptian swimmer, whose sideline mission in life seemed to be rescuing Channel damsels in distress. Helmy played the role of big brother to Trudy and others, and his merry disposition and good sense of humor helped make them close companions. Helmy would spend four summers on the Channel, making six attempts himself before finally making it across in 1928, to great fanfare in his native country. The privileged son of a famous Egyptian general, Helmy had grown up in an era when the Egyptian sporting life was profoundly influenced by the British, and, like his father, he was preoccupied with Egypt's honor.

One of the more handsome men of his time, Helmy was often described as having a massive physique, and he towered over the other swimmers while posing for photos, which he loved to be in, especially if there were women with him. As a swimmer, though, Helmy wasn't the perfect fit to train with Ederle. His combined breaststroke and side stroke was slower than that of the American girl, something that eventually prompted Burgess to ban them from swimming together. And for a swimmer, he had an odd fear of what was alongside him in the water.

Ederle was in the Channel one day, pacing Helmy in calm waters, when about two hours into the swim a school of large fish swam between the pair. Burgess and Pop Ederle were in the accompanying rowboat and thrashed wildly at the fish with their oars to disperse them, while Helmy swam in a panic to the boat, panting for breath as he clambered aboard, finally safe from attack. The next day at lunch, he was still shaken, even though Burgess tried to explain they were porpoises, not sharks.

"No shark's going to make a meal out of me," Helmy said.

"They won't bite you, Helmy, and if they did, they'd bite you gently," Burgess assured him.

For Trudy, it was a grim reminder of the sharks she had seen the year before hanging up in the village, and it didn't help that a few days later while on a walk with Burgess they happened upon the troubling sight of fourteen sharks lined up onshore in the next town, one of them over nineteen feet long. To top it off, the local fishermen were spreading rumors than an octopus was in the vicinity.

The sharks weren't the only negative image from the previous year that would haunt Ederle. She was shocked when she and her father ran into Wolffe in Boulogne on July 12, a meeting that was awkward until Pop invited the former trainer to lunch and everyone put aside their differences.

Wolffe, who, Trudy said, was now "so chubby that he makes Pop look as slim as a chorus girl," was ostensibly there on vacation with his wife but was actually looking for a swimmer to train. He told the Ederles he had received a cable from Barrett, who had asked him to train her, but he was disturbed that he had not heard from her after sending her a return cable.

Wolffe thought as the days went on that Barrett—who, unbeknownst to Wolffe, was already on the English side of the Channel, preparing for her attempt—might have been kidnapped or seduced by the lure of Paris. He had been told the American woman was six feet tall and weighed two hundred pounds, so he spent much of his time walking up and down the unpaved roads outside Cape Gris-Nez, staring at every large woman who passed by on the off chance it might be her. Mrs. Wolffe joined in the hunt, and Wolffe reported that he spent five pounds in his search, a huge sum for him when translated into francs.

Though the hatchet had been buried, Trudy wasn't pleased when

Wolffe said he and his wife planned to stay at her hotel for their vacation. She wasn't interested in their itinerary, just worried that Wolffe would try to interfere with either Burgess or her as she prepared for the swim.

Swimmers, meanwhile, were arriving almost by the hour, lured by the promise of improving conditions and the glamour of being the first to cross the Channel since Enrico Tiraboschi had three years ago in the record time of sixteen hours and thirty-three minutes. Among them were Omer Perrault of Canada, Corson, and the old woman of the Channel, forty-nine-year-old Jeanne Sion of France.

And then there was Itchy Gook, the mythical Eskimo swimmer, who constantly complained that the waters were much too hot and who feared sweating to death like a lobster in the Channel. Gook was actually a famed hoax concocted by bored newspapermen the year before, though the *Paris Herald* solemnly reported one day that he had postponed his Channel try because the water was too hot for him.

Eskimos were about the only ones not represented on the French coast this summer. There were Argentinean, Norwegian, Japanese, French, Egyptian, and American swimmers, and on most Sundays, they would all go into the Channel for a goodwill swim together before assembling on the veranda for tea and cakes.

Across the Channel in Dover, Barrett trained with her companion, Miss Leister, at her side at all times, while Corson swam with her husband nearby in a rowboat. Both were becoming more familiar with the Channel by the day, and on July 11, Corson showed she was in shape by swimming from Dover to Ramsgate, a distance of twenty-two miles, in six hours and twenty minutes, just six minutes off the pace set by British amateur star Frank Perks a year earlier.

Trudy, meanwhile, was becoming increasingly irritated by the weather, which delayed training and caused interruptions in her schedule. The same day Corson was swimming twenty-two miles on the other side of the Channel, Trudy had planned to race Helmy and Burgess from Cape Gris-Nez to Wissand, four miles away, giving them a forty-minute lead. But the swim was canceled because the swimmers wouldn't have been able to find their way through the heavy rain and fog.

Instead, Ederle went to the old trawler washed up on the shore to see if it would be a suitable starting point for the swim. She had to do something with her time, and doubts about whether she would ever make the swim were creeping into her mind.

"What am I living for anyway?" a morose Ederle would ask Meg and Harpman as she waited day after day.

"To swim the Channel and be the most famous girl in the world," they would reply.

Other times, she would wander off and climb the hill that led to the lighthouse high above the Channel. It was quiet there, and she could stand in the strong winds that usually raked the area, gaze at the Channel, and try to get a glimpse of the white cliffs of Dover on the other side. On clear days, they stood out and seemed deceivingly close. It was as if they were mocking her, saying, We're close, but just try it.

Trudy would raise a clenched fist at them and vow to make it. Strolling back to the hotel, she would remind herself that five men had done it, so why couldn't a woman? It would probably take her longer, because men were naturally stronger, but Trudy didn't care if it took a week. The goal was to be the first woman across and discover whether a woman had the perseverance and courage to take anything the Channel could throw at her.

If she did make it, she knew she would strike a blow for women everywhere. "I'll bet all the women in the world will celebrate that night," she said.

The monotony of training was interrupted when word came from London that Frank Perks was going to make the first attempt of the summer despite the cold, which was keeping swimmers onshore. He was supposed to arrive in France on July 13 and plunge into the Channel at midnight, so Harpman, Trudy, and Meg went to the nearby town of Audinghen and bought a large supply of fireworks to set off from the rocks along the shore to give him a proper send-off.

A good-size crowd that included Burgess, Wolffe, Helmy, Meg, and Trudy waited in the cold, along with several newspaper correspondents, for Perks to arrive, but as midnight passed and he did not appear, they went home disappointed. The fireworks didn't go to waste; they were set off the next night, Bastille Day, a national holiday in France and also Helmy's twenty-eighth birthday. Later that night, Perks entered the water to make his attempt.

Unfortunately for Perks, the water had cooled noticeably in just one day, and he lasted just nine hours, at which point fog, chill, and choppy waters finally got to him. On the motorboat that accompanied him was Corson, who had volunteered to cook for the British swimmer in order to get a feel for the Channel conditions.

Ederle was waiting for warmer waters before she made her attempt, and she was encouraged by the fact that more cars carrying vacationers were heading toward the coast, a good indication that the few weeks of fair weather she needed for the water to warm were just around the corner. She wanted to go to Paris and enter the seven-mile swim on the Seine as a warm-up, but she was disappointed to get a telegram telling her that the swim was for amateurs only.

Meanwhile, Harpman got the biggest scoop of the summer, one that would play big when Trudy returned to the United States. On a walk one warm day, Trudy confessed that one of the big reasons she wanted to swim the Channel, apart from gaining fame and honor for herself and country, was to get a red Buick roadster she desperately wanted. Her father had promised it to her if she was successful, but the *Daily News* wasn't going to pass a marketing idea by, and Patterson immediately authorized Gallico to order one, and printed its likeness in the paper. The *Daily News* would have the car waiting for Trudy if she was successful.

Trudy wasn't alone in her longing for a car. Americans were buying them by the millions, and the automobile business was the main force driving the go-go economy of the 1920s. Americans weren't supposed to drink, but they could drive, and the number of cars on the road multiplied from 7 million in 1919 to 23 million just four years later. Now they were coming out in more than one color, and Trudy had her heart set on the red one she had seen before leaving home.

The days of training droned on, meanwhile, punctuated by some fun times on the beach. As always, Trudy was reading. This time, the book was *Road to Love,* by Elenore Meherin, a novel that caused her to weep about Katy the crippled girl.

"I had hoped she would get well, marry and live happily ever after, but anyway the story ended nicely," Trudy said.

What Trudy had no way of knowing was just how her story was going to end.

6

A Promise from Pop

Channel swimmers faced three big issues before they even dipped a toe into the water in the summer of 1926, and these didn't include the sheer amount of nerve it would take merely to take a stab at the nasty, chilly stretch of water.

For all swimmers, there was a raging debate over the question of what or what not to eat, and crazy theories abounded as to the relative merits of gorging oneself on things like chicken legs and chocolate in the water to maintain energy or relying instead on just some sugar cubes and fruit to keep nourished as the long hours piled up. Trudy was one of those who thought, from her experience the year before, that eating too much led to seasickness, but some trainers insisted their swimmers dine in the water as if they were having Sunday dinner at home.

Eyewear was the second prime topic of conversation when Channel aspirants got together. The goggles of the day tended to leak profusely, and for some swimmers the salt water that burned their eyes was sometimes the toughest thing the Channel could throw at them. Ederle herself compared it to acid being poured into her eyes, and said she had hardly been able to see when her goggles leaked badly the year before.

Finally, for any woman trying to make it across who had a problem with the idea of walking naked onto a beach in England with hundreds of people watching, there was the subject of what to wear, something that became a big topic in 1926. Most men didn't bother with a bathing suit, swathing themselves only in protective layers of grease and going into the water as naked as the day they were born. Those who did cover themselves chose swimwear that consisted mainly of some shorts and an undershirt.

For women, it was another matter. Though suits had come a long way in the last decade and they didn't have to fight the Channel covered from head to toe in elaborate waves of material, the one-piece suit was still uncomfortable and restrictive over long distances. The times were changing, but they had not changed so much that any self-respecting woman was going to dive into the English Channel in her birthday suit.

A year earlier, Trudy had worn a one-piece suit with a high-cut neck, which badly chafed her body and hung down on the bottom, dragging her into the water as she swam. The baggy part also ballooned, making it harder for her to make progress, even with her strong stroke. There was little wonder, then, that the suit was on her mind from the time she boarded the *Berengaria* for France. In one of her first bylines for the *Daily News* and the *Chicago Tribune,* she wrote that she was undecided about whether to wear wool, which would be warmer, or silk, which was softer and less grating. She took along both suits and planned to make long swims in each while training.

On cold days, when training was impossible, Trudy would huddle with Meg and debate different forms of swimwear. Reporters and others said, "Wear nothing. Who will see you?" But for a religious daughter of German immigrants, this was not an option. Not even God was going to see her on the beach in anything that might be considered immodest, much less see her swimming with nothing on.

Just the suggestion gave her nightmares. She envisioned making it all the way across the Channel, only to walk up on the beach in England without a stitch on. But Trudy also knew that swimming the Channel was going to be hard enough without adding suspect swimwear into the equation, and she searched for ideas about what to do. A solution came to her one day on the beach, and she suddenly leaped up and cried, "I've got it. I've got it, Meg." What she had was an idea before its time: She would use the twelve-dollar silk racing suit she had worn as an amateur in an entirely new way.

Why not cut up the silk suit into a "panty and sort of brassiere" effect? she proposed to Meg. She would clip off the modesty skirt from the suit, put an elastic band through the top of the panties to hold them in place, and then use the remaining material to make a formfitting brassiere that would close in the front with large hooks that could be easily removed if the silk top started chafing her.

Ederle had come to France to make history by swimming the English Channel. Little did she know she would also make it by inventing a two-piece bathing suit that would show off her grease-slathered midriff.

The two sisters got to work, and soon the new suit was created. Not only was it far more comfortable but there was no dragging or heaviness, since the water went right through instead of gathering inside the material. Even with the extra weight of the American flag stitched on one side and the WSA club emblem on the other, it felt almost like she had nothing on.

Trudy was ecstatic, and she wasn't the only one. The tabloid photographers knew they would have no problem getting their pictures published when they first saw Ederle standing on the beach in the two-piece suit. Even though she was caked in grease, the pictures of her showed so much skin that they were almost scandalous by the standard of the times. But times were changing quickly in the go-go 1920s, and now this daredevil swimmer stood in what amounted to a sports bra and silk shorts, ready to take on the English Channel.

The debate over what nourishment she should take as she made her way across the Channel wasn't solved as quickly. One thing Trudy knew was that it wasn't going to be "beef tea" or anything similar to what Wolffe had given her on her previous attempt. She wasn't so sure she needed much of anything at all to make it across, but Burgess belonged to the old school, which favored nutrition, even at the cost of nausea.

Burgess didn't approve of the beef tea, either, and while Trudy suggested chicken might be the thing to eat, he thought chocolate, egg yolks, and thick-skinned grapes, eaten in no particular order, would make for good dining in the water. Burgess himself had been fed every half hour on his successful swim years earlier, but Trudy wanted to eat only infrequently and only when she felt a need for food. One thing they both agreed on was that they would not follow Helmy's diet, which included both coffee and brandy—a choice that may have had something to do with the swims he could never complete because of stomach trouble.

"I do not approve of dope for a swimmer and I call brandy dope," Burgess said.

Burgess wanted to test a variety of foods during several strenuous training swims that would mimic conditions Ederle would face crossing the Channel. The day before the final practice swim out into the Channel in late July, the water was terribly rough. Burgess wanted to postpone the training session, but Ederle was anxious not only to swim in difficult waters but to see if she got sick by eating solid foods as she went along.

The decision nearly cost Trudy her life.

Meg cooked a chicken, Burgess got some grapes from a local farmer, and they drove down the coast to the bay at Audresselles, where they hired a fishing boat to take Burgess, Pop, and Meg along on the swim, despite pelting rains and high waves. Trudy was swimming with Helmy when a big gust of wind hit the boat and took it farther out into the Channel, and soon Helmy and Trudy were all alone in terrifying conditions in the open sea.

They tried to swim close together and head for shore, but the sea tore them apart and tossed them up and down like corks. Trying to make headway in the furious waves, Trudy thought she was going to drown, and she worried that the boat carrying her sister and father had capsized with them in it. Still she managed to fight the elements with all the strength she had, making it four miles back to Cape Gris-Nez, where she then had to contend with the fear of being dashed to pieces against the huge rocks as she made her way to shore. She was trembling with fright as she went slipping and falling over the slimy rocks, all the time searching the stormy seas for the boat carrying her family.

Helmy, meanwhile, had somehow made it back to the boat, where he gave Pop Ederle the bad news that he and Trudy had been separated. Henry Ederle thought for sure his daughter had drowned, and he sat crying as the boat was tossed about in the turbulent seas.

Onshore, fishermen tried to get Trudy in dry clothes, but she refused to budge. She stood there, fear in her heart, scanning the horizon. After what seemed like an eternity, the boat finally appeared, with everyone safe aboard.

The chicken and grapes went uneaten, but nobody was in any mood to care.

By now, Burgess had pretty much given up on telling his swimmer what to do about almost everything. He was more of a cheerleader than anything, having come to the realization that his advice was going to be more crucial out in the water as he helped lead Ederle across the Channel than it would be during preparations for the swim.

Ederle was left alone to come up with a solution to the final problem that had bothered her ever since her first Channel swim, when she'd been nearly blinded by the sea. She thought she had solved it even before leaving for France, when she had wraparound goggles specially made at a Fifth Avenue optometry shop. Rather than the spectacle-type of goggles she had worn in the past, which had two lenses, these had one straight piece of glass that covered both eyes. The new goggles looked good and would be a forerunner of later models, but in test swims they hadn't worked as advertised.

The glass was bound with metal and leather and was supposed to be waterproof, but Trudy hadn't been in training long when she found the goggles leaked around the bridge of her nose. Water would seep through until the salt made her eyes smart so painfully that she was forced to stop and take the goggles off. To make it across the Channel, she needed to be able to see, and as the day of the swim approached, she had found nothing that would work.

Inspiration struck at the oddest time, just two nights before she would take on the Channel. Sitting at the dinner table at the hotel, she watched wax drip from the candles that provided the only illumination for the meal, and the thought struck her that perhaps candle wax could be used to seal the leak in the goggles. Trudy went to work that night on them, melting wax on the inside of the frame, and the next day she took a dip in the Channel to test them out. Much to her surprise and relief, they allowed no water to reach her eyes.

"I was intoxicated with joy," she recalled later. "None too soon had this greatly dreaded fear been eased out of my mind."

In just a few weeks, she had created the two-piece bathing suit and pioneered the first use of wraparound goggles.

Could becoming the first woman to swim the Channel be far behind?

Men had tried swimming the Channel long before Webb made the first successful crossing in 1875. Local legend had it that three men fleeing political convictions under Napoléon had rushed into the water near Calais at the turn of the nineteenth century and made a desperate swim toward England. It was said that one drowned on the way, another died after collapsing onshore, and the third had washed up onshore and lived several years after as an expatriate in England.

The first official attempt, though, was made in 1872 by an Englishman, J. B. Johnson, who did it after making a bet of thirty pounds, with a promise of collecting one thousand pounds if he made it across. Johnson wasn't shy about promoting his swim. He put placards up around London, promoting himself as the "hero of London Bridge and champion swimmer of the world," and fixing the date of August 23 to make the attempt.

Most thought Johnson had no chance at all of making it to France, given the nature of the currents, which would turn the twenty-one-mile swim into one at least twice as long. But that didn't stop a curious crowd of several thousand people from gathering at the Admiralty Pier in Dover to see Johnson, his entourage, and a group of reporters board the steamer *Palmerstown,* which took him about two hundred yards off-shore. There, he stood on the paddle box and made a grand dive into the Channel, much to the delight of the huge crowd.

Johnson, his suit adorned with medals from about two dozen smaller conquests, made the first two miles in about thirty minutes, but then he ran into a strong tide, which slowed him down and prompted him to ask for some port wine for fortification. He drank that, and about ten minutes later, he drank some more, before deciding that swimming to France might be more difficult than he'd previously thought. He climbed aboard the *Palmerstown* just a little more than an hour into the swim, thirty pounds poorer but much wiser about the difficulties the Channel presented.

Webb, the son of a naval officer, had achieved notoriety a few years before his swim by diving into the mid-Atlantic off Cunard's *Russia* while working as a seaman on a voyage from New York to Liverpool and saving a guest who had gone overboard. He took a more scientific approach than Johnson before he dived into the water from the Admiralty Pier on August 24, 1875. Since he had failed in his first attempt to swim the Channel a few weeks earlier, Webb researched the tides and plotted a course before setting off for France this time. On his second attempt, he was accompanied by a lugger (a small sailboat) and two row-boats.

One of the boats rowed in front of Webb to set the course, while the second held an expert diver just in case he should falter and need assistance. He used a steady breaststroke throughout the day and night, eating nothing, but partaking of ale, beef tea, brandy, and coffee to keep him going. Webb took advantage of the warm weather and a calm sea to make good progress, though he stumbled at one point when bitten on the shoulder by a jellyfish. He was more than halfway across and in sight of the Cape Gris-Nez lighthouse in the early-morning hours when he began tiring and the diver took off his clothes to be ready to jump in and save him. But Webb was bolstered by a big gulp of brandy, and the diver was able to get dressed again.

The tide pushed Webb away from his intended landing area, and after dawn his diver jumped into the water to swim with him for a bit and give him encouragement. Webb kept drinking coffee and beef tea to maintain his energy, but the wind came up and the tide was strong. Those aboard the boats didn't think he could make it. Webb, though, got a bit of luck about 9:30 A.M., when a large rowboat with eight people aboard came out to cheer him on. He was able to use the craft to shelter himself from waves that were now breaking over his head as he fought on. After swimming against the tide for two hours, he was within a mile of the beach at Calais.

When Webb reached shallow water, he stood up, and those in the boats jumped in the water to hug him in delight. The crowd that had gathered in anticipation of his arrival cheered, and a carriage was brought down to take him to the Hôtel de Paris, where he was given a massage before downing four glasses of port wine and then falling into a sound sleep. He made the crossing in twenty-one hours and forty-five minutes, a record that would last forty-eight years.

Webb's swim made him famous, but it didn't exactly set off a wave of new Channel swimmers. Most people felt the proper way to get across the water was in a boat, if they had to at all, and it wasn't until after the turn of the century that the Channel craze began for real—and just as in 1926, it was the newspapers that made it happen.

In July 1904, Sir Alfred Harmsworth, a London newspaper owner who advocated that every boy and girl should learn how to swim at school, offered one hundred pounds to anyone who could swim the Channel, and said he would put up money for their expenses in Dover. That prompted three newspapers, including the Harmsworth's *Daily Mirror,* to sponsor contestants, and though all three contenders failed, the publicity campaign by the papers on behalf of their swimmers made Channel swimming suddenly hot once again.

Burgess was among the competitors in 1904, and he would come back the next year, only to fail once again in the race that featured Kellerman. It would take Burgess thirteen tries before he finally became the second man to swim the Channel successfully, which he did in 1911, making it across in twenty-two hours and thirty-five minutes. That same year, Wolffe made the closest of his twenty-two attempts, coming within just a few yards of shore before tides forced him to abandon his effort.

Another dozen years would pass before anyone else successfully swam the Channel, and, when it happened, the victors came in rapid succession. Henry Sullivan started off the 1923 season by becoming the first American to swim the Channel, landing in Calais twenty-six hours and fifty minutes after he began. Sullivan won the Channel Swimming cup and a one-thousand-pound prize from the *Daily Sketch.* Using a combination trudgeon crawl and breaststroke, he had battled heavy tides on his seventh attempt at the Channel, and it was estimated that he swam a total of fifty-six miles to get across. A week later, Argentina's Enrico Tiraboschi became the first man to swim from France to England, and set a record that made the westward route the favored course from then on.

Boston's Charles Toth tried to swim the Channel in the opposite direction the same day Tiraboschi set the record, but he couldn't make it, and a few weeks later tried it again and failed. Not ready to quit, Toth then went to France, where he hooked up with Burgess as a trainer. On September 9, he headed from Cape Gris-Nez toward England. Accompanied by the tug *Alsace,* he made it in sixteen hours and fifty-four minutes, just off the record set by Tiraboschi.

The summer of 1923 had been the greatest so far for the Channel-swimming craze, even bringing the best attempt ever by a woman when Corson nearly made it across. Now, three years later, no one had come close since, and the Channel once again seemed as formidable as it had been when Webb became the first man to conquer it a half century earlier.

After the long weeks of waiting and experimenting, everything finally seemed to be coming together for Trudy, and now it was just a question of waiting for the right water and tide conditions, and hoping someone didn't beat her across. On July 25, she declared herself satisfied with both her training and her body after going to the English pharmacy in Boulogne and weighing in at 156 pounds, exactly what she had weighed for the swim the year before. She had gained seven pounds since leaving home, in the hope the added weight would help her endurance.

Bookies in Paris were tipped that Ederle and Cannon both might try at any time to swim, and they put out odds of 6–1 that neither American swimmer would be successful. Pop Ederle had earlier gone to London, reportedly with $22,000 in cash, to place a bet of his own after hearing that the odds there were 50–1 against his daughter making it. But when Lloyd's of London offered only 5–1 against her, he refused the bet.

Back home, thoughts were mixed about her chances. Always ready to find a new way to promote its swimmer, the *Daily News* went out with its inquiring photographer and asked people between West 181st and West 191st streets on St. Nicholas Avenue what they thought of Ederle making it across.

"Such a feat is impossible for a woman," George F. Lacker, a crew manager, declared flatly.

Insurance agent Jack Toale said if any woman could do it, it would be Ederle, while college student Blanche Berkowitz was rooting for someone of her own gender to make it across and was impressed with Ederle's determination.

"What is mostly in her favor is that she herself feels certain that she can do it," Berkowitz said.

They were rooting for her across the Channel, too. Actually, the British were rooting for anyone who could take their minds off their own misery—if only for a short time—by emerging from the water and stepping onto the shore near Dover.

The country was still recovering from the Great War, which had taken not only a huge human toll but also a financial toll on the British Empire. The Brits owed huge debts to the United States, and one London newspaper started a campaign that summer to get the war debt canceled. But while there were occasional grumblings about the United States, there was also mutual respect for a country that had played such a big part in winning the war.

More pressing in everyday life, though, was the ongoing coal strike, which would last seven months and become the most protracted, costly, and bitter labor dispute the country had ever seen. In May, there had been a ten-day general strike in sympathy for the coal miners—the only general strike in Britain's history, one that caused the government to bring tanks out in the streets to control the crowds, and left four million workers idle.

The Brits needed something to cheer about, and they found it in the brassy women who weren't afraid to pose a challenge in an arena where only men had tread before. As July turned into August, there was constant chatter not only about Ederle's chances but also about those of her fellow competitors, who were just waiting for their chance to make history.

Even better for the home fans was that they had someone in this fight. Gleitze, the London typist who failed in 1922 and 1925, would be the first woman to make the attempt this season and only the second swimmer behind Perks when she took off July 24 from Cape Gris-Nez. But Gleitze lasted only about five hours before the wind and waves came up, drenching people in the motorboat following her and finally forcing her to give up her swim.

Cannon was training off the same coast as Ederle, under the direction of Weidman, who wanted her to swim around the first of August. Sion, who had fallen short the two previous years, was preparing to give it another try, and Corson was keeping to herself in England, patiently waiting for just the right conditions to make her swim.

Barrett wasn't about to wait for any of them, even if it meant swimming the Channel from Dover to France, now thought of as a tougher task than doing it from the other direction. The hulking schoolteacher had gotten the least attention of any of the female swimmers, but she understood as well as any of them what being the first woman to swim the Channel would bring in both fortune and fame.

Barrett had originally planned to use Wolffe as her trainer, or so he surely thought, but he would cost money, and she had a better offer. Though she had written Wolffe seeking his services, she also wrote British Olympic coach Walter Brickett and convinced him to come aboard at much less than what Wolffe was charging. Brickett, who took a week off work to guide her efforts, was amazed at Barrett's ample physique and predicted that she had what it took to make it across.

"She may surprise all," Brickett said. "I consider her good for 20 hours."

Barrett turned out to be good for that, and more. She set off on Tuesday, August 3, at 8:00 A.M. from under the celebrated Shakespeare Cliff in Dover with just the small motorboat she had rented for seventy-five dollars to accompany her. She had been anxious to go for days, and the fact she was running out of money and had Brickett only for the week made her decision to leave even more urgent.

"Doesn't it look near? And yet how many have tried and failed," Barrett said a few days before her swim. "I feel in perfect condition and full of pep. I feel I could get in the water right away and swim all day."

Barrett swam not only all day but most of the night, too. With Leister, her faithful companion, urging her on from the motorboat, she battled currents and waves and kept plodding relentlessly ahead as day turned into night. Barrett didn't need to be reminded to eat; she dined on beef essence, oranges, and chocolate, all the while chatting away with Leister as she steadily made her way across.

Barrett looked for a time like she was almost certain to make it, but the Channel had many ways of defeating its would-be conquerors. In this case, a dense fog settled in, making it almost impossible to see, which was what did in the schoolteacher so agonizingly close to her finish. Barrett was within two miles of Cape Gris-Nez when she was pulled, exhausted, from the water at 5:35 A.M., twenty-one hours and thirty-five minutes from the time she'd left Dover.

Barrett may have come up just short, but her near miss and the story of her underdog effort won her wide acclaim. She was bombarded with telegrams of support, and a woman in New York said she would give Barrett $500 for her next attempt. The New Rochelle Rotary Club raised $233 to help Barrett meet her expenses.

Leister told reporters that offers of help, including boats and tugs, were pouring in and were greatly welcomed, but said that she and Barrett did not want to call too much attention to themselves.

"We are not out to make a show and get all possible publicity," she said, clearly taking a dig at the newspaper-sponsored campaigns of both Ederle and Cannon and the crusade for motherhood and sainthood that Corson was trying to pull off.

Barrett returned to Dover to prepare for another attempt, taking a day off to go on a shopping trip before returning to her little inn. Gazing out the window on a sunny day and seeing the white cliffs of France beckoning from what seemed just a short distance away, she pondered the significance of what might have happened if she had somehow made it those last miles.

"If only we had seen where we were and there had been no fog," she told Leister. "How different it would have been, Gracie."

Ederle was astonished by the endurance of Barrett, who had set a new record for the time a woman had spent in the Channel. She was also increasingly edgy about her own swim, and shocked that Barrett had come so close to stealing her thunder. Adding to her anxiety was not only the long wait but the knowledge that Sion, Cannon, and Corson might enter the water for their own tries at any time.

She was sick of waiting, sick of training, and sick of the constant talk about the Channel and the dangers that it posed. She remembered that her friend Paul Berlenbach, the German-American boxer, had told her that during his training for the light heavyweight title the year before with Jack Delany (a fight Berlenbach would win by a fifteen-round decision after first being knocked down), no one ever spoke about the fight. On the coast of France, all anyone ever talked about was the treacherous Channel.

At every meal, the order was given that there be no Channel talk, but before the first course was served, someone would look out the window and invariably say, "The wind's changing. It will be a good night, tonight."

"All you hear is talk of wind, weather, tide, Toth and Tiraboschi," Ederle said. "It has reached the state where I bring a book to the table and when I am not eating I sit with my fingers in my ears burying myself in Zane Grey's *Heritage of the Desert.*"

Mostly, though, she was sick at the thought that someone else might beat her across the Channel while she sat idly waiting for just the right weather and tides. Still, there was too much at stake to chance misjudging the seas and the tides, and Burgess insisted he wouldn't allow Ederle to cross unless both the tides and winds were favorable. But there weren't many good wind days on the French side of the Channel, and the first day the tides were supposed to be favorable was on Friday, August 6. Trudy had a few more days to fret, and to hear about the horrors of the Channel, before she would even have a chance to go.

While the tug captains didn't think much of Ederle's chances, Burgess thought she could succeed if the conditions were just right. He drilled the thought into her as he gave her a daily massage, but also gave her lectures on the vagaries of the Channel and the different things she could expect from it. By the time she was ready to go, Ederle understood almost as well as the grizzled old swimmer himself what would be in front of her all the way across.

As the window of opportunity approached, Ederle walked the rocky French shoreline with her father. She wanted him to make sure there was no repeat of the previous year, and that there would be no one who would pull her out without her permission. She wanted his word.

"Don't let anybody take me out of the water unless I ask," she told him. "Promise me."

The attempt by Barrett gave a new sense of urgency to the preparation, and the day after Barrett was pulled from the water in the soupy fog, the decision was made. Trudy would take to the water on Friday, weather permitting, leaving at 6:45 A.M. to take advantage of a westerly tide. The old veteran and his young swimmer figured that with Trudy's powerful American crawl, it would take between twelve and fourteen hours to make it across, a time unheard of in the previous five Channel crossings by men.

With the date now set, there was a flurry of final preparations. Louis Corthes, the captain of the tug *Alsace*, was notified in Boulogne that his services would likely be necessary, and Harpman set about making sure that the Marconi wireless she had arranged for would be installed on the tug, so that the story of the swim could be relayed as it unfolded. The *Daily News* and the *Chicago Tribune* also had airplanes on standby to carry photographs from the beaches of France to London for processing and transmission on the incredible new Bartlane photo system.

The other newspapermen weren't about to be left behind. They rented their own tug and their own Marconi set. The *Daily News* and the *Tribune* might have had their exclusive contract, but now all bets were off. They were going to cover the swim from the deck of the *Morinie*, and they were going to be there if she made it across for the biggest sports story of the summer.

The day before the swim, Trudy made sure her two-piece suit was just right and applied more wax to her goggles, while Meg tried to calm her own nerves by walking two miles to the shrine of the Virgin Mary at Audresselles, where she lighted a candle in the tiny cave beneath the Virgin's statue and said a prayer for her sister's safety. Although the family was Lutheran, she wasn't taking any chances.

Neither was attorney Dudley Malone, who wired Ederle some words of encouragement from New York on the eve of her swim. "I do not think that you will give up before you reach the English shore, but if such a feeling should come to you, think of your Irish lawyer and make the English shore," he wrote.

The Channel was choppy most of the day, but the winds quieted, and by evening a clear calm hung over the little fishing village as everyone gathered around the dinner table at the inn. The waters were as placid as a mirror when Burgess walked in at 10:00 P.M. and announced, "If the weather continues as is, tomorrow we start!"

A great cheer went up, and Pop Ederle ordered a round of drinks for the assorted townspeople, reporters, and Channel watchers who had gathered in anticipation of just such a moment. Trudy and Meg had grenadine, while everyone else toasted with cognac before smashing their glasses into the fireplace in celebration.

Suddenly, it was bedlam in the inn, with people dashing about to take care of their final tasks. Madame Blondiau and her mother-in-law would stay up all night to cook a chicken and broth, while the reporters and photographers arranged for cars to get to Boulogne, where the *Morinie* was waiting.

Burgess gave Trudy a massage; then everyone kissed good night. A mixture of tension and excitement filled the air as the realization sank in that in just hours Trudy would embark on a swim for redemption and for the record books. It was one she was so determined to win that she was almost willing to bet her life on it—and had already risked her life for it.

"I could never face people at home again unless I get across," she said.

Outside the little inn, the Channel was calm and silently waiting. Trudy headed upstairs for bed, confident she had done everything she could to get ready.

In just a few hours, she would step off the beach for the start of what W. O. McGeehan would later describe as "in my opinion, the greatest sports story in the world."

7

"Come out, Gertie."
"What for?"

The swim a year earlier had been sabotaged by problems with Ederle's trainer, her own inexperience, and her failure to take charge
of the swim, as only the person who was making it could. Even so, Trudy
never doubted she would make it across, until Wolffe made the ill-fated
decision to pull her from the water at a time she thought she was still
swimming reasonably well.

By contrast, everything had gone right this summer of 1926 in France,
or almost everything. Trudy had savored her weeks with her family and
swimming friends at Cape Gris-Nez, and even the near tragedy of a few
weeks earlier, when she thought she might drown or be crushed on the
rocks, had been pushed far back in her mind.

Now, on the eve of the swim, she felt strong, both mentally and
physically, and eager to take on the Channel once again.

"I feel as if I could lick Jack Dempsey," she said.

Dempsey already had an opponent, so that would have to wait. The
Manassa Mauler was in training for a September 23 fight in Philadel-

phia against Gene Tunney for the heavyweight championship of the world, and though it would be the biggest fight ever, he was as interested in what Trudy was doing overseas as she was in what he was doing to get ready for Tunney.

Burgess, meanwhile, had added a new wrinkle. He told reporters who were wondering about Trudy's chances of making it that he thought not only that she would but that she would break the record set by Tiraboschi three years earlier in the last successful Channel swim. It was the first time such a thing had been mentioned, though few among the assorted reporters gathered in France were convinced that a woman could beat a man in any event.

Burgess wanted Trudy in the water four hours before high tide, at 6:45 A.M., and planned to have her follow the course set by Tiraboschi. A good route was important, because there was no way to swim the Channel straight across, due to the vicious tides that came from seemingly every direction and would pull a swimmer one way or another. Swimmers had to figure ways to ride the tide when it was favorable, and try to miss most of the tides that would work against them. But it was an inexact science at best, dependent upon charts that were not known for their accuracy and on the memories of men who had spent their lives on the Channel.

The plan for Trudy was to get as far out toward mid-Channel on the first tide without being swept down the French coast toward Boulogne. She would make her way toward the North Sea as the tide shifted, hoping to get to the edge of the Goodwin Sands in time to catch a third, usually favorable, tide, which would help her toward the English coast.

It was a good plan on paper, but the Channel had a way of making good plans go bad. It was twenty-two miles from the beach near Cape Gris-Nez to the beaches of Dover, but like all Channel aspirants, Ederle would swim much farther as the tides played havoc with the Strait of Dover. Still, Burgess understood what Wolffe couldn't have the year before: He had a fast swimmer who might be able to use her speed to neutralize the tides like no swimmer had done before.

"If she can last 14 hours, Gert will have a splendid chance of getting to England," the grizzled trainer told reporters.

As usual, Trudy slept well. Meg woke her at 4:00 A.M., and Trudy smiled before asking, "Do we go?"

Told that this was the morning she had been waiting for ever since her swim had been aborted the year before, Trudy jumped from bed and looked out the window at the new moon and morning star.

"Isn't it beautiful?" she said. Then she looked at her sister again, this time with determination brimming in her young eyes. "England or bust," she declared.

Downstairs in the old hotel, there was a meal laid out fit for a Channel swimmer. Madame Blondiau had spent the night getting things ready for her young guest, and Ederle sat in her pajamas, eating cornflakes with milk and half a fried chicken and drinking a cup of coffee diluted with milk. She topped it all off with a peach, a decision she would come to regret.

Trudy wasn't the only one up early that morning. Half the village was waiting to see her walk into the water, and so were friends and supporters, who got on a rickety bus headed for Boulogne, where they would board the tug *Alsace*. Among them were Pop Ederle, Helmy, and assorted guests and dignitaries. The tug was piloted by Corthes, a grizzled veteran who could neither read nor write but knew the Channel better than anyone, and who had accompanied more Channel swimmers than any other tug captain. Ederle was happy with the choice of tug, especially after hearing that Corthes was so skilled he could pilot it to within three feet of her and keep it on course the whole time.

Corthes had it stocked with rations, a first-aid kit, and the wireless that would be used to transmit reports of Trudy's progress. Flying above the *Alsace* were both the French tricolor and an American flag that had flown when Toth followed the same tug across three years earlier, something Trudy thought would bring her luck. The tug would leave Boulogne once everyone was aboard and churn its way toward Cape Gris-Nez, where Corthes would anchor offshore and await the small boat that would bring Burgess, Meg, and Harpman once Trudy stepped into the sea.

Her meal finished, it was now time for the most distasteful part of the swim for Trudy—the application of the grease that was supposed to keep her body temperature up in waters that had now warmed to about sixty degrees and prevent the dreaded jellyfish from biting her. Ederle had planned to bring her own special grease this year, rendered lamb fat offered by meat packers her father did business with, but they hadn't come through, so now she was on her own. She worried about the grease, because on her first swim it had worn off, leaving her shivering in the cold water.

The job of applying the grease fell to Meg and Harpman, who slathered her first with olive oil, letting it sink in for a half hour, then with a heavy yellow-white coating of lanolin. Burgess would top it all off on the beach with a thick coating of Vaseline and lard, making Trudy the most slippery fish that would be in the Channel that day.

Burgess was staying in a house in the village at the top of the rocks, and Harpman walked up to help him get everything together. He gathered a crate of green grapes, an extra pair of overalls, and an alarm clock before starting off for the beach with her. Just as they were leaving the hilltop, they heard the siren of the *Alsace* as she came around the rocks—perfect timing for a perfect morning.

Indeed, the water was calm and as warm as it would get, tides were favorable, and the conditions they had waited two months for had finally arrived. Now the sun had just started to peek its way over the farmland beyond.

"Looks like a good day," Burgess said.

Several photographers and reporters were already on the beach when Ederle came down from her hotel, and a movie camera on a tripod recorded the scene. There would be Marconi wireless sets on two different tugs, and more than fifty reporters and photographers would follow her across. The story of the summer was about to unfold on the first Friday of August on the English Channel, and it would be well documented.

Instead of going off rocks as she had a year earlier, Ederle would wade in from the beach, which meant almost a mile more added to the swim. She had been leery of the rocks to begin with, and the frightening incident where she felt she was going to be smashed against them in the storm had scared her even more. She would have to swim a mile longer, but she liked the idea of going from the beach much more. Trudy now stood on the beach, arms and legs spread apart, as Burgess applied one last layer of grease. A funny little black-and-white dog that had followed the townspeople down to the water licked some that had dropped from her arms. A crimson sun rose above the dark waters as Burgess kissed her on the cheek before heading to the rowboat to get out to the *Alsace.*

Trudy went calmly toward the Channel, now suddenly all alone on the water's edge. People in the crowd yelled out, "Cheerio, Trudy," and she said a little prayer, asking for guidance along the way.

It was 7:08 A.M., and the Channel was calm, at least for the moment. Trudy turned to yell "Cheerio" back to the crowd before wading into the chilly water and beginning her swim with a slow, even version of the American crawl. Onshore, an American flag was waved at the *Alsace* to signal the swim had begun, and the ship replied by sounding its siren.

Trudy was easy enough to spot, with her red diving cap and the one-piece goggles of yellow glass. She certainly looked like no other swimmer in her improvised suit of black silk trunks and a narrow brassiere of black silk. Fortunately for the modest swimmer, she wouldn't have to remove these because of chafing.

The morning start was timed four hours before high tide to give Ederle the benefit of the westerly tide so she could conserve strength during the middle stages of her journey. There was a slight southerly breeze and a gray haze—normally, indicators of a hot day to come—and it seemed like all the waiting had paid off with a perfect day to go swimming in the Channel.

The *Alsace* puttered a few hundred yards offshore as it waited for Ederle, as well as for Meg, Harpman, and Burgess. On the side of the tug, someone had scrawled in chalk an arrow pointing forward and added "This Way Ole Kid" to it.

Everything seemed perfect as she swam from shore, but this wouldn't last long. Barely fifteen minutes into the swim, Ederle began getting severe cramps in her stomach, the result, she thought, of the peach she had eaten at breakfast. For a few brief moments, she thought she might have to abandon the swim almost before it had begun, but the more strokes she took, the better her stomach began feeling.

The pace was quick, mostly because Ederle didn't know how to swim any other way, though Burgess had tried his best to slow his young charge down. Trudy was two miles out in just forty-five minutes and settling into a good rhythm when those onboard saw a dispiriting sign. The sands beneath the South Foreland Lighthouse on the English side—where Marconi had conducted his wireless experiments—were clearly visible, which usually meant there was high wind in the middle of the Channel.

On the deck of the tug, Harpman took note of that as she looked up from the typewriter on which she was writing dispatches to give to the wireless operator for transmission. The term *play-by-play* hadn't yet entered the lexicon of American sportswriters, and her constant updates and those of other newsmen on the *Morinie* might have been the first time such coverage was used.

"This doesn't look so good, does it?" she asked Burgess.

"No, but don't let Gertie know. I told her not to look up toward the English shore until the ninth hour and I don't want anyone to let her know before then that we can see the cliffs."

Ederle was oblivious to it all as she settled comfortably into her American crawl, averaging twenty-one strokes a minute, even as Burgess implored her to slow down. Corthes told Burgess he had never seen a swimmer go off so fast in all of the Channel swims he had been on. The swimmer herself was in high spirits, calling jokingly to her father on the tug to join her in the water, saying she was going so slowly that even he could keep up. She then looked up to Helmy and started singing "It's a Long Way to Tipperary," and soon everyone onboard except the captain himself was joining in the chorus.

Burgess had carefully mapped out a course he thought would be ideal, but it would soon become a matter of guesswork as the tides kept changing, the wind picked up, and Ederle was forced much farther toward the North Sea on the second tide than Burgess had planned. He knew from experience that she would have a problem regaining her route to get around the treacherous Goodwin Sands—an area filled with wrecked steamers, warships, and boats of all sorts—by the tenth hour, as planned.

The *Daily News* and the *Chicago Tribune* were, of course, sparing no expense. In addition to the wireless, they had a motorboat from Dover, with Don Skene of the *Tribune*'s Paris bureau onboard to take Sorenson's first photographs and rush them to London. Trudy waved to Skene as he jumped from the boat to the tug and back again with the photographic plates.

Arriving about the same time was the *Morinie,* the tug hired by other press and photographers, who had waited to see Ederle begin her attempt before piling into their vehicles and driving to Boulogne to take the tug out into the Channel.

Onboard both tugs, the wireless machines were being put to good use. Wire services put out hourly updates on her progress, and those paying close attention on the receiving end could see that each one seemed to carry even more warning that the seas were becoming treacherous and the winds blustery. The Friday-afternoon newspapers in New York would all have front-page stories announcing Ederle was partway across the Channel, along with crudely drawn maps showing what they thought was her progress.

Among the reporters on the *Morinie* was an interested observer. Cannon had joined the group on the tug and sent word that she would be glad to swim with Trudy for a stretch if she wanted, a mark of good sportsmanship. Trudy had also invited Vera Tanner, the champion woman swimmer of England, to swim with her as she had the year before, and Trudy had been disappointed when Tanner didn't respond. Sion and Perrault also both refused because they planned to try the Channel themselves a few days later. That left only the slow-moving Helmy and Meg as swimming companions during the long swim, so she was happy that Cannon had decided to come along.

The first hour was the worst for Trudy, who, although not nervous, was acutely aware that she either would make this swim or never try it again. She had long ago decided that fear was her greatest enemy in the Channel, and she was determined not to let it interfere with her attempt.

"Swimming the Channel is all in the mind," she said. "You have to make up your mind that you're going to punish yourself. You can't give up as soon as the water gets a little rough or the wind gets bad. I think maybe that's why it's difficult for most women to swim the Channel. They don't want to punish themselves."

To those onboard, it looked like the punishment was beginning early. As the fourth hour of the swim began, the tide changed and the sighting of the sands of South Foreland proved prophetic, as now a high wind whipped the sea into a fury. But Trudy calmly plowed her way through the waves, telling those onboard to let her know when it was noon so she could have a bite to eat.

Ederle was going against conventional logic of the time, which was to eat a lot to retain warmth and energy. She didn't want to waste valuable swimming time eating and wasn't particularly hungry when in the water. Still, lunch would provide her the first change of pace, and she took it a bit early—at 11:35—when chicken broth was fed to her from a baby's bottle on the end of a pole held by Burgess. She also ate a leg of chicken, but she wasn't happy about resting in the water, even though she was about an hour ahead of schedule. When she resumed again, Burgess kept putting out his arm as a signal for Trudy to slow down, but she had been through that before with Wolffe and wasn't in any particular mood to listen this time around.

"If I go any slower I will sink," she said. "The water is wonderful. I could stay in it a week. Earlier it was cold."

On deck they played the phonograph for Ederle, using big needles to produce the loudest sound. Unlike the previous year, there was no band, which was probably good news to the tug captain, who wouldn't have to put up with seasick band members. When they played the song "No More Worrying," Trudy looked up, grinning, and said, "There won't be if we get to Dover tonight."

While the mood in the water was good, the mood on the tug was growing as dark as the skies overhead as the wind became gale force in the early afternoon and the sea grew terribly heavy. Trudy was thirteen miles into the swim, benefiting from the tide and making over two miles an hour, but still she was only ten miles from the French shore.

The weather, which had been so good just a few hours before, had now worsened to the point that some of the guests on the tug were leaning over the rail, seasick, and waves dashed over the deck. Burgess went to Harpman and suggested for the first time that Trudy should abandon her effort because the sea was simply too rough for anyone to swim through it.

"Gertie will have to come out. It's not humanly possible to go on in a sea like this," Burgess said.

Harpman replied that Ederle was still swimming strongly, and reminded Burgess of the promise everyone had made to her not to let anyone take her out unless she asked to get out herself.

"I won't take the responsibility of telling you to take her out," Harpman told the trainer. "She'd never forgive me."

As the sea raged, so did the argument. Harpman went to Corthes, who was having a tough time keeping to windward, where the tug could partially shield Ederle from some of the wind and waves without causing her to change her stroke or her pace.

"Is there any chance, Captain?" she asked.

Corthes shook his head sadly.

"No, no human being could do it today. Miss Ederle is the most wonderful swimmer I've ever seen. She's gone farther than any other swimmer ever went in the same time and she's had worse weather than any swimmer ever had. The only chance is when the tide changes. If she can last that long and the wind drops then, there may still be hope."

Burgess thought otherwise.

"It is madness to keep on," he said.

Meg, meanwhile, had entered the water to swim with her sister, a practice that was acceptable in the fluid rules of Channel swimming. But she, like the other companion swimmers, wasn't greased and she could swim for only a short time in the chilly water before climbing back aboard the tug and sitting, teeth chattering, under a pile of robes, trying to get warm while she drank hot coffee.

Harpman walked over and told her what Burgess had said, and she was going to have none of it.

"Oh no," Meg said. "It will break Trudy's heart to take her out. We promised and we must keep our promise. We will wait and see what happens when the tide changes."

More people on the tug were getting miserably seasick as it rolled and bucked across the waves. The water temperature was sixty-one degrees, but the seas were so high that the tug was being rocked by waves crashing over the deck, and Ederle was being forced to dodge driftwood carried high by the cresting waters. The only good thing about the rough seas was that the jellyfish didn't stick around long enough to bite.

Those onboard who weren't busy vomiting over the rails busied themselves with trying to keep Trudy's spirits up. The phonograph broke, so they started singing every song they could think of. Despite the sounds of the rough seas and the tug and her own difficulty in hearing, Trudy heard the choruses and particularly liked the rendition of "The Sidewalks of New York" because she could set a good rhythm to it with her stroke.

"Let Me Call You Sweetheart" was still her favorite, though, and those on the boat sang it endlessly, stopping only to exchange worried glances among themselves. As the storm raged, it was Ederle trying to keep everybody's spirits up from the water, and every time she stopped swimming for a moment, she laughed, because they would all jump up, worried that she was quitting.

Earlier in the swim, Sorenson had taken off his shoes and climbed out on the narrow steel rim running around the outer edge of the tug, about a foot above the water, and clung there like a monkey, drawing silly pictures on a small blackboard, which he lowered toward the tumbling water for Trudy to read. Now he drew pieces of the red roadster she dreamed of, shouting at her over the din of the sea, "You've got two wheels of that roadster now. Keep on, Trudy, you're sure to get the four."

Meg tried a different kind of inspiration after finally warming herself enough to get out from under the pile of robes. On the blackboard she wrote, "Think of Mother," drawing a laugh from Trudy, who replied, "Always and always." Trudy was even happier when messages came in on the wireless from her mother, which Meg would read to her.

The conditions continued to deteriorate, with huge waves tossing the tug about and making it difficult for Corthes to keep his pace. The waves were far worse than the previous year, when Ederle had been pulled from the water after a particularly strong wave smashed into her. But as the storm raged on for four hours, those onboard kept reminding themselves of the many times Trudy had begged them never to allow her to be taken out unless she was drowning.

She looked like she almost was at times, gasping for a breath as waves crashed over her and the tug bobbed dangerously only a few feet away. The difference this year was that Trudy was still in control of the swim, and those onboard knew exactly how she felt about keeping going until she either made it or collapsed trying.

"I won't drown," she'd told them repeatedly before the swim. "If I go down once, I'll be sure to come up again, and that will be time enough to take me out. But never, unless I ask you to, allow anyone to touch me. I'll faint before I ask to be taken out. And I never fainted in my life."

Touching, of course, was rule number one in the unwritten code of Channel rules. If a swimmer was touched by anyone while in the water, he or she would be immediately disqualified. That had happened to Trudy once, and she wasn't about to let it happen again if she had anything to say about it.

Still, it wasn't easy to watch as the huge waves tossed her about and it seemed like she could go under with each one. Everyone onboard the tug had a stake in either Trudy or her swim, and as they huddled on deck, they felt helpless as they watched her fight on.

New Yorkers jamming subway cars and street trolleys on their way to work on that Friday morning had no way of knowing the drama unfolding overseas. The morning papers spoke of a possible attempt by Ederle, but it would not be until the early-afternoon papers came out that they would have an idea how she was doing.

The Ederle family had better information. Her mother got an early phone call from the *Daily News* that the swim was under way, and sister Helen and brother George went down to the newspaper office to read the wireless cables from Harpman as they came in. The information was then relayed by phone both to the summer house at Highlands and to the butcher shop on Amsterdam Avenue, where Uncle John was leading the cheers.

Mrs. Ederle stood in her front yard of the summer home, leaning against the fence as she waited for bulletins about her daughter's progress, while neighbors gathered around, ready to celebrate at the slightest bit of good news. Inside, charts and maps of the Channel were spread around and Trudy's progress was charted with each new cable that came in.

The *New York Telegram,* which didn't have the benefit of someone covering the swim, reported in its afternoon final edition that just prior to the close of the stock market there were rumors on Wall Street that Ederle was within a few miles of the English shore. Brokerage houses received many inquiries, mainly because they had taken money at 3–1 odds on her making the swim, a practice that was legal at the time. The biggest bet was reported by J. S. Fried & Co., which had taken six thousand dollars to two thousand against her chances.

At 2:05 P.M., Burgess declared Ederle's position marvelous, though it turned out she had already gone farther north than planned because of strong tides heading out to the North Sea. The fate of the swim now hung on the next change of the tide in about an hour, and Trudy swam on as the waves rolled over her, sometimes burying her head deep beneath the water.

While Corthes struggled to shield her from the brunt of the winds with his tug, the second tug, carrying the other press people, came dangerously close four different times, and the backwash added to the problems Ederle was already having. Pop Ederle was almost beside himself as he screamed at those on the other tug.

"You loafers. If I had a gun, I'd shoot you," he yelled. "Keep back. Don't you see you're trying to kill the child?"

Trudy looked up from the water with a bemused look on her face.

"Why, Pop," she said, "what will people think of you?"

The humor wasn't forced. Ederle would later say that she was happy the entire swim, even when the sea raged around her. She had always been comfortable in the open sea and liked rough water anyway, and both the one-piece goggles and the two-piece swimsuit were working perfectly. Trudy was eating little, as was her plan, but she drank some hot cocoa and had a block of chocolate. Sugar seemed a key to keeping up her energy, and she ate sugar cube after sugar cube, delivered on the end of a long rod from the boat. With no touching allowed, food delivery via a fishing pole was the preferred method of nourishing Channel swimmers.

Helmy joined her in the water, and those onboard the tug held their breath as the two swam through a cloudy mass of the dreaded jellyfish, but both escaped without being stung. It might have been his fear of more jellyfish, or simply because he was a plodding swimmer in with a greyhound, but Helmy didn't last long with Trudy before bidding her good-bye and swimming about 150 yards over to the *Morinie*, where he asked Cannon if she wanted to take his place.

Burgess rowed over to get Cannon from the other tug, and when he returned, he brought a surprise. Also on the boat was a bronzed American by the name of Louis Timson, a Massachusetts swimmer sent to England by the American Legion to take a crack at swimming the Channel. Timson had been at his Dover training quarters when he heard that Trudy was in mid-Channel, and he'd boarded a motorboat to go out and watch.

By now, the tide had shifted and the current was taking Trudy southwest toward England, just as Burgess thought it would. Rain came on and off, but the wind was still very strong and the waves continued to crash over Trudy's head. Under these trying conditions, Trudy was more than delighted when Cannon joined her in the water.

"Hello, Lillian," she said. "We seem to be fifty miles from nowhere."

"Why, my dear, you are almost there," Cannon replied. "Keep it up."

Cannon's willingness to help Trudy was admirable, considering the Baltimore swimmer wanted to become the first woman across the Channel almost as badly as Ederle did, and that the two had begun the summer locked into a dispute over their trainer. They had reconciled during the long days of training, and not only had Cannon wished her luck on the beach in France but she swam for about an hour in the turbulent Channel, giving Trudy a welcome respite from having to go it alone.

Timson followed Cannon in the water, but, like Helmy, he didn't last long. He was a breaststroker, and after only a few minutes he realized that he could not keep up with Trudy and her speedy and efficient American crawl. He returned to the tug and settled into a new role as cheerleader, with his loud, powerful voice and encouraging smile lifting Trudy's spirits even more. For what seemed like hours, he kept shouting, "Take it easy, Trudy" and "You're wonderful, Trudy, wonderful." Timson was also a good singer, which helped on a boat full of tone-deaf people.

In the water, Ederle was doing some singing of her own, mostly to her favorite tune of "Let Me Call You Sweetheart," which she'd played continuously on her hand-wound Victrola at the Hôtel du Phare. Now she hummed it as the hours went by and she swam one stroke at a time toward England.

Ederle kept up the pace, swimming relentlessly, though she had no way of knowing just how well she was doing. At 4:30, she asked how near she was to the East Goodwin Lightship and was encouraged when told it had been sighted. The lightship marked the eastern edge of the Goodwin Sands, the graveyard of many sailors and ships because of its nasty currents and tides, but being able to see it meant that Trudy was making progress toward England.

The South Calliper buoy was also to the northwest of the swimmer, giving assurance to both Corthes and Burgess that Trudy had reached a good position north of Dover and to the east of Deal, where the final current should help bring her in. Burgess, who had feared they had headed too far north toward the North Sea, showed Trudy the chart and she paddled in place while studying it. She asked Burgess how much longer he thought the swim would be, and he replied about five hours.

"Don't let me ever give up," she said, shaking a fist in the air for added emphasis.

It wasn't going to be easy. Mountainous waves, gray with crests of foam and cresting twenty feet high, beat against the deck of the tug. The wind shrieked, the sky was darkening, and Corthes thought the weather was so bad that he wouldn't be able to land the tug at Dover and might have to put in at Deal, which would require an additional four hours of maneuvering to cut through the waves and current. Most of those on-board were terribly seasick, and the mood was growing as somber as the skies as they contemplated hours more at sea. Burgess, who had been briefly optimistic only a short time earlier, again grew doubtful about her chances, and for one of about a dozen times that day, he insisted Trudy be taken out of the water.

Pop Ederle was going to have the final decision, and he wasn't sure what to do. Burgess certainly knew the Channel and the conditions, but Pop wasn't sure the trainer knew his daughter. Pop Ederle walked away to a corner of the tug by himself, where he broke down, crying in despair at what might happen to his daughter. After a few minutes, he went to Timson, his eyes brimming with tears.

"Mr. Timson, will you give your word of honor to stand here [at the steel railing at the edge of the deck] so that if you see Trudy weakening you can jump in?"

"I'll not move from here," Timson replied, "but she isn't weaken-ing. She's marvelous."

Timson was true to his word, remaining at his post and leading the cheerleading efforts. The cheerleading proved vital because Ederle could see that almost everyone else on both the tug she was following and the tug filled with reporters was growing increasingly despondent as the swim went on. Cannon and Helmy were both too seasick to go back in the water, but while Meg had a stinging pain in her side, she insisted on going back into the water, if only for a while.

If things on the boat were bleak, Trudy wasn't aware of it in the wa-ter. She felt not only happy but strong and in control as she swam along with no change in her stroke, her red cap disappearing beneath the wa-ter, only to reappear a few seconds later. Harpman saw her grit her teeth and thought she was suffering, but Ederle would tell her later that she did it merely to keep the salt water out of her mouth.

By 6:00 P.M., the sea was still frightful, yet Trudy plowed on. This was a critical time in the swim for many Channel swimmers battling both weakness after long hours in the water and the elements of the Channel. More than a few had given up with fewer miles to go than they had already traveled, but Trudy was determined not to be one of them. Again, Burgess suggested that it would be wise to take her out, but Meg told him in no uncertain terms that the promise they had made to her sister not to let anybody touch her unless she was drowning would be kept.

Indeed, Trudy hadn't given a thought to quitting when she heard someone yell from the boat that she should. The suggestion angered her, even though the cliffs occasionally visible through the waves to the north of Dover still seemed mighty far away.

Burgess was equally determined not to have a drowning on his watch. He had grown fond of the young American girl, and besides, it would be bad for business. At 7:11 P.M., he told Harpman that he would not take the responsibility of waiting for a sign from Trudy indicating she wanted to quit. Instead, he leaned over the side of the tug and made his case directly to the swimmer.

"Come out, Gertie. You must come out."

An astonished Ederle looked up and yelled back, "What for?"

Those aboard the tug cheered wildly, forgetting for just a moment that their stomachs had been turned upside down and that Trudy's victory was still not a sure thing. There was still the treacherous Goodwin Sands to get past, where the tides shifted rapidly and the wrong turn of the current could mean disaster, but Trudy's response gave them hope that maybe, just maybe, it could be done.

Burgess himself seemed taken aback by her pluck, and he told Harpman that he had never seen anyone so marvelous in the water. Instead of worrying about the waves and the wind, he began focusing on the possibility she just might make it, telling Ederle to take her time as she passed the South Goodwin Lightship, which saluted her with its siren. The sea was still vicious and the winds icy, but now Ederle was only a few miles from the English shore. She knew now that she was making good time, though the grease was wearing off and she was feeling cold for the first time.

The lumps of sugar she kept eating stimulated her, and as she crept close to England, she had some slices of pineapple and some pineapple juice. The plan was to ride the last tide onto shore, but it turned an hour and a half too soon, and instead of being swept toward shore, she had some of her hardest work just to make progress as the sky grew darker.

But make progress she did, and when she was only about a mile off the coast, she could make out bright lights onshore, which came from bonfires set by a crowd that had gathered quickly after getting word that the American was nearing the beach a few miles north of Dover.

"Is that England?" she asked Burgess.

"Yes," he replied.

"Then let's go."

Trudy swam strongly in the last stretch and was about three hundred yards off the coast when the tug could get no closer to shore. Burgess, Pop, Timson, and Sorenson got in a small rowboat to accompany her in the oncoming darkness. She stopped swimming and took off her goggles because she could not see through them, then swam toward the boat to hand them to Sorenson. Burgess, knowing that the current near the shore could still stop her agonizingly close to the finish, yelled at her to keep going and toss the goggles in the water, but Trudy was determined to keep them as a souvenir.

"Just swim," Burgess yelled out. "Swim."

In the boat, Timson held a lantern up high, and Trudy followed it in with a finishing sprint that drew hysterical shouts from both those on the tug and onshore.

Some of the reporters and photographers on the *Morinie* were determined not to be scooped on the historic moment when Trudy set foot onshore. They piled in a rowboat and tried to follow her in, but it sprang a leak and began filling fast. They had to be plucked from the water and put back on the tug, very wet but rescued just in the nick of time.

One reporter, Ralph Barnes of the *New York Herald Tribune,* was determined to get his scoop. The wireless on the *Morinie* had failed an hour earlier, and he didn't plan to wait in line to send his story. He swam ashore and ran two miles into Dover to find a phone, where he then relayed his story to the London bureau in time to get it in the next day's paper.

It was a wild scene on the beach, where people were lighting flares and dancing in joy before bonfires of driftwood. Trudy sprinted toward the shore, a spotlight from the *Alsace* trained on her, and about fifteen feet from the water's edge tried to stand up. But the water was too deep and she went to the bottom, then had to start swimming again, keeping on this time until her hands touched the pebbles offshore.

People on the beach screamed in delight as she stood up, then paused to adjust her brassiere, which had gotten tangled because of the grease and heavy waves. Her father had already reached shore in the boat, and he ran up to her with a wrap, but she told him to stay back, knowing she had to get a foot out of water before her victory would be official.

Trudy had made a mental list of things she would need to do if she made it, and that was the first item on the list. The second wasn't far behind.

"Pop, do I get that red roadster?" she asked.

Whistles went off, giant cheers roared over the beach, and several women went running into the water, getting their skirts wet, to kiss Trudy as she came ashore. One woman put her arms around Ederle, not seeming to mind the grease that still covered the swimmer's body.

With the first scrape of her hands on the rocks in the fading light, she made history. Fourteen hours and thirty-nine minutes after leaving the rocky shore of France, she had become the first woman to swim the English Channel. Stunningly, she had fulfilled Burgess's prophecy by doing it in record time, smashing the mark set by Tiraboschi three years earlier by an hour and fifty-four minutes.

Burgess later calculated the swim at thirty-one and a half miles and said Trudy had taken 100,000 kicks and 22,000 arm strokes to make it across. Trudy would later say it was closer to thirty-five miles, and ten hours of the swim had been made while battling various storms.

Amazingly, Ederle wasn't particularly fatigued, though the boost she got from what she later said was an "intoxicating feeling of elation" on hitting the beach most likely played a part in that. Her achievement reminded her of a childhood dream or fantasy, but this was all so real. Trudy wasn't onshore long, much to the dismay of those in the crowd, who wanted to celebrate with her. Pop put a towel and dressing gown around her and she had to fight her way through the adoring crowd to the rowboat for the trip back out to the *Alsace,* which would take her to the dock in Dover.

There were hugs, congratulations, and tears of joy on the tug, where everyone tried to make her as comfortable as possible. Ederle wanted some pineapple for her tongue, which she said "felt like a scenic railway," but that and a strained ligament in her right wrist from shaking so many exuberant hands on the beach were her only injuries from the swim. Burgess gave her his coat to keep warm and the tug took off through the choppy waters, where the girl who had so gallantly made her way across the Channel promptly became seasick. The water had calmed enough to dock in the Dover harbor, but the tug had to wait for a large barge to be moved, so the *Alsace* didn't get to shore until around midnight.

One more bizarre scene awaited, as a quite proper English customs official wouldn't let Trudy in because she didn't have her passport. After much questioning, he produced an official document and made her stand up on deck while cross-examining her for her name, her father's name, and their family history.

The rest of the group got the same treatment before the official made a grand announcement that they would be permitted to enter England, but only on the condition that they be back at ten o'clock the next morning with their passports. The dockhands witnessing it all cheered Trudy and booed the customs official mercilessly.

At Dover, they checked into the Grand Hotel, where Meg and Harpman gave Trudy a bath, her first since leaving Paris two months earlier. They brought her some ham sandwiches, and she ate four before going to bed.

The reality of her new celebrity hadn't yet begun to sink in. But it was clear something had changed.

"I was tired, awfully tired, and I couldn't understand why people wouldn't stop making a fuss over me and let me go to sleep," she would say later. "It was at least five hours after the swim was completed before I was quietly in my room and then I was overtired and could not sleep."

While Trudy was looking for a place to sleep, the world was just finding out about her stunning accomplishment. The Associated Press sent a bulletin proclaiming her victory.

> KINGSDOWN, England (AP)—Gertrude Ederle, American girl swimmer, landed here tonight, successfully swimming the English Channel from Cape Gris-Nez, France. She made the crossing in spite of unfavorable conditions.

Word had gotten back quickly to Ederle's family in the United States via the dispatches from the *Daily News* offices. Mrs. Ederle was so nervous, she hadn't been able to sleep the night before, knowing her daughter was in the water, and she hadn't eaten in twenty-four hours. When the phone rang with the fateful news, she was too nervous to answer it and delegated the task to Trudy's cousin, thirteen-year-old Elsie Ederle.

"Gertrude has won!!" Elsie yelled.

The street in front of the Ederles' Highlands home was soon crowded with hundreds of neighbors who came to celebrate, while Mrs. Ederle held court in her front yard. She told reporters she'd known Trudy would make it because her daughter was determined to make up for the previous year—and she desperately wanted a red roadster.

"I am the proudest and the happiest mother in the world tonight," she said. "But I knew she would do it this time. She left here with her mind made up to let nothing keep her from her goal and she has won it."

At the butcher shop on Amsterdam Avenue, Uncle John stood outside, handing out free strings of wieners to every youngster in sight, in front of a homemade sign celebrating her success. MISS EDERLE SWIMS THE ENGLISH CHANNEL IN 14 HOURS, it read.

At the Ritz-Carlton, Jack Dempsey called the United Press from his suite to see how the swim had gone.

"Say, can you tell me how Miss Ederle made out in the Channel swim?" he asked.

"She made it? That's great."

Dempsey was as pleased as if he had just knocked out Gene Tunney, and he celebrated with his managers and trainers.

"I didn't think she'd make it," he said, grabbing manager Doc Bagley in a playful headlock, "but I'm tickled to death she did."

8

The Celluloid Web

The news reached Boulogne from the deck of the *Morinie*, which
pulled into its home port about 6:00 A.M. Saturday, after steaming five hours overnight through heavy seas to carry its weary and weak-
stomached cargo of reporters, photographers, and swimmers back to
France. Hundreds in the city had stayed up all night to find out what
had happened, and they were in the harbor to greet the tug.

"Where is Miss Ederle?" they yelled as the tug approached.

"She is across!" came the reply.

Rutherford wrote in the *Times* that no one aboard the tug looked all
that happy, except for the newspapermen and photographers. They were
grateful not only for a big story but to be finally ashore after navigating
the Channel across and back again in vomit-inducing seas.

Cannon was on the tug as it returned, the question running through
her mind whether she should even make her own attempt now. But while
she had to have been disappointed she would never have a chance to be

the first, she never let on to reporters that she was anything but thrilled with Trudy's successful swim.

"She is wonderful," Cannon said. "No other person, man or woman, could have accomplished the feat. She used a powerful stroke and meant business. I was so pleased to accompany her part of the way. I swam for an hour and found the water very cold. How great she is!"

Rutherford reported that there was a lot of discussion among swimmers and others in Boulogne about the future of Channel swimming now that Ederle had not only made it across but also struck a stunning blow for her gender by setting a new record in the process. Most expected Cannon, Corson, and other swimmers to go forward with their plans anyway, but now they also had to face a new record, one that was thought impossible to beat. Rutherford handicapped the remaining contenders by noting that Cannon was frail in comparison to Ederle, was not speedy, and could not stand a severe buffeting in the water. As for Corson, the mother of two who was trying her own swim, he was slightly more optimistic, saying she was "very persistent, but the Ederle record also stands before her, even if she is successful."

Across the Channel, the sun was coming up and Ederle was awakening to a world that, for her, would be changed forever. She had slept fitfully, and she took a second bath before going down the hallway to wake up Meg and Harpman for some breakfast.

Outside the hotel, crowds were already beginning to gather in hopes of getting a glimpse of the woman who had beaten the men at their own game. Reporters gathered to hear the story of her triumph, but they would have to wait for Trudy to get a rubdown from Burgess before getting the scoop from the swimmer herself. Pop Ederle, a cigar in his mouth as always, wasn't shy about filling up the time in between by describing to everyone just how the swim had gone and what a courageous swimmer his daughter was.

"She'll get that roadster and everything else she wants," he said.

Corthes, the tug captain, told reporters that Trudy would have made it four hours earlier if the weather hadn't gotten so bad, while Helmy chimed in with a comment that would prove strikingly prophetic.

"The first woman Channel victor? The first kid, you mean," the

Egyptian swimmer said. "There will be another Channel victory next week, but never another like this."

Ederle wasn't as much of a kid as they thought. When she swam in the Olympics, she was said to be seventeen, most likely because Epstein shaved a year off her age to make her appear even more of a child wonder than she really was. She was actually born on October 23, 1905, making her just short of her nineteenth birthday in the Olympics, but Epstein had a knack of getting publicity and wasn't above making up a little white lie about her swimmer's age.

Ederle never corrected her age publicly, and when she tried to swim the Channel the first time, she was widely described as an eighteen-year-old. Now, instead of being nineteen, as every newspaper article described her, she was actually nearing her twenty-first birthday. She would live the rest of her life with the younger age, and even when she died, there were conflicting reports about how old she was.

The trip to see the customs man to clear up the passport issue didn't prove necessary. Apparently, the bureaucrat had gotten word from higher-ups that he better not ruin the party, and he arrived at the hotel early to make a cursory check of the documents and congratulate the Channel queen himself.

Burgess wanted Ederle to go back into the Channel for a light swim to limber up her muscles, an idea that didn't particularly thrill her after she'd spent more than fourteen hours in it the day before. But it was a chance for photographers to get pictures of her in the daylight on the English shore, so she dutifully got back into a swimsuit—this one a more traditional one-piece outfit—and prepared to head out to the beach. First, though, she held a brief session with reporters eager for quotes to fill their Sunday newspapers.

Ederle told them she would never swim the Channel again but would be glad to take a boat across as soon as she could. And while she didn't seem to grasp the enormity of the moment, she did seem pleased that she was the first of her sex to have conquered the raging waters.

"Well I am the first woman who did it, am I not?" she said. "It's up with the women and down with the men."

The first real details of the swim came courtesy of Burgess, who was more than glad to share some of the glory, since he'd never really gotten any when he became the second man to swim the Channel. He told reporters that the first two hours were all right but that the wind had churned the sea up and he'd had to take her off course so the tug could help shelter her. To do that, Trudy had had to swim east at one point, he said, and crowds watching from shore must have thought she was crazy.

"I know very well if we had been wrong in our calculations and Trudy had been forced to give up, her handlers would have been drummed around the world as a band of boneheads," Burgess said. "Instead of steering northwest we were driven northeast. By the seventh hour out, the north wind got so bad we were steering almost directly east heading for the North Sea."

Burgess credited his swimmer with never having wavered, even while being forced to take a zigzag path because of heavy seas and to keep clear of numerous wrecks on the Goodwin Sands. Burgess also gave himself some credit for coming up with the idea not to eat much on the swim, even though he had initially opposed it, saying, "Our starvation plan was the best treatment as most swimmers get seasick in such rough waters, but Trudy didn't."

The successful crossing was only a few hours old, but suddenly everyone wanted a part of Trudy. She walked through Dover arm in arm with Burgess, Sorenson, and the dashing Helmy, followed by large crowds on her way to the beach, where she delighted everyone by showing off her stroke for about fifteen minutes.

Corson was training on the English shore for her own attempt and came to the beach to pay homage to Ederle. She had made the mistake of waiting too long to swim, and now she had to be resigned that she would never be the first.

"I congratulate you, but you're a naughty girl," she told Ederle. "I wanted to be the first woman to swim the Channel, but now I am determined to be the second."

After Trudy's swim, Helmy and Timson carried her through the streets of Dover on their shoulders, followed by large and admiring crowds. Trudy had brought along extra clothes just in case, and she changed into a skirt and tie with a blazer to pose before a statue in town devoted to Captain Webb. The mayor of Dover and his wife joined her in paying tribute to the man who had first conquered the swirling waters, while bands played and people shouted her name.

The town's postal service was flooded with telegrams and cables of congratulation, including one from President Coolidge, which reached Trudy before she left the hotel. She had no way of knowing, but the reaction at home was almost as hysterical as it was in Dover, especially among the New York tabloids, all of which were eager to make her a national heroine.

Thanks to modern technology and the time difference, the news had already swept over New York City before the sun went down the day before. Work was suspended at the sausage factory on Amsterdam Avenue as Uncles John and Ernest ran through the shop, telling the twenty-seven employees of the success. Neighbors waiting outside knew Trudy had made it when her uncles came out with a telegram in one hand and huge hunks of bologna in the other.

At the Polo Grounds, which, like other parks of the time, didn't have a public-address system, the announcer went around to the different stands and used his megaphone to trumpet news of her triumph. Fans stopped watching to cheer, then were doubly pleased when the Giants pulled out a 6–3 win over the Cincinnati Reds.

Harpman's account of the swim would be published the next morning in the *Daily News,* thrilling readers with her detail about how Ederle had refused to give up, despite the treacherous waters. In the same edition, Gallico became the first to seize on the "What for?" comment made by Trudy when Burgess tried to get her to quit the swim.

"And thus, with two words, Miss Gertrude Ederle disposed of the English Channel. No wonder it couldn't lick her. She destroyed it utterly," wrote Gallico, who in the typical flowery style of the time went on to compare her success to childhood stories of fairy princesses who shattered the forces of evil in the time of danger.

"I like to think of Trudie's great adventure that way," Gallico said. "She slipped into the grip of the enchanted waters and struck out for the pots of gold that lay at the end of the journey."

Ed Sullivan wasn't as flowery in his praise, but just as effusive. The man who would introduce the Beatles to America nearly four decades later declared that Trudy had "stamped herself as the greatest girl athlete of all time, far greater than [tennis players] Suzanne Lenglen, Helen Wills, [golfer] Glenna Collett or any of the other girl athletes, who have stamped themselves and their records upon the scroll of sports.

"For Gertrude Ederle yesterday proved that the female of the species is far greater than the male."

Most extraordinary was that the first photographs of the swim were printed in Saturday's *Daily News,* a feat that was almost as unimaginable as a woman swimming the Channel. The first picture was of a greased-up Ederle standing on the beach at Cape Gris-Nez just before entering the water for her swim, and the second purported to show her arm sweeping across the water as she began her swim. At least that was what the reader was told, for the pictures were so grainy that Ederle looked more like a creature from outer space than a swimmer.

Still, it was a spectacular coup for the tabloid that billed itself as New York's "Picture Newspaper," and it didn't come cheap. The photographs were obtained via the new Bartlane process, a technological wonder of the 1920s that allowed images to be put on perforated telegraph tape and transmitted over wires before coming out as a picture of sorts when the same tape was run through a machine at the other end.

The pictures had been rushed from mid-Channel by boat to Dover, then driven by motorcycle to London before being sent to New York by cable and made into plates at the newspaper. The *Daily News* proudly declared that just nineteen hours had elapsed from the camera's click until the photos appeared in the paper.

The *New York Times* had its own photo spread, entitled "Miss Ederle in Action and in Repose," showing photos from her swim the year before and one taken of her holding a doll upon her return from that failed attempt. The *Times* would have to wait another week for photos of the actual swim—and even then it would be scooped once again by the *Daily News.*

The paper also reported for the first time that it had backed Trudy for $5,000 if she failed the swim and $7,500 if she won. America had its first true female sports hero, and the *Daily News* was going to ride the wave of adulation every step of the way with her.

The rest of the world joined in the cheering, marveling at the accomplishment while expressing grudging admiration for the pluck of Americans, who seemed to have a knack for daring to do things that others wouldn't.

"Young America has again startled the world," the *London Observer* said. "Twenty years ago no woman would have dreamed of attempting such a feat. Even now its accomplishment verges so nearly on the incredible that further details of the record time cease to surprise."

The London papers devoted pages to Ederle, though she had to share space with the eminently quotable Anita Loos, the famed American screenwriter and author who was riding the success of her first book, *Gentlemen Prefer Blondes,* published a year earlier. Loos had arrived in London the same day Ederle was swimming the Channel to watch rehearsals of her 1923 farce, *The Whole Town is Talking,* and gave interviews to almost every paper about most everything, except Channel swimming.

Loos was attractive, sophisticated, and wittier than Trudy. She was also no stranger to controversy, and there was talk that censors would ban the play based on her book if she tried to produce it in London, because it made scathing references to British royalty. That didn't happen, but two months later the play *The Fall of Eve,* which Loos wrote with her husband, John Emerson, was banned by the British censors because the plot involved a married woman who drank too much and took her husband's best friend to bed with her.

By contrast, Trudy was the all-American girl, a young woman devoted to her mother and father, and the complete antithesis of the flapper girls, whose short skirts and penchant to party seemed scandalous to the higher echelons of British society. She was an immediate favorite with the London press, though it surely didn't hurt that the stories were accompanied by pictures of her in a swimsuit.

The *Illustrated Sunday Herald* ran a full front page of photos, one show-ing Trudy swimming the Channel while her father and Burgess watched from the tug, and another of her on the beach in Dover with a large crowd of people looking on. The *Daily Sketch* bannered the story with the astonishing headline THE CHANNEL CONQUERED BY A GIRL.

The more sedate *London Times* offered a rather stuffy view, saying, "To be the first woman to swim across the Channel and to swim it faster than anybody else has ever done before is an achievement of which Miss Ederle may well be proud."

And then there was the *London Daily News*, which was forced to eat crow after an ill-timed editorial published on Saturday proclaimed that women would never be equal to men and "even the most uncompromising cham-pion of the rights and capacities of women must admit that in contests of physical skill, speed and endurance they must remain forever the weaker sex."

The editorial was written before Trudy's remarkable swim became known, and the paper came back on Sunday to congratulate her in its own way.

"Miss Ederle is evidently a superwoman," the paper said. "Her per-formance is felicitous and is a pointed retort to our comment, and, while it fails to affect the integrity of our statement as a generalization, we offer our defense without enthusiasm and in the chastened spirit of true humility."

Papers in France were more generous with their praise, and they were almost beside themselves in Berlin, where they made note of Trudy's German heritage and implied that she had won not just for her-self but for the fatherland, too. The paper *Nachtausgabe* called her feat "one of the greatest athletic achievements of all time," while *Achtuhr-Abendblatt* said that "incontrovertible willpower combined with tran-scendent ability and a well deserved stroke of good luck helped achieve this masterpiece in the art of swimming."

Sir Herbert Barker, a prominent British surgeon, tried to explain it in medical terms. He said women tolerated cold better than men and had greater endurance than men did. He ended by saying that the evolution of the swimming suit played a big role by allowing Ederle to swim the Channel without the risk of drowning in her garments.

Back home, the swim was quickly becoming a rallying cry for both the women's movement and those who believed that it ushered in a new order in the world of sport. Writers opined that it showed women were equal to men, with the *St. Paul Pioneer Press* going as far as to say the practice of separating men and women in sports was now "patronizing and condescending in the present practice of classification of women in sports."

Ederle's fellow female athletes were ecstatic about the possibilities ahead. Collett, the woman golf champion, knew she wasn't going to play against Bobby Jones, but she thought that there might be a woman someday who could compete against a man.

"I suppose the men will have to try again now to get that record back," Collett said. "It just goes to show that women can even beat the men if they try hard enough."

Lenglen, the great French tennis player, said in Paris, while on her way to take a ship to the United States for the U.S. Open, that Ederle "must be a superwoman, that's all. I consider Miss Ederle's feat the greatest any individual athlete has accomplished for a decade."

The longtime coach of the Northwestern University swimming team said that Ederle could never have done what she did thirty years ago because corsets and other "ridiculously unnecessary clothing" deprived women of the muscular freedom necessary to be a good swimmer. Now, Tom Robinson said, physical education was a driving force in helping women become equal with men.

"It has taught her how to dress sensibly and comfortably, it has taught her to think more freely, and it has helped her to enjoy life as she never had a chance to before. As a result, it has brought a new race of women athletes."

The shock and magnitude of Ederle not only making it across the Channel but shattering the record set by a man couldn't be overestimated, considering the times. Women were still getting used to the idea of being able to go behind the curtains of a voting booth, and they were expressing their rights in ways that could never have been imagined a generation earlier.

The flapper girls got the attention, but women were now not just voting but being elected to office. More women were playing sports, and they were competing for and winning medals for their country in major events like the Olympics. Trudy exemplified the spirit of the newly freed female's ability to do anything men could do, and feminist leaders were quick to embrace her success.

"It's a far cry from swimming the Channel to the days to which my memory goes back, when it was thought that women could not throw a ball or even walk very far down the street without feeling faint," said Carrie Chapman Catt, founder of the League of Women Voters.

Catt remembered the first speech she had heard from a feminist forty years earlier, who predicted that women's freedom would go hand in hand with her bodily strength. Now, she said, that was being proven true by women everywhere.

"Today the American woman is a far better physical specimen than she was two generations ago and she is ashamed to be ill."

Mrs. Raymond Brown, the managing director of *The Woman Citizen,* the magazine of the suffrage movement, said, "The beauty of these spectacular achievements by any one woman is that they kill off a lot of bugaboos that hinder the rest of the women. People still say silly things about women being weaklings, despite public school athletes and the sports in which women of all ages indulge so generally. It takes a good drama like this to teach the world a lesson."

The world needed the lesson. Henry L. Sullivan, who three years earlier had taken nearly twenty-seven hours—almost double Ederle's time—to become the first American male to swim the Channel, echoed the thoughts of the time.

"I hardly thought it possible for a woman to do it," Sullivan said.

Most New Yorkers didn't, either. But they loved the fact that an American woman had done it, and predicted that it would change women forever. At least that was the view of Jacob Hirschey, an usher from the Bronx, who was caught by the *Daily News's* inquiring photographer on East Fourteenth and Broadway.

"The slim type of girl will go out of fashion," he predicted. "The athletic type is bound to be the type most admired."

Ederle's stay in Dover was short, much to the dismay of the thousands who followed her to the beach for her brief swim and back to the Grand Hotel, where she tried unsuccessfully to say a few words to them from the balcony of her suite. Still shy about public speaking, the size of the crowd both frightened and overwhelmed her in a way the Channel never could. She did stay long enough to dine at the hotel, which had a menu that must have pleased both her and her butcher father. The luncheon featured oxtail soup, roast ribs of beef, Yorkshire pudding, and a cherry tart and custard for dessert.

All of Dover was bedecked in the Stars and Stripes, bands played, and excited shouts reverberated down the town's streets when there was word of a Trudy sighting. When the Ederle party gathered to leave on the 4:00 P.M. steamer for Boulogne, a row of cars followed them down to the dock, where local residents crowded around to give her one final send-off.

The trip back across the Channel was a lot quicker than the swim over, and once again, an excited throng awaited Ederle as the Channel steamer *Biarritz* made its way into the harbor. Even before it docked, harbor craft gave her a noisy welcome, with flags flying from their mastheads and sirens and horns wailing. Among the welcoming craft was the *Alsace,* which had accompanied her on her swim, and Captain Corthes's young daughter greeted Trudy with a huge bouquet of flowers.

With thousands cheering her every move, Trudy and her party went to the home of the American consul at Boulogne, William Corcoran, for what would be the first of many receptions. At one point, Corcoran cried out, "Hooray for Prohibition" as he served champagne to all in a toast to Ederle, a move that would later prompt some Prohibition leaders in the United States to call for his removal from his post.

The celebration would be more raucous that night at the Hôtel du Phare in Cape Gris-Nez, where townspeople who had watched Trudy train for two months gathered to welcome her home. Pop Ederle was in a mood to party, even if his daughter just wanted to go to bed, and he held court in the lobby, greeting a stream of well-wishers while popping cork after cork from some seventy bottles of the best champagne around for nonstop toasts and speeches.

Pop had every right to be happy. Not only had his daughter made it across against all odds; there were reports he had profited by putting a large sum at Lloyd's of London on his daughter's chances. He had also insured her swim with Lloyd's, and he stood to make 2,700 pounds just because she'd made it across.

Wolffe was among those enjoying a bit of the bubbly, telling anyone who would listen that he greatly envied Burgess for being the trainer but had always known that Trudy could swim the Channel. "Miss Ederle had everything against her," Wolffe said, "and she won. She is an athletic phenomenon and I do not believe her Channel record will ever be beaten."

Trudy, meanwhile, was desperately trying to get off a telegram to her mother, which she had been unable to do in Dover. The cable that eventually went out from Boulogne would have made any mother cry.

"My dearest loving mother," it read. "We did it, the trick is turned, and aren't you just so proud?"

By this time, Ederle was beginning to get an idea about the enormity of what she had done. If the crowds who followed her every move weren't clue enough, the telegrams and cables that poured in from around the world by the hundreds were. The first offers to cash in were among them, with the Columbia Theatre sending an offer of one thousand dollars a week for Trudy to appear, while the Shuberts doubled that to two thousand.

There were also bids from radio networks to broadcast Ederle's personal story of her swim, while a chewing-gum company wanted her to endorse its product. A car company offered a roadster, but it wasn't the red Buick she wanted, so she refused. Buick wasn't far behind, sending a man by airplane from London to tell her that the company would present her with a car when she got home, though the *Daily News* had already taken care of that.

"I guess we will sell the business now," Pop Ederle said as the offers kept coming.

The money was huge at a time when the minimum wage at Ford plants was $6 a day, a car salesman might bring home $200 a month, and a ready-to-build house could be bought from the Sears catalog for as little as $800. A Dodge touring car was advertised new in Morristown, New Jersey, for $795, and gas to fuel it was $.18 a gallon.

Trudy vowed not to endorse any of the products she didn't actually use or approve of. There would be no cigarette ads and nothing that even hinted of the risqué. She wanted to be herself, though she was coming to the realization that what she was had suddenly changed in the time it had taken her to make it from France to England.

"I never dreamed that being a celebrity entailed so much," she said in a bylined story for the *Daily News* on Sunday, August 8. "Since I set foot on the sands of England Friday night, I haven't had a moment of my waking time to myself. I have to fight the question that now and again vaguely forms in my mind, the question whether in the end success in a great endeavor is worth quite all the grief."

Indeed, the next day Trudy was forced to dodge two men from Paris and one from London who had come to offer her public appearances. It wasn't an easy task in the tiny fishing village, where she also tended to doing the laundry she hadn't done for three weeks and began packing to leave. That by itself wouldn't prove to be an easy task. The robes, sweaters, and other garments worn by Meg and Pop on the tug were so soiled with grease that they were being shipped home in a big box, and the family sorted through two months' worth of possessions to decide what to take on the return home.

Ederle wanted to leave as soon as possible. She was eager to get home to see her mother, get her new red roadster, and get to Philadelphia to watch the much-anticipated heavyweight-title fight the next month between Dempsey and Tunney.

"I wish we could go home immediately," she wrote. "I have a will to get there and get into that roadster Pop is going to give me for having made good. And, by the way, Pop seems to be getting more kick out of the whole thing than any of the rest of us. At times he's almost irrational with joy."

Trudy would have one last good look at the Channel before she left. On Tuesday, she got up early to go to the shore to see her friend Helmy and Georges Michel, the enormous Frenchman who had won the Paris Marathon two weeks earlier, try to swim the Channel themselves. Trudy had planned to swim some of the way with Helmy, but the crush of expectations now on her precluded that, and so she merely wished them good luck.

The *Alsace* accompanied Helmy, a good-luck sign for the Egyptian. But both he and Michel, who swam adorned only in grease, had to abandon their swim thirteen hours after they'd entered the water, because the sea got too heavy and they had stopped making progress. Harpman wrote about the failure, and said there was "a general impression here that nobody but Trudy will conquer the Channel this year."

There was one more bit of business before leaving France. American consul Gaston Smith, who represented the Cape Gris-Nez area, was holding a reception in Ederle's honor on Wednesday, and the swimmer and her entourage made their way up the coast for one last tribute. All the men who worked at the giant shipping yard in Calais stopped what they were doing to gather around the administration villa, where Trudy was received by the wife of the sporting editor of the *Paris Tribune*.

Ederle seemed confused and overwhelmed as she got out of the car and saw men gathered on nearby rooftops, on the tops of automobiles, and even on top of the villa itself to greet her. They yelled her name, and cheered and whistled as she went by.

"What am I going to do? I can't face all these men," she said.

Somehow, Ederle got through it, even going so far as to shake hands with a few of the well-wishers. But she was so overcome by emotion that she could only nod her head in thanks when presented a silk scarf in honor of her accomplishment. From there, it was on to City Hall for a reception with the mayor, but Trudy wanted nothing more than to just get out of town, scarf in hand.

"I guess this will be for my wedding dress," she said.

When it came time to leave France, New York wasn't the destination. Henry Ederle had planned all along for a visit to his mother's home in Bissingen, Germany, where Trudy and her sisters had almost drowned in the town lake on their previous visit twelve years earlier. There would be no disappointing the seventy-six-year-old so eager to see the granddaughter who was causing such a commotion.

The trip home would have to wait. It was off to Paris, then to Germany by train, even though Lufthansa had offered to fly the Ederles from Paris to Berlin and from Berlin to anywhere in the country. Trudy may have been brave in the Channel, but even she had her limits, and she wasn't about to take a chance on the rudimentary propeller planes of the day.

A theater in Berlin sent her an offer for an appearance there, but Trudy declined, saying she wasn't going to appear anywhere before she appeared in her hometown.

"If I'm making a mistake, nobody will suffer but myself," she said. "Anyway, grandmother would be offended if we shortened our few days visit with her in order to appear in Berlin."

The mistake wasn't turning down an invitation to perform in Berlin. It was going to Germany in the first place, a move that delayed her return to New York for nearly two weeks. Henry Ederle insisted on it, and his dutiful daughter wouldn't dare have argued, even if she was now the Queen of the Channel.

But the delay would haunt Ederle the rest of her life.

9

Channelitis Strikes
Cape Gris-Nez

The Germans greeted Trudy as one of their own, which indeed she was. Her parents had been born in this land, she had spent time there as a child, and now she was returning as the long-lost daughter who had made good. Thirty thousand people jammed the train station at Stuttgart to see her arrive, and she was mobbed in a motorcade that went off through the city streets as people pushed forward in a never-ending line, trying to get close enough to see her or maybe even shake her hand.

Her father and sister were with her, along with Harpman, who chronicled the postswim tour for the readers back home in the *Daily News*. But Harpman didn't have this playing field to herself, as newspapermen and photographers from around the Continent vied to get a scoop or a photo that would satisfy the seemingly insatiable demand for anything that had to do with the girl who had swum the Channel.

Dudley Malone, meanwhile, arrived in Europe on the liner *France* with fifteen telegrams in hand offering Trudy different endorsements and employment. Disembarking at Cherbourg, he used the occasion to warn the press who greeted him to stop writing stories that their papers made look as if they were written by Ederle—unless they came up with some money for the rights to her personal pieces.

"One thing I want you boys to get straight right now," he declared to reporters, "there was only one newspaper agency directly associated with and behind Trudy on her swim to fame—the *News* and *Chicago Tribune*. They are the only ones authorized by me to use signed stories by Trudy."

Not for much longer they weren't. Malone hadn't gotten to be a rich lawyer by overlooking contractual details, and the deal with the newspapers called for them to get firsthand stories and photos only through the conclusion of the swim itself, something the papers had somehow overlooked in their haste to hitch their star to Ederle's. With demand great for anything related to the swimmer, Gallico was dispatched to see Malone before he left for Europe to try to get an extension of his newspaper's deal.

Gallico was a better sportswriter than he was a negotiator, and he was outmatched when it came to Malone. It didn't help that all the newspapers were offering was a small pittance to keep the right to exclusive material, while Malone knew a hot property when he saw one. He demanded several thousand dollars, a figure Gallico had no way of agreeing to, and soon it was a free-for-all for the media wanting to tell Trudy's story.

Malone would make mistakes—and a lot of them—in the coming months, but his initial instincts were correct that Trudy should go home on the earliest boat and strike while things were hot. The playboy mayor of New York, Jimmy Walker, had already committed to a welcoming ceremony, and Malone knew that the time to capitalize on all the endorsement offers was when the hysteria over her accomplishment was at its zenith. Even as he traveled across the Atlantic, there were others trying to swim the Channel, and Malone knew that any sudden rush of success by others or a successful attempt by Corson would take some of the bloom off of Ederle's rose.

Trudy was just as impatient to get home for reasons of her own, but there was no way she could speak out against her father, who had promised his mother during a side trip to Germany earlier in the summer that he would bring Trudy to visit if she was successful. And there was no way she could be the proper granddaughter and not visit her elderly grandmother when she was just a country away.

"I must see grandmother," she said. "But I can hardly wait until I get home. I want to sail as soon as we can make our visit to Germany and I want the captain to step on it when we start."

The town of Bissingen had never seen anything quite like this, and various officials, athletic clubs, and singing societies turned out to greet Ederle and offer her their personal congratulations. Her grandmother was somewhat of a celebrity in town herself; she was the mother of nearly two dozen children, owned an inn, and still personally managed her farm and guesthouse. The year before, she had crossed the ocean to see her children and grandchildren in their new land, a remarkable feat at her age.

Trudy arrived, to find Grandma Ederle seated on the steps of her hotel, a white-haired woman with gaps between her teeth and a lined face that made her look even older than her years. A crowd of enthusiastic villagers engulfed the two as Trudy got out of her car and kissed her grandmother, tears running down her cheeks. Henry Ederle, who had left home at the age of sixteen, beamed proudly as many of his surviving twenty brothers and sisters, along with fifty grandchildren and seven great-grandchildren, joined the happy scene.

"I never dreamed the name of Ederle would achieve world fame," Grandma Ederle told German reporters.

Trudy and Meg explored some of the places they had seen on their trip twelve years earlier, including the mountain lake where they had almost drowned after slipping in, something that had cost both a spanking. Ederle, warned now by Malone that everything had to be for pay, didn't give any exhibitions, but she was the guest of honor in a parade given by swimming clubs, and she spoke to them about how proud she was of her German blood.

Earlier, Ederle had received a telegram from Oberwager at the United German Societies of New York. He told her of his plans for a celebration "in the form of automobile parade and banquet upon your arrival" back home, while another German society that claimed Henry Ederle as a member sent a cable saying, "The Manhattan Council of the Steuben Society of America is proud that the first woman Channel conqueror is a German American and the daughter of a Steubenite. Congratulations."

Germans on both sides of the Atlantic wanted to claim Trudy as their own, and there were wildly inflated stories in German newspapers that Henry Ederle was a millionaire butcher in New York and one of the biggest meat purveyors in the country. The stories about Trudy were remarkably similar in both German and English, though, and so were the thoughts of her supporters.

"You'll get married soon now," suggested one good German haus-frau.

"No, I'll not get married yet," Trudy said, laughing. "I'm going to settle down to work for three or four years. I have no desire to get married. I've never seen any man who could make my heart flutter and I guess I won't for many a day."

Trudy was still getting letters and cables by the dozens in this small town, but now many were coming from people who had nothing to offer but who wanted something from her. One man asked that his train fare be paid to Berlin so he could see a prizefight, and several girls sent photos of themselves, asking Trudy to take them with her to the United States. One persistent man tried to get her to intercede with the American consul in Bissingen to send him to the United States, saying he had quarreled with his wife and wanted to get "as far away as possible."

It never seemed to stop, and any idea Trudy had that she was going to have a vacation in Germany was quickly shot down. She was exhausted, not by the swim of the Channel, but by the constant crush of people who wanted to talk to her, shake her hand, ask her if she was getting married, or see if she would tell them what it was really like in the dark, cold waters between France and England.

"I thought I was going to get some rest here," she said. "But if this keeps up, I'll have a nervous breakdown before I get home."

Henry Ederle had made his plans carefully, booking passage on the *Berengaria* to sail back home on August 21, leaving enough time both for the family visit in Germany and a few days in Paris before returning. But while he was good at selling meat, he had no idea that the delay was costing Trudy money by the day. His daughter had aroused enormous excitement around the world, but three weeks would elapse between her swim and the time she'd step ashore in New York, and in this case, time really did mean money.

Gallico wrote that it was good of Trudy to go see her relatives, and he correctly predicted that three-fourths of the offers she was getting were probably phony and that she probably wouldn't do anywhere near what Malone thought she would do in terms of endorsements and performances. There were reports of a half million dollars in endorsements and offers, but Gallico had seen it before and was skeptical.

"What became of all the Red Grange offers?" he asked. "Red was a flop in the movies. He never collected near the money he was reputed to have been paid."

Gallico said the only endorsement he ever saw for Grange, the Galloping Ghost, who had signed for a reported $100,000 to begin his pro career in the NFL the year before, was for some kind of drink that would help people score touchdowns for life. Trudy would fare better, he said, "but she will have to work for it."

The publicity machine that was the *Daily News* kicked into high gear in the days following Ederle's swim. Not only did the paper have the fuzzy Bartlane photos the next day; it had something its competitors couldn't match—Harpman, who was with Ederle every step of the way. Even though the *News* didn't have an exclusive contract anymore, Harpman had become close friends with Ederle in the two months they'd spent together, and she continued to convey her thoughts and feelings in stories that ran every day on her trip through France and Germany.

Publisher Joseph Patterson knew what sold newspapers, and apart from coverage of sordid crimes and tales of wayward starlets, this was the best front-page stuff he had ever seen. The only thing missing were good photos of the swim, and he dropped into Gallico's office the day of the

Channel crossing to find out how soon the paper was going to get them. He told Gallico, who was serving as managing editor while the usual editor was on vacation, that he would be satisfied if the paper got the pictures at the same time as Hearst's *Mirror* and the *Evening Graphic* but would not be happy if beaten by competing tabloids for them.

Gallico knew the two liners bearing film were due to arrive on the same day, so he decided to split up the numerous film taken by Sorensen, on the off chance that one liner might get in early. The biggest problem was that they were to drop anchor at the quarantine station off Staten Island early Sunday morning, too late for the photos to be the centerpiece of the widely read Sunday paper.

There was a third liner steaming the same day from England, the *Empress of Britain*, which was scheduled to dock Saturday night in Quebec, and that got Gallico thinking. A glance at the map showed the snow-white ship would be at sea for just four days, making landfall at Cape Breton, Nova Scotia, on Friday before making its way across the Gulf of St. Lawrence and up the St. Lawrence River to its final destination. Gallico decided to put some of the film on the *Empress*, then began trying to figure out a way to get that film back to New York in time for Sunday's paper.

Money wasn't a concern, because Trudy sold newspapers, and besides, the paper had already just invested another fifteen hundred dollars in a car for her. So Gallico called his troops together and began brainstorming on how to get film from the *Empress* to New York in time for the Sunday-morning newspaper. It had to be done by plane and by sea, a feat that seemed impossible even for the newspaper and a country that thought nothing was impossible.

The first piece to the puzzle was getting a seaplane to fly out to the *Empress*, and it was tough finding a seaplane in the wilds of Canada. In addition, there would be night flying, in an era when flying at night was done only by those without much concern for their welfare. Finally, there was no plane that could fly such a long distance without stopping numerous times for maintenance, and such delays would result in missed deadlines.

It seemed impossible, but so had the idea of a woman swimming the Channel. And it wasn't long before Gallico came up with a plan to score a big scoop, a daring hopscotch effort to snatch the film from the *Empress* after it entered the Gulf of St. Lawrence and ferry it one thousand miles by relay all the way to New York in time for the Sunday paper.

The plan was fraught with peril, and Gallico knew it could collapse at any point. But on Thursday, Capt. M. D. McFarlane, coinventor of the Bartlane system; Joseph Surzel of Pacific & Atlantic photos; and Harry Schumacher, assistant sports editor of the *News,* gathered in Quebec and began making arrangements for one of the most audacious news-gathering efforts ever.

There were no seaplanes in Quebec, but millionaire paper manufacturer Frank Clarke, who depended on the *Daily News* to buy tons of his product every day, stepped in to secure one piloted by Captain Robinson at Seven Islands. Robinson headed out the next day to rendezvous with the ship, but the *Empress* wasn't where Robinson thought it would be and he had to fly around looking for it. He finally located it in choppy waters just off Anticosti Island in the Gulf of St. Lawrence. On having spotted the ship, he had to wait more than two hours before the steamer got to the leeward side of the island, where the seas would be calm enough to land. When it did, the pilot signaled the ship and swooped in to pick up a waterproof packet containing the film taken by Sorenson.

From there, the plane flew to Rimouski, a town on the St. Lawrence River, where another seaplane and a biplane were waiting. The contents of the pouch were divided, given the very probable chance that at least one of the planes would not make it, which turned out to be a good move, because the land-based plane was forced down by fog at St. Eloi. But the seaplane, flying just a few feet above the waves, reached Quebec, where it was refueled and serviced before heading out again.

The plane flew through heavy fog before landing on Lake Champlain at Plattsburg, just inside the U.S. border in upper New York State. There, the film was transferred to a land-based plane piloted by W. H. MacMullen, a former British war pilot, who flew it to New York at 112 miles per hour, landing early Saturday afternoon at West Side Park (renamed Lincoln Park in 1930) in Jersey City.

At 3:00 P.M., McFarlane sauntered into Gallico's office, his mission accomplished.

"Here you are, old chap," he said, dropping the precious film on the desk.

The paper would trumpet it as one of the greatest beats in journalism history, and indeed it was—for as long as it lasted. One large picture that would grace almost the entire front page showed Burgess applying grease to Trudy's legs as she stood on the beach at Cape Gris-Nez, with a small dog in the foreground and a movie cameraman grinding away in the rear. Other photos showed Trudy in the water, and still others showed her father, Meg, and Burgess leaning over the railing of the *Alsace*, urging her on.

Sorenson had done his job well, and the photos would become the iconic images of the swim. To get them a day ahead of the other newspapers and in the big Sunday paper to boot was beyond even Gallico's wildest expectations.

Gallico was so excited that he put the best photos in the early pink edition, which hit the street at 8:00 P.M. Saturday. The best the opposition could hope to do was head down to the pier Sunday morning to pick up film and have their pictures in time for nice layouts in Monday's editions, by which time the several million people who read the *News* would find them old hat. Indeed, when Gallico checked the pink edition of the rival *Mirror* that night, there were no pictures of the swim anywhere to be found.

A check of the replated *Mirror* a few hours later, though, showed something entirely different. The *Mirror* had the very same picture of Trudy being greased up on the front page, and other pictures inside. Editors at the *Mirror* had simply taken the early edition of the *News*, pinned it to a board, and photographed it. The paper then triumphantly called the photos its own. Anything was fair game in the tabloid wars, and the *Mirror* could worry later if the *News* tried to sue.

One of the greatest beats ever came undone because the *News* was simply too eager to get its paper out.

"If I had any brains, I'd have held back my precious scoop until our two-star final, which came at midnight," Gallico would say later. "By that time, there wouldn't have been anybody left at the *Mirror* plant big enough to make the decision to swipe our shot. Editors go home early on Saturday night."

The decision would be mostly forgotten the next day, because even bigger news intruded on the front pages. Rudolph Valentino, the silent-movie star, had collapsed in his apartment at the Hotel Ambassador and was then operated on for appendicitis and a gastric ulcer at Polyclinic Hospital.

America's favorite screen lover, star of *The Sheik* and *The Four Horsemen of the Apocalypse*, and the biggest celebrity of his time, was listed in guarded condition at the hospital, where three surgeons and a renowned specialist were called in to try to save his life. Peritonitis set in, and for a week the country breathlessly picked up newspapers every morning to read the latest on his condition and hope for his recovery.

Valentino died eight days after he was stricken, and the nation mourned his passing. Eulogies poured in from around the world, and Dempsey paused from training for his fight with Tunney to pay his respects. Dempsey had met Valentino during several movie productions, and Dempsey's wife, Estelle Taylor, was scheduled to play opposite the romantic actor in his next movie.

"I liked him tremendously," Dempsey said. "The screen has lost a dandy fellow and a talented actor."

The body of Valentino, who came to the United States from Italy in 1913, was put on display at the Frank Campbell Funeral Parlor Church on Broadway at Sixty-sixth Street for two days, and an estimated 75,000 people filed through to see him for a final time. When viewing was finally cut off late the second night, several thousand people who couldn't get in became unruly and police had to move in and disperse the crowd.

A city that had been celebrating was now a city in mourning. But it would be only a few more days until Ederle came home and began making New Yorkers feel better about themselves.

The inevitable backlash about Ederle's victory didn't take long to form, and it came from the very country where Trudy had been feted as a hero just a little more than a week earlier. The British press had spent a few days thinking about this American girl who had bested their Channel, and it wasn't long before they went on the attack. Trudy was still in Germany when word quickly spread of the accusations being made in the London papers.

Most of them centered on Ederle's use of the *Alsace* for her swim, or, more specifically, the role it had played in protecting her from the elements as she battled in high seas and horrible conditions. One paper accused Ederle of having "hugged the lee of the tug" when the water was most turbulent, then added to its indignation by questioning her use of a "modern stroke" in making the swim.

The *Westminster Gazette* went to the scene for its report, quoting fishermen and boatmen from both sides of the Channel as questioning the role played by both the *Alsace* and the *Morinie* in helping her across. Other papers joined in, saying the swim may have been successful but that it was not as sporting as other efforts to cross the Channel because Ederle was helped by the shelter of the tugs.

"Ederle probably swam in the water all the way across, but I don't call that swimming the Channel," snorted one old seaman.

Trudy's camp replied quickly to these charges, defending their young swimmer, and they had some powerful weapons. Corthes had been accompanying swimmers across the Channel with his tug since 1902, including ten attempts by Wolffe, four by Helmy, three by Lillian Harrison, and the successful crossing by Toth. No one was going to question his seamanship or his integrity, and he declared that he "did no more for Miss Ederle than I have done for any of the other aspirants, and I did no more than any accompanying tug ever does for a swimmer."

Burgess wasn't pleased, either. He had made it across the Channel himself and trained many others to try the same, and he told the papers that everything was done in the proper sporting matter. The swim, Burgess noted, was witnessed by more people than any other successful swim, and one of those witnesses was Cannon, a fellow competitor, who would have "had something to say if unfair aid had been given Miss Ederle in any manner."

"It was a good, clean swim," Burgess said. "I would take an oath on it any time."

The Associated Press correspondent wrote that he was on the *Morinie* for the whole thing and that it was a fair swim under the most trying of circumstances. And Rutherford wrote an open letter, saying that Ederle had followed the rules of Channel swimming, though the only real rule was that once touched, a swimmer was done.

Clemington Corson, the husband of Ederle's rival, chimed in to say he thought the tugs helped shield Trudy from the ferocious storm that swirled around her but that there was nothing in the rules against that. And those onboard the *Alsace* issued a statement sworn to in front of the American consul in Boulogne that she "abided by all rules of Channel swimming and international sportsmanship."

The strongest defense came from the *Daily News* itself, which wasn't about to allow the swim to be questioned. The paper had a lot invested in making Trudy a star, and it let loose with both barrels at the cowardly English press for even suggesting something was amiss. On August 20, Gallico wrote that Trudy laughed when told the swim was being challenged and "for this reason I am hardly inclined to froth at the mouth because of the magnificent display of sportsmanship on the part of the British press that attacked the girl." Gallico belittled the British writers as stuffed shirts who rarely left their offices to see what was really happening in the world and were simply jealous that the American girl made it.

"The good gentlemen who wrote the stuff and printed it made themselves elegantly ridiculous, as they were tucked away in their little coverlets each night they went to sleep soundly and secure in the thought that no woman could swim it. It eased them through the long nights and then along came an American girl who not only did it, but broke every record doing it. The fact that they couldn't keep their mouths shut is their hard luck. Not alone, Trudy, but the whole world is laughing at them."

The *Daily News* backed up Gallico's column a few days later by running a series of six photos taken from movies shot on the *Morinie*, with the heading MOVIES PROVE TRUDY'S CRITICS ABSURD! The paper reported that a sold-out crowd watching the premier of the movie the day before at the Rivoli Theatre had risen to their feet, cheering three times.

Ederle herself said that the *Morinie* actually made it harder for her: "The wash was fearful, it almost took me down."

There was other grumbling going on that had as much to do with sour grapes as anything that might have happened on the Channel. The mother of Clarabelle Barrett told reporters in New York that she hoped her own daughter would not try swimming the Channel again because Trudy's record-breaking swim made it pointless to try. "What's the use?" she asked.

Mrs. Nathan Barrett had other things to say. She claimed her daughter, who had come agonizingly close to making it a few days before Trudy, would have been the first woman to swim the Channel had she had the tugs and other luxuries that Trudy had. Barrett's operation was so low-budget that when she made her attempt from the English side a few days before Ederle, only to fail just two miles from Cape Gris-Nez, she had just a small motorboat and a rowboat to guide her along the way.

"Clara hasn't had the backing of people with wealth and of newspapers in her attempt and so is still an amateur," her mother said. "I doubt if any woman could have stayed in the water as long as she did and still feel as little fatigue as the papers report she felt."

And then there was Burgess himself, who was stung by the fact the Ederles had not invited him to the big reception in Calais after the return to France and disappointed that he was not getting more credit for helping Trudy across, given the fact that her trainer the year before had failed. Burgess had waited until the last minute, expecting to get the invitation to travel to Calais, then spent the rest of the day in bed, a disappointed old man.

"Miss Ederle got over, I got my pay—no bonus—just an old rowboat that wasn't usable anyway, so I have no further interest in the matter," said Burgess, who conveniently didn't bring up the fact that Harpman had doubled his pay earlier that summer when he was insisting on training Cannon along with Ederle.

Henry Ederle gave Burgess the rowboat they had used during training as a farewell gift, but Burgess was upset that he got no bonus, especially when Corthes got five thousand francs extra for his role in captaining the *Alsace*. Burgess was so unhappy, he decided he would rejoin Cannon, in hopes she would not only make it across the Channel but beat Trudy's record.

On August 17, Cannon entered the water at Cape Gris-Nez shortly after midnight for her attempt. Villagers and tourists gathered to light flares to see her off, and she took off, confident in both her abilities and the fact that she had the same tug captain and the same trainer as Trudy had on her swim. As Cannon swam on an almost-straight course toward England, the Channel was remarkably calm as her supporters on the *Alsace* sang songs to her.

Two-and-a-half-hours later, though, a huge storm struck and the going got so bad that Corthes stopped the tug for about thirty minutes to see if it would pass. In the din of the storm, Cannon didn't know what was happening and had to tread water, while being careful not to touch the tug, and on several occasions those on the tug thought they had lost her in the darkness. Finally, Corthes refused to go any farther, saying he feared for both the safety of the swimmer and the people on the tug as the storm continued to rage and the boat tipped up and down at crazy angles.

Like Trudy, Cannon didn't want to quit when Burgess told her she had to come out of the water.

"I am all right and I don't want to come out," she said.

"You must," responded Burgess. "It is impossible to go on."

"Oh dear," cried Lillian. "I feel fine. May I have another try?"

Trudy, meanwhile, had left her grandmother's home in Germany and was in Paris, where her arrival was greeted by huge crowds at the train station. In a few days, she and her family and friends would board the *Berengaria* for the trip home, and she longed for some quiet at sea. She told reporters in Paris that she had no interest in swimming the Channel again, despite reports of offers of up to twenty thousand dollars for a race between her and other swimmers. She didn't have much else to say, and newspapermen grumbled among themselves that she was declining interviews and was not forthcoming when she did talk.

There was a reason why, as they soon found out.

"Papa told Gertrude not to talk to reporters anymore," Meg told them. "If any talking is going to be done about Gertrude's plans or the contracts that have been offered her, Dudley Field Malone will do it in New York."

The strain of instant celebrity seemed to be getting to Trudy, and on a shopping trip with Harpman, she suddenly began crying.

"I don't know what's the matter with me," she said. "I don't know why I should be like this. I never did anything so foolish before. I don't want to cry, but it doesn't seem that I can help it."

Harpman urged her to go back to the hotel and rest, but Trudy refused.

"I'm all right. I guess it's just because we've all got the hives," she said. "It's time we were going home."

There was still hope among the few remaining Channel swimmers, even as Trudy and her party boarded the *Berengaria* and headed across the Atlantic for New York. Though the general feeling seemed to be that no one else would make it across the Channel that summer, there were still plenty of swimmers waiting for just the right weather and proper currents to try.

Ederle's crossing only seemed to spur public interest in the remaining swimmers, all of whom had different claims to the Channel. A few days after Trudy made it, Corson, Barrett, and Timson frolicked in the waters off Dover for the movie cameras and the thousands who had gathered to watch them train. The German challenger, Ernst Vierkotter, quietly waited in the wings for his attempt.

Of all the swimmers, Corson probably still had the most to gain from making it across. The mother of two had been beaten by rough seas after fourteen hours in the water three years before, and while she was an accomplished long-distance swimmer, it was hard for both bystanders and the newspapermen to get over the fact that someone who had given birth to children would have the energy and determination to swim the dreaded Channel.

Corson, a professional like Ederle, made it clear she was in it for both fame and money. She would have had a lot more of both if she had been the first one over, but she still held the motherhood card in an era where being a mother was considered among the most noble of things, and when motherhood was celebrated in the arts and in real life.

Corson didn't shy away from constantly taking advantage of her particular attraction—bringing up her small children, whom she had left in America for the summer.

"You bet I will swim your Channel," she had said upon arriving in England in early June. "What do you think I came over here for? What do you think I left my home and two children for?"

While Corson waited for just the right moment, others weren't so shy about plunging into the cold waters to give it a try. On August 23 alone, with Trudy safely on the *Berengaria*, headed home, there were five attempts, four from the French side and one from England, creating a near traffic jam of would-be Channel conquerors in the sliver of water that separated England from the Continent at its narrowest point.

From England came Barrett, the underfunded but determined swimmer, with Leister on the boat beside her for her second attempt after the heartbreak of her near miss. As Barrett took off again under a broiling sun from Dover, she made it a point to keep the small motorboat following her several hundred yards away. If it seemed like she was making a statement, she was: She would be the first woman to swim the Channel without the aid of any tugs sheltering her from the angry sea.

The swim was doomed from the start. A boat carrying photographers, newspapermen, and Leister took on water as it left shore and then sank, forcing its waterlogged occupants to have to walk back to Dover in search of another boat. The misadventure convinced several of the newspapermen that this would be a swim better suited to cover from shore, but Leister was determined that she get another boat to follow Barrett across.

On her last attempt, Barrett had made it twenty-one hours and thirty-five minutes through darkness and fog, only to be stopped just two miles short of the French shore, but this swim wasn't going to last nearly as long. She became seasick early when the seas kicked up, and when the Channel steamer *Stad Antwerpen* came too close and swamped her a few hours into the swim, she swallowed so much water that she felt she could go no farther.

Barrett called to the boat that she wanted to give up, but those on-board pleaded with her to stay her course and see if the nausea would wear off. Leister, in particular, was so dismayed that Barrett wanted to quit that she began arguing with her as the swimmer treaded water in the Channel. But Barrett, knowing the stakes weren't as high on this attempt, had already made up her mind.

"I am not swimming for anyone except myself," she yelled out. "If I don't want to swim, I won't."

As the argument continued, Barrett edged closer to the motorboat, finally touching it and disqualifying herself. She had lasted only four hours and twenty-five minutes in the water, but she didn't seem all that upset about it when she got in the boat. Her main worry was that the remaining members of the press realize she was quitting because of illness, not because she was a quitter, and that she might try it again the next year.

"Let Ederle, Cannon and Corson do as they will," she said. "Anyone is entitled to full credit for swimming the Channel in those conditions."

Across the Channel, swimmers were almost bumping into one another as they plunged into the waters near Cape Gris-Nez with their eye on the white cliffs on the other side. Cannon was making her second attempt, while Germany's Otto Kemmerich and Ernst Vierkotter joined French sailor and marathon swimmer Joseph Ledriant in the Channel.

Corson came by in a motorboat to watch Cannon start at night, giving her fellow American some extra inspiration, because the two were fierce rivals and not terribly friendly toward each other. But Cannon, whose heart never really seemed into the swim after Ederle made it, would last a mere two hours and thirty-five minutes before a terrible pain in her side convinced her that she had appendicitis and forced her to quit.

The others didn't last long, either. Kemmerich, who raised eyebrows among newspapermen because he carried an oxygen tank around while training and used special webbed gloves in his swim, quit after more than four hours because of bad weather and the possibility of sharks, while Vierkotter made it ten hours before quitting. Ledriant was the feeblest of all, swimming only fifty-nine minutes before he was pulled from the chilly Channel.

The colony of swimmers at Cape Gris-Nez had now dwindled to a few. The summer was coming to a close and it seemed like Ederle just might own the Channel by herself.

Onboard the *Berengaria,* Trudy finally had a chance to reflect on some of what had happened in the few short weeks since she'd turned the still-young world of female athletics upside down and shattered myths about the superiority of men. She grew melancholic, worrying about what the future held for her now that she had accomplished such a big feat at such a young age, and wondering what she would have to do to cash in on her fame.

'Well, what am I living for now?" she asked Harpman. "You swim the Channel and you die. Well, I guess I'll go to work for two or three years, and after that I can have a good time. I guess I'll have to start work the very next day after my arrival."

Even on a ship plying the Atlantic, the young star couldn't get away from adoring crowds. She spent much of her time reading mysteries to try to avoid curious passengers who wanted to talk to her about the Channel and her swim. One book she particularly liked was *The Black Orchid,* so much so that she heaved a great sigh every time her reading was interrupted by autograph seekers. For four nights, she even refused to go to dinner, partly to escape wearing evening clothes and partly to avoid people who wanted to shake her hand, spending her time on deck instead, eating chicken sandwiches, olives, ice cream, and nuts.

As the liner steamed toward New York with its special cargo, the city awaited her arrival with increasing eagerness. The *Daily News* was still leading the cheerleading, with Harpman filling reports via wireless from the ship, and the paper sent its roving photographer to Fourth and

Flatbush avenues in Brooklyn to ask residents what kind of homecoming they thought she should get.

Most wanted a mayoral reception and a parade, but all agreed that they were excited she was finally on her way.

"A queen's welcome wouldn't be too good for her," said Mrs. Anna Johnson of Herkimer Street. "In fact, I think it would be quite appropriate because she is the queen of all athletes."

Joseph Lessner, a store manager on Union Street, said the welcome should be hearty.

"All the city authorities have to do is to make the arrangements. The New Yorkers will do the rest when they see her," he said.

Little did Lessner know how right he would be. Trudy was headed home, and the city was ready to put aside its mourning over its favorite actor and celebrate its favorite girl instead.

10

A Hero's Welcome

The voyage home was a rough one, with North Atlantic storms making even the colossal *Berengaria* toss and turn. The swells were so high the day before her arrival that the bathing pool couldn't be filled and Trudy did not take her daily swim, much to the disappointment of her fellow passengers, who liked to sip a soon-to-be-forbidden cocktail and watch the free daily show put on by the newly famous Channel swimmer.

There was plenty more to do on the luxurious ship, which boasted a grand social hall, a huge sunroom, and luxury accommodations for those in first class. The *Berengaria* was the third-largest ship in the world and the flagship of the Cunard Line, part of the line's "Big Three," along with its sister ships the *Mauretania* and the *Aquitania*. It had begun life as the *Imperator* in Germany, where it remained during the war, after which it was used to carry home American servicemen—both dead and alive. The British later claimed the ship as war reparations for the sinking of the *Lusitania*, and it was refurbished and rechristened the *Berengaria*.

As the ship approached the United States, Ederle fretted that she might cry at the welcome, and wondered what was about to come. The day after her triumphant swim, she had received a telegram from Mayor Walker, promising her a royal reception on her return, but she was not sure what that really meant.

The tumultuous receptions she'd gotten in England, France, and Germany after her swim gave Ederle an idea of the excitement surrounding her victory, but she still wasn't sure how it was playing back home. That changed some in Paris when, before their departure, Harpman showed her a copy of the *Daily News,* with the front page headline screaming EDERLE SWIMS CHANNEL.

"That's what I've prayed to see for over a year," she told Harpman. "Ever since the failure of the first attempt when the papers all announced in big, black type, 'EDERLE COLLAPSES.'"

The girl who had returned home subdued and near tears a year earlier was coming home happy and victorious, and New York was more than eager to welcome her back. The day before her arrival, residents and shopkeepers on Amsterdam Avenue between Sixtieth and Sixty-fifth streets got the neighborhood ready. Every house for blocks was dressed up like a Christmas tree, while the five-story brownstone building at 108 Amsterdam, adjacent to the butcher shop, was a mass of red-white-and-blue bunting and American flags. The filling station at the corner of Sixty-fifth Street was strung with festive pennants, and crude signs were hung in the window of both the Ederle Brothers Meat Market and the butcher stores down the street to greet Trudy upon her return.

Inside the Ederles' shop, a sign announcing a bargain sale of pork chops and sausages was nearly hidden by signs welcoming Trudy home. Even the peddlers' pushcarts that lined both sides of the street were decorated with signs welcoming her.

People in the neighborhood had so many different plans to celebrate that no one was really sure what would take place, or when. Even the family seemed confused, though the day before her arrival, Uncle John sliced liver pudding and weighed out frankfurters while telling reporters that the family planned to go to the Ziegfeld Follies the night of her return.

Everyone wanted to get into the act. The neighborhood of immigrants had a true American hero, and there was no shortage of stories about the wonderful young woman they knew. At the Meyer and Kaner drugstore at 94 Amsterdam Avenue, the social hub of the block, Jack Shaff stood behind the counter and proudly described getting a postcard from Trudy the day before her swim that said she was having a grand time but couldn't get ice cream in Europe like she could at home.

"Strawberry marshmallow frappe," Shaff said. "That's what she likes and I'll tell the world she can eat three times as much as the ordinary girl."

Trudy was eager to see the old neighborhood, and even more eager to make her way to Highlands and the family's summer cottage on the Shrewsbury River. Summer was fading, and she wanted nothing more than to return to the place where she'd learned to swim before the season came to an abrupt end. More important, she wanted to get there for the end-of-the-summer dance at the neighborhood club.

"I am delighted that my return home will be in time for the Twin Lights club ball, which always marks the end of the season for The Alley at Highlands, where my family summers," Ederle wrote in the *Daily News*. "We call the row of bungalows where we and our friends have passed many summers The Alley."

Highlands had big plans for their favorite daughter, but it would have to wait until New York took its turn celebrating her return. Everyone, it seemed, wanted a piece of Trudy, and everyone wanted her first.

Magistrate Oberwager of the United German Societies of New York was so determined that German-Americans play the biggest role in honoring Ederle that he paid a visit to Ma Ederle, giving her a huge bouquet of roses, one of which she pinned back on his lapel while photographers swarmed around taking pictures.

Oberwager asked to accompany Mrs. Ederle on the city's welcoming boat out to the *Berengaria* when it docked at the quarantine station. He promised that bands and thousands of club members would march in front of Trudy in a parade from the docks to City Hall for her meeting with Walker. Ma Ederle needed little convincing, because these were her people, but Oberwager offered further encouragement anyway, reminding her—and any reporter within earshot—that the society had warmly embraced her daughter after her failed attempt the year before, when her return hadn't been such a big deal.

"The United German Societies welcomed your daughter last year. She came back a little disheartened. But she knew she could conquer," Oberwager said. "She told me many times that she would succeed. That spirit was befitting your daughter. When, in the angry Channel, they directed her to come out, she made that now famous query: 'What for?' That, too, was fitting in your daughter."

It would not be the last time the theme of the fatherland was introduced. The Great War in Europe had been over barely more than a handful of years and emotions were still raw, both among the hundreds of thousands of immigrant Germans who populated the city and those Americans whose families had made great sacrifices in "the war to end all wars." The two sides coexisted peacefully, but there was still an edgy undercurrent of suspicion and mistrust.

The German community was both large and active. By 1890, there were a half million immigrants from Germany living in New York City, and while the war had caused a backlash against anything German, there were large areas of New York where German was not only spoken at home but in the butcher shops, bakeries, and shoe stores of the neighborhoods. Pop Ederle was a proud Steubenite himself, and a prominent member of his own German-American social club.

Oberwager wasn't about to let the mayor interfere with his idea about what the celebration should be like—not when he and other German-Americans were welcoming one of their own kind.

Before leaving Paris, Trudy went shopping, buying gifts for the family at home, and a powder blue hat for herself. She giggled as she anticipated the thought of her family trying to spot her on the *Berengaria* by looking for the hat she had left home with.

"I'll fool them all at home," she said. "They'll be expecting me in that red hat I wore away, but I'll sail up the bay in a blue one."

Ederle caused a stir as she took the boat train from Paris to Cherbourg for her return home. Tourists clambered between the swaying train cars to try to get a glimpse of the swimmer, offer her a few words of praise, or even shake her hand. By now, Trudy was getting used to the constant attention, and she was in a merry mood as she got off the train at Cherbourg with her prized ukulele in one hand and a balloon in another.

She and her father and sister were among the eleven hundred passengers in first class, a group that included some other celebrities of the time. But passengers were so taken by the Channel swimmer that they barely paid any attention to American actress Peggy Hopkins Joyce, who was as famous for her scandalous affairs, marriages to wealthy men, and lavish lifestyle as she was for her work on screen and stage, or Jean Borotra, the French tennis player who was going to the United States to represent his country in the Davis Cup matches.

The mayor of Cherbourg gave a brief speech, wishing both Ederle and Borotra well. Then Trudy and her family boarded the ship, which blew its whistles as it steamed out of port and into the very Channel she had conquered only a few weeks earlier.

The trip seemed excruciatingly long, and was made even more so by the turbulent seas. But the *Berengaria* steamed steadily toward New York City, and on a warm Thursday night in late August, it was closing in on the harbor. Much of the city slept, but before heading to bed people had eagerly scanned the evening papers, which said the ship had radioed in and would reach the quarantine station in the harbor sometime Friday morning. There were stories outlining the various celebration plans, and city officials urged people to come to City Hall or line the streets of lower Manhattan for the parade to welcome their young hero home.

Four other ocean liners would dock in New York Harbor that day, carrying both society's elite on the upper decks and the latest batch of immigrants down below. The *George Washington* of the United States Lines was to dock at Fourth Street in Hoboken after a journey from

Germany; the French Line's *De Grasse* was coming in from Le Havre; and the Holland America liner *Nieuw Amsterdam* was steaming in from Rotterdam. Two other liners, the *Lancastria* and the *Zeeland,* would be leaving the harbor at midnight, heading for England.

New Yorkers, though, had eyes for only one ship. The *Berengaria* was scheduled to dock at the foot of West Fourteenth Street, and the city was all made up and ready to meet its most famous guest.

The party began before Trudy ever got ashore. As the steamship approached New York Harbor, billowing dense black smoke from its three huge stacks in the morning mist, the captain sent word to Ederle to make her way to the upper deck.

"The planes want to welcome you. They want to drop flowers down," she was told.

"You're kidding, aren't you?" Ederle replied.

It was no joke, just a preview of things to come. Two biplanes circled above the *Berengaria,* their loud engines heard even above those of the ship as it made its way into the harbor. One was from the *Daily News,* with a message welcoming Trudy painted underneath its wings, and both planes took turns dropping welcoming wreaths of flowers on deck. As the ship edged its way toward the quarantine station, the harbor erupted in a mass of noise and activity, with boats of all shapes and sizes tooting their horns and whistles, while the fireboats saluted the ship with sprays of water pointed toward the sky.

Captain Rostron of the *Berengaria* had vowed to get the ship into port early enough for the party to begin, and though delayed by fog, the vessel reached the quarantine station at 11:18 A.M., just a few minutes later than planned. While health officers went aboard to make sure there were no passengers with communicable diseases from overseas (the devastation from the 1918–1919 Spanish flu pandemic, which had killed an estimated 50 million people worldwide, with 675,000 dying in the United States alone, still had officials on the alert), a fleet of boats raced through the harbor to greet the *Berengaria*—a welcoming the likes of which New York had never seen. There were lobstermen aboard their boats, fishermen in their craft, and even people in canoes craning for the first glimpse of their returning celebrity.

Among the boats was one chartered by a delegation of meat dealers in honor of Ederle's butcher father. The Ye Olde New York branch of the National Association of Retail Meat Dealers was represented by a large group of men of the trade, who carried a big sign that read BUTCHER'S SPECIAL.

America's girl was dressed for the party of her life. Trudy wore a blue suit coat, along with her blue felt Reboux hat. She also had on a blue-flowered scarf, tan gloves, tan stockings with green garters, a blue blouse, and patent-leather shoes. In one hand she carried a gold vanity case made in Paris, and with the other she somewhat innocently clung to a doll she called "my Channel Sheik."

The city's official welcoming boat, the *Macon,* took Mrs. Ederle, Ober-wager, and other family members out to the quarantine station to be the first to greet Trudy and escort her back to shore. Also onboard were dozens of reporters, eager to get the first words from Trudy, even before she made it to land. Together, they searched the railings of the liner for the swimmer as the boat, with a welcoming sign attached to its flank, pulled alongside the *Berengaria*.

Amid the din of roaring engines, Ma Ederle couldn't wait any longer. From the top of the *Macon,* a high-pitched woman's voice sounded: "Trudy, Trudy, Trudy." Soon others took up the call, and high up on the ship's side a head and arm were thrust out of a promenade-deck window, the arm waving a small American flag. It was Trudy, with her father and sister next to her. One of Trudy's uncles was so excited on seeing her that he jumped up and down on the deck of the tug and fell through a skylight onto the tug's lower deck. But hardly anyone noticed in the turmoil of the homecoming celebration.

Gallico was there and set the scene:

"There she was, hanging half out of the port, waving madly and with every wave of her arm releasing new torrents of sound. The *Macon* began emitting mad whoops, the airplanes thundered and roared overhead . . . and all because of one little girl. Was it any wonder that one's heart crept into one's throat at the sight?"

On the *Riverside,* another city boat, a band played "The Star-Spangled Banner" and other patriotic tunes as Ma Ederle scrambled up a rope ladder onto the *Berengaria* and soon was hugging and kissing her daughter in her stateroom.

"My girl, New York is giving you a wonderful welcome," she said.

"How wonderful," Trudy replied.

As everyone in the harbor strained to get their first glimpse of their returning hero, Trudy and her family, amid many more hugs and tears and excited shouts, were transferred to the *Macon,* where reporters were waiting to talk to her about her great conquest. Gallico could do little but marvel at a moment the likes of which he had never seen.

"And then, just as Trudy stepped onto the *Macon,* the sun burst thru the gray mists and glittered and shone until the white and silver seaplanes looked like jewelry in the sky, and its radiance was reflected in the face of Trudy," he wrote.

Gallico might have been overdoing it, but not because of a lack of perception. Indeed, he saw something little noticed in the flurry of the reception: a young woman who seemed to be struggling to understand what was happening to her, trying desperately not to be overcome by the moment.

"Every line of her face showed the struggle between laughter and tears as her mother held her in her arms, and still the brass throats of a hundred ships sounded their salute to young courage. Her lips and chin trembled. Tears welled to her eyes and then, even as the sun had shattered the gray mists from which Trudy had come, her smile and laugh would break through her tears, to give way again a moment later as her emotions overcame her," Gallico reported.

While the celebration continued above, Trudy went down into the salon of the *Macon,* where newspapermen, family, fellow swimmers, and anyone who had been able to wrangle an invitation aboard the boat were there to greet her. Ma Ederle stood next to her daughter, fanning her in the heat and bringing her water, as reporters quizzed her on her historic swim.

The controversy raised in England over the tugs helping her swim was mentioned, but this was a day for celebration, not for investigation.

Trudy told reporters she had gained seven pounds before the swim, lost four or five making it, and had trained by walking and swimming one hour a day and taking a three-hour swim once a week.

They were more interested, though, in whether she planned to marry.

"I'm in no hurry," Ederle told them.

"Have you had any proposals?"

"I'm not interested in proposals. I never give them a chance."

A writer for the *New York Journal-American* took it upon himself to critique her looks for his readers.

"Ordinarily Trudy is not what would be styled a beautiful woman," he wrote, "but today she seemed filled with the admiration and loyalty all around her and her brown eyes danced with eagerness. Her red lips untinged with rouge were bright as cherries, and her cheeks aflame with color."

In addition to the reporters and city officials, the *Macon* was crowded with Ederles of every shape and size, many of them speaking German amid the din of the homecoming. There were forty-two of them all together on the *Macon* and *Riverside,* including Trudy's sisters Helen and Emma, her brothers George and Henry, and her uncles John, Jacob, and Ernest. Ma Ederle entertained reporters with stories of how she had taught her daughter to swim in the river at Highlands when she was just eight.

'I tied a rope around her and let her down in the water off the pier head. She did a little dog paddle," Mrs. Ederle said. "After two or three days she learned to swim. It was hard to get her out of the water. She always liked to paddle in the bathtub, too."

Trudy's swimming family was there, too, a large party of women in bathing suits, including Helen Wainwright, Doris O'Mara, Aileen Riggin, and Lillian Stoddard. Charlotte Epstein was on board, along with Viets, Trudy's chaperone from the first swim.

Among the well-wishers, of course, was Oberwager, who immediately caused some tense moments when he launched into a glorification of the fatherland while greeting her on behalf of the United German Societies.

"When you failed in your attempt to swim the Channel last year and returned, we of the United German Societies were the only ones to greet you. We have stood by you all along and are ready to stand by you," Oberwager said. "And while we are proud of your achievements because of your Teutonic origins, we also know that you are a proud little New Yorker."

"You bet," snapped Trudy.

Malone didn't like what he was hearing from Oberwager, who by now was droning on about Trudy's German upbringing and how much she owed to her heritage. He surely didn't see the economic benefits of linking her swim with Germany, which was what Oberwager was intent on doing.

"Cut it out," Malone told Oberwager.

Oberwager wasn't paying attention, or maybe he, like Trudy, couldn't hear amid the chaos and commotion onboard the city boat. But reporters quickly told him that Malone wanted him to shut up, and he indignantly threatened to cancel all German participation in the parade if he didn't get an apology.

"It was the Germans of New York who first organized this reception," Oberwager said. "The mayor's committee only came in at the last minute, and we've got a right to honor this girl of German parents as we wish to."

On the deck above, Oberwager asked Malone if it was he who had cut off his remarks.

"Yes I did. I said it when I saw that the racial and national element was injected into this reception," Malone told Oberwager. "I stopped it because I am responsible for this little girl. She's an American and is not going to be made the center of any controversy. This is purely an American celebration and anything alien to an American celebration will not be tolerated."

That settled, for the moment at least, the boat headed toward Pier A, where it seemed all six million of New York's residents were on hand to celebrate Trudy's return.

◌◍◌

Coming out of the pier shed, Trudy suddenly stopped short, a bewildered look on her face. In just a few short weeks, she had become increasingly accustomed to attention following her wherever she went, but this went beyond anything she had seen so far. Before her stretched a throng of some fifteen thousand people pushing and crowding one another on a steamy summer afternoon just to get a glimpse of the girl in blue.

White faces and waving arms moved in every window of the adjacent Whitehall Building, men perched on iron fences for a better view, and the L station was lined with people cheering. Beyond the pier, high up in the Custom House, tiny figures scampered on the top ledges to see Ederle as she made her way to the waiting car with Grover Whalen.

Whalen, a top executive for Wanamaker's Department Store, had been the city's official greeter since the previous mayoral administration of John Hylan, who hadn't been much for crowds or big events. It was Whalen who had invented the institution of the New York City ticker-tape parade and had organized huge civic receptions for returning war veterans and their commander, Gen. John Pershing, as well as for President Woodrow Wilson when he returned from Versailles. Whalen had also been there for parades for North Pole hero Cmdr. Richard Byrd and for the Prince of Wales, thus earning the moniker "Mr. New York."

Whalen's job was both to put the parades together and to ride in the open cars of those being honored. Dapper and handsome in his straw hat, he always did it well. On this day, though, even Whalen seemed overwhelmed by what he saw as he and Trudy walked through surging crowds to get to their car.

A hundred policemen strained to hold back the crowd, with mounted officers riding their horses like cossacks in charges against the surging lines. Trudy made it into the back of the open car, and Whalen and Malone were just getting in with her, when a few dozen people broke through and reached the vehicle. Men's hands caught the edge of her blue serge suit coat, and for a moment it seemed they would drag Trudy off the back of the folded convertible top that served as her seat.

Others grabbed Trudy's sleeves and the lapels of her coat, reaching for her hands as she drew away in fright. Just then, four mounted policemen rode toward the car, hitting the men furiously with clenched

fists and catching them by the backs of their collars and throwing them
to the ground. Ederle half-fell back into the car as the police swatted
the last of the men away, and the parade of vehicles lurched unsteadily
away from the pier.

Ahead of the car carrying Ederle, Malone, and Whalen marched thousands of members of the United German Societies, followed by Boy
Scouts, a band of trombones, and delegations from her home neighborhood, whose members sported bright blue badges signifying their im-
portance. Behind them was a delegation of Swiss yodelers in green vests
and shorts with tassels, followed by more delegates, another band, and,
finally, the car carrying the woman of the hour.

Gallico was there to cover the story, but he had another mission—to
present Trudy with the red Buick roadster she so wanted. She saw the
car gleaming in the sunshine, but the crowd was so massive and unruly
that there was no way she could stop for the presentation, and Whalen
wouldn't have allowed it anyway. The car ended up following at the end
of the procession, and someone ran into it and crumpled a fender.

A smile returned to Trudy's face as the convoy headed past the skyscrapers of Lower Manhattan, a route that would later become known
as the Canyon of Heroes, on its way to City Hall. The crowds were huge,
with some two million cheering, screaming people—a full third of the
city's population—lining the street. Broadway was decorated in a mass
of flags and brightly colored bunting with welcoming banters strung
from light pole to light pole, and store windows were decorated with
bright lights.

It was the biggest reception ever, bigger than the one General Pershing or the Prince of Wales had received, and even bigger than the frenzied welcome given to the Twenty-seventh Division when it had returned
from the war in 1919—all this for a young woman who clutched her
"Channel Sheik" doll with its fake pearl necklace as if it were the only
friend she had.

Truck drivers abandoned their trucks as far west as Greenwich Street
and walked over to Broadway to see her, and they were hardly alone. She
was a girl of the city's neighborhoods, and they all came out to see her in

the biggest turnout the city would ever see for one of its sports heroes—
and a woman at that.

Ederle sat high on the rear seat, waving to the crowd and smiling
broadly as the procession crawled up Broadway. So much confetti rained
down that it seemed like New York was getting a summer blizzard. Down
from the top of the skyscrapers fluttered streamers, confetti, hats, newspapers, typewriter ribbons, and even toilet paper. Each great office building seemed to be vying with the others in terms of the amount of paper
they could throw down from the windows.

The various bands in the parade were also trying to outdo one another by constantly playing "Let Me Call You Sweetheart," the song that
Trudy had hummed to herself as she made her way across the Channel.

Gallico wasn't far away, pen in hand, chronicling the scene unfolding before him.

"In the triumphal march up Broadway, she stood in her car like a
young goddess and tried to take all of New York into her arms. Her parade plowed through a solid mass of cheering humans packed so closely
that they opened only for the passing of Trudy and then closed behind
her immediately," he wrote.

Trudy kept waving, a smile frozen on her deeply tanned face, which
was half-hidden underneath a hat and a head of boyish bobbed hair
bronzed by salt water and sun. The blushing girl seemed to be getting
more comfortable with the adulation directed her way, laughing as they
bellowed what had already become her signature phrase. "What for,
Trudy?" they cried. "What for?"

Two bluecoats rode on each running board of Trudy's car, and near
Wall Street one was forced to use the bottom of his shoe against the
chest of a souvenir hunter. Others were on another kind of hunt, taking advantage of the press of humanity to commit a little larceny as Ederle's motorcade went by. Police arrested several pickpockets, including
one brazen thief who took a roll of bills totaling thirty-five dollars from
the pocket of New York Telephone Company worker Walter Jackman
just as he tried to shake Ederle's hand.

The motorcade moved slowly toward City Hall, where the crowd was
so thick that trolley cars were stalled and men in straw hats piled on top

A view of the crowds surrounding the Ederle motorcade in the Canyon of Heroes homecoming parade in August 1926. (*Library of Congress, New York World Telegram Collection*)

Standing in her car, acknowledging the crowds in her parade. (*Library of Congress, New York World Telegram Collection*)

Trudy in the water during the 1926 swim.
(*Gertrude Ederle personal collection*)

At home with her parents, circa 1922. (*Gertrude Ederle personal collection*)

Trudy's mom at her Highlands home with a telegram announcing that her daughter had made it. Henry Junior, Trudy's younger brother, and Emma, a sister, stand beside her. (*Gertrude Ederle personal collection*)

After winning her first big race, the Joseph P. Day swim from Manhattan Beach to Brighton Beach, in 1922. (*Gertrude Ederle personal collection, Paul Thompson Photo*)

With her first trainer, Jabez Wolffe, prior to her first Channel attempt in 1925. (*Gertrude Ederle personal collection, Herbert Photos*)

Setting sail for France in 1926 with her sister Meg and her father. (*Gertrude Ederle personal collection, Keystone View Co.*)

Playing her ukulele, 1925. *(Gertrude Ederle personal collection)*

A postcard showing the Olympic women swimmers in Paris in 1924. Ederle is at far left. *(Gertrude Ederle personal collection)*

PARIS - JEUX OLYMPIQUES - 1924 -
Équipe américaine - Nageuses

U.S. women's swimming team in Paris, 1924. Ederle is at far right. *(Gertrude Ederle personal collection)*

Trudy and Johnny Weissmuller with noted swimming coach Arthur Bachrach between them. *(Gertrude Ederle personal collection)*

Ederle, second from left, flexing muscles with fellow WSA swimmers Helen Wainwright, Lillian Cannon, and Aileen Riggin. *(Gertrude Ederle personal collection, Herbert Photos)*

Heading into the water for a historic swim, 1926 *(Gertrude Ederle personal collection, International Newsreel Photos)*

Being given something to drink during the 1926 Channel swim. (*Gertrude Ederle personal collection*)

Martha Melchner, sister Helen, and brother George at the *Daily News* newsroom, looking over bulletins on the swim as they came in, 1926. (*Gertrude Ederle personal collection*)

The prized red roadster given to her by the *Daily News*. *(Gertrude Ederle personal collection, Underwood & Underwood)*

With director Clarence Badger on the set of *Swim, Girl, Swim* in Hollywood, 1927. *(Gertrude Ederle personal collection)*

On the set of *Swim, Girl, Swim* with Lila Lee, left, and star Bebe Daniels, middle. *(Gertrude Ederle personal collection)*

Learning how to play golf while on tour, 1927. (*Gertrude Ederle personal collection*)

Trudy in a pose to attract swimmers at the Bronx Dale swimming pool, circa 1931. (*Gertrude Ederle personal collection*)

"Join Me At"
THE BRONX DALE SWIMMING POOL

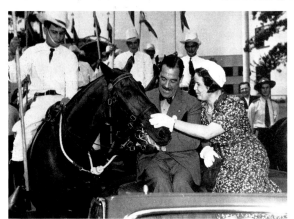

With Grover Whalen at the New York World Fair's parade on the thirteenth anniversary of the Channel swim, 1939. (*Gertrude Ederle personal collection, Acme News*)

Working in an aircraft-instrument factory during World War II. (*Gertrude Ederle personal collection, American Overseas Airlines*)

of the cars for better viewing. Police lines shifted and wavered at City Hall, where police motorcycles managed to move enough of the crowd out of the way to get Trudy's car to the front steps. Whalen assisted Trudy from the car and she held his arm as they mounted the steps to be greeted by the mayor.

The official ceremony was to be held inside, much to the displeasure of those who had come to join in the celebration. As the doors closed behind Trudy and her delegation, the crowd surged toward the building, and an iron rail under the windows of City Hall broke, causing people in the front to fall forward. Others rushed from behind and trampled them, while outnumbered police desperately tried to keep order. Women screamed in fear and men swore in anger as mounted police tried to control the crowd by riding among them. One officer, Inspector Joe Kuehne, said he had never seen anything like it in his thirty years on the New York Police force.

"There was an old woman about 85 years old in the front of the crowd, which stormed the doors," he told a *New York Times* reporter. "I was afraid she would get hurt and tried to assist her to a safer place. She became indignant and protested."

Six people were injured, among them eleven-year-old Herbert Kohler, who suffered a sprained left foot, and thirteen-year-old Adla Paplia, who was overcome by heat and exhaustion. Also falling victim to the heat and excitement was Ellen Mitchell, a twenty-seven-year-old, who received first aid and went home after reporting the loss of a watch she valued at two hundred dollars.

City Hall was draped in bunting, thousands waved flags, and the noise upon Trudy's arrival was deafening. She was led up spiraling stairs into the rotunda, above which hung an oversize picture of her being swathed in grease by Burgess on the shore of France before beginning her swim.

Whalen had gone all out for the celebration, and now Trudy stood between the mayor and Malone under a canopy of American flags in the rotunda. On each side, she was flanked by army and navy officers and members of the mayoral committee. On the balcony of the chamber, a band played patriotic hymns, and Miss Virginia, Chate Pinner, sang the national anthem. The welcoming ceremony was broadcast by the municipal radio station, WNYC, and fifty amplifiers installed especially for the occasion relayed the remarks to those outside.

Whalen formally introduced Trudy to the mayor, telling him that the parade showed "there was that human touch that struck the populace and they turned out in millions. It is my privilege to turn over this precious treasure from Amsterdam Avenue to the kind consideration of your honor."

Walker, whose time in office would be known for his tolerant attitude toward speakeasies and his pursuit of chorus girls, jokingly asked Ederle for a kiss before presenting her with a scroll commemorating her swim and a key to the city. Walker had been elected for the first time just months earlier, and he was clearly reveling in the moment as he launched into some mayoral hyperbole that sounded as if it had been lifted from the sports pages of the day.

"When history records the great crossings, they will speak of Moses crossing the Red Sea, Caesar crossing the Rubicon, and Washington crossing the Delaware," he told Trudy. "But frankly your crossing of the British Channel must take its place alongside all of these."

Walker also made it clear that he was in Trudy's corner when it came to any questions about the legitimacy of her swim.

"I do not know much about this controversy about the tug, but mayors are supposed to be practical and I have this in mind; that the old Channel is still there and there are a lot of tugs to be hired by anyone who wants to try it and this mayor will be the first volunteer to refuse to try it."

The hot, stuffy room went quiet as it became Ederle's turn to respond. She spoke nervously, seeming dazed and bewildered by the events of the last few hours, and repeated herself as she tried to thank everyone for the reception. She told the mayor she had done it for her country and thanked both New Yorkers and German-Americans for their support. She said she didn't have words to express how happy she was. "It's wonderful. Everything is wonderful," Trudy kept saying. "It's all so wonderful."

As speeches go, it wasn't much. But it came from Trudy's heart, and for that she was given a loud and long ovation.

The mayor escorted Ederle back down the stairs, and the parade of people marched through the rotunda and out the front door to the large porch. They quickly realized they had made a mistake, as the crowd by now had reached the steps and the entire front of the building was blocked. Trudy took a step forward and was bounced back by the policemen in front of her, who were wrestling with the crowd and accidentally bumped her. She cried out, and patrolman John Donovan lifted her in his arms and carried her back into the building. Someone else pushed the mayor, and he also retreated to the relative safety of the rotunda.

They all gathered inside the mayor's office and waited, hoping for the crowd to thin a bit. In the meantime, Inspector Kuehne asked police headquarters to rush one hundred additional reserves to City Hall, one hundred extra traffic men to Fifth Avenue and Thirty-fourth Street, and another one hundred recruits to Amsterdam and Fifty-seventh, where the parade would be heading. No one had anticipated the size of the welcome, or the fervor of the crowds. On this hot summer day, Broadway looked as if it had been the center of a winter blizzard, City Hall was in danger of being overrun, and Trudy hadn't even made it to her home next to the butcher shop yet. New York had its first genuine female hero, and New Yorkers wanted to see her, touch her, and listen to her speak.

Men were the ones who had been expected to welcome her home, because most worked in the area, but it was the huge turnout of women that surprised everyone. They came from their homes, from their jobs, and from their schools to see one of their own, a woman who had bettered both the Channel and the men who had swum it before her. It was a stunning sight for women, many of whom had marched these very streets just seven years earlier with placards carrying a million signatures urging that they be given the right to vote.

After about thirty minutes, word was given to make a break for it, and the swimmer and her party hurried out of City Hall, posed for pictures with the mayor on the steps of the building, and then walked briskly to her waiting car. Trudy climbed onto the folded top in back, Whalen joined her, and two officers jumped on the running boards of each side of the convertible. It was 2:30 P.M. and a steamy city was getting steamier by the minute as the parade began anew, this time heading up Lafayette Street, with its eventual destination the Ederle home on Manhattan's West Side. The crush of humanity wasn't as thick as it had been on Broadway or at City Hall, but cheering crowds still lined the way and made it slow going as the parade worked its way north.

Some of the delegates from Amsterdam Avenue had dropped out at City Hall because the distance was proving hard on their feet, but a band or two remained and played determinedly as the parade resumed. At Ninth Street, the cars turned west toward Fifth Avenue, and an employee of John Wanamaker's huge department store ran out to present Trudy with a huge cluster of American Beauty roses on behalf of the shop.

Berlenbach, the German-American boxer and friend of Trudy who had lost his light heavyweight title a month earlier, joined the parade as it started the long march up Fifth Avenue, horning in with his green roadster, which was loaded with his friends. Trudy was already much farther up the avenue, but the remaining crowd wasn't too hoarse from cheering her on to give the fighter a rousing ovation, too.

The stores on Fifth Avenue were ready, with workers running out with packages to drop in her car. Elaborate bouquets of flowers were tossed her way, including one from Saks. A Miss Rose Meune ran up on behalf of other merchants to give her a large silver loving cup and another cluster of flowers. Even the pigeons paid attention. As the motorcade passed the public library at Forty-second Street, they flew out from under the eaves of the huge building as if to greet her, circling the car until she passed by and then returning to their perches.

The drive from City Hall took about an hour, while thousands of neighbors, fans, and gawkers crowded Amsterdam Avenue, waiting anxiously to greet Trudy when she arrived home. Her arrival about 3:30 P.M. was announced by the motorcycle advance guard, and by a youth who had climbed the roof of the tallest building on the block to spot the motorcade as it turned onto the avenue. "Here she is," he shrieked, send-ing the already-excited crowd into even more of a frenzy.

The extra reserves called out earlier from City Hall arrived in time, and now there were about three hundred policemen on horses, foot, and motorcycles in the streets around her home. As her moment of ar-rival neared, they drove all but the immediate neighbors from the block, urging them to move along and prodding them with the bottom of a shoe if they didn't get the idea the first time. For the cops, it wasn't bad duty. In the basement of the Ederle Brothers Meat Market, two clerks made pork sandwiches on rye bread, and police and neighbors took breaks to go below and eat them. Though Prohibition was still in effect, the police looked the other way when an occasional celebrant walked by drinking from a "growler," a small pail used to carry beer home from the pub.

Amsterdam Avenue was awash in a sweaty sea of humanity, gaily fes-tooned in red-white-and-blue streaming, and filled with the native languages and accents of its immigrants. A jazz band played in the mid-dle of the street, a loud siren roared on a balcony, and bells rang as the motorcade carrying the neighborhood hero turned the corner onto Amsterdam. The crowd surged forward to get a better view, and al-though the police held most of the people back, some broke through to greet the motorcade.

"Easy men," a stout sergeant called to his platoon. "Look out for the women and children."

There was no rhyme or reason to the decorations, which included lodge emblems, the star and crescent of Turkey, and symbols of other homelands. Signs were everywhere, proclaiming AMERICANS CAN DO ANYTHING, TRUDY SWAM THE CHANNEL; THE FIRST WOMAN OF THE WORLD; and, of course, WELCOME HOME TRUDY.

The five-story tenement where the Ederles lived next to the butcher shop was swathed with flags and bunting, which covered almost every inch of the first few floors. American flags were everywhere, but there were also German, Italian, and Irish flags in abundance. This was all new to Trudy, because on a normal day the only decorations would have been a large billboard for Sinclair Opaline motor oil three stories high on the side of the brick structure and a clothesline filled with laundry running from above the butcher shop to a second-floor window.

One newspaper called the building, "typical of most of the streets on New York's West Side, where friendliness and good neighbors count more than fine appearances."

All the shops had signs welcoming Trudy, but the numerous butchers in the neighborhood took particular pride in the fact that she was one of their own. They all had pictures of Ederle, bearing the news she was the daughter of a butcher and that she ate meat three times a day. The most elaborate display was in the window of her father's shop, where there was a lifelike imitation of the English Channel built out of cardboard, with bright green waves moving up and down quickly and Trudy hitting the water at sixty strokes per minute. It was operated by a lever attached to a small electric motor, and beneath it was this verse:

> Pop Ederle by cutting meat made for himself a dame.
> His daughter Trudy by cutting the waves won victory and fame.
> You see her, how she fights the sea and how she puts it over.
> Hurrah for her, first of her sex to swim from France to Dover.

As the official car pulled in front of the Ederle home, a small girl got through the police line and presented Trudy with a gilt crown symbolic of the Amsterdam Avenue community. Ederle wasn't going to put it on, but the girl insisted, and so Trudy put it on her head for a moment, along with a sash that read QUEEN GERTRUDE THE FIRST. The crowd had Trudy surrounded, and she was helpless in the car. Though they meant well, the sheer crush of people frightened her, just as it had since the moment she stepped off the *Macon* at the harbor. Now police on horses pushed their way through to help her out of the car and clear a lane to the curb. Trudy looked around for a moment, answering greetings, then stepped from the car with Whalen and rushed across the sidewalk and up the dark stairs to her second-floor home.

The family dogs greeted her at the door, and she rushed inside, followed by Pop Ederle, who was nearly buried under huge bouquets of red roses he had collected on her behalf. It had been less than five hours since she came ashore, but what a five hours it had been.

"It's so wonderful, so wonderful," she kept repeating to the dogs.

Trudy had barely had time to sit down when she realized the medal the mayor had given her was missing, and Uncle John was dispatched to the city car, where he found it on the floor of the backseat. Any thoughts Trudy had of staying inside evaporated when a bright red roadster drove up, and she went down to see the one prize she so wanted, delivered by the *Daily News* to her door. She climbed into the driver's seat and was photographed in the car while everyone cheered her good fortune. By now, she was wanted upstairs again to receive the neighborhood welcoming committee, which had been waiting in the butcher shop for hours for her return.

Oberwager was in charge once again and, back among his own people, he wasn't going to waste the chance to applaud her Teutonic heritage. This time, though, he seemed to get the message and offered Trudy up as a unification figure of sorts, someone who could help heal the scars of war and make people forget the atrocities on both sides.

"It proves that all distinctions with respect to national feeling and race prejudices resulting from the war have disappeared," he said. "Gertrude is a German-American girl, her father and others were born in Germany, and they continue their German associations with all the vigor of the Teutonic race. This demonstration may be considered as a public reunion of all the people for it is the first time since the war that such a great and wonderful demonstration was held in which the Americans of German descent played such an important part. We are proud of Trudy the American girl, born in this city of a father and mother who first saw the light of day in Germany."

Outside, the crowd wasn't going away. They chanted Trudy's name and called her to the window, and she went over two or three times to wave and smile at them. Finally, Pop Ederle volunteered to do the window duty, while he and his wife stood waving until the crowd eventually thinned out and four police stood guard over their front door. Trudy was exhausted, but her day was not done.

The mayor's welcoming committee had planned a dinner to salute

Trudy that night, and people began milling about on the street in the early evening hours, hoping to sneak a peek at her when she came out for the event. There were some four thousand people jammed onto the block, and the crowd surged forward on several occasions, only to be pushed back by police when they heard a cry of "Here she comes!"

Whalen would be returning to accompany the Ederles to the Hotel Roosevelt, where the dinner was to be held, but he was late and the crowd was getting agitated. Vendors on the street tried to sell WELCOME HOME TRUDY buttons, but people were so boisterous and so closely jammed together on this Friday night that many just took what they wanted without paying.

The city sent a car, which arrived at 7:30 P.M., accompanied by a shrieking motorcycle escort. Whalen had not yet arrived, so cops on the street suggested the chauffeur drive around the block until he got there. The driver circled the block four times, stopping each time in front of the Ederles' home. Each time the car halted, a crowd of several hundred approached it, many clinging to it and peering inside before yelling out loudly that it was empty.

On the last pass, the crowd, now maintaining some semblance of order, marched solemnly behind the vehicle, eight to ten abreast. About then, Whalen appeared wearing a topper and a flower in his buttonhole, doffing the hat to a roar of cheers. The Ederles quickly joined him in the car, prompting hundreds of people to surround it and try to touch Trudy. One man ran around screaming, "That's the girl who owns the Channel!"

At the Roosevelt, there were sixty places set, and the family mingled with both close friends and members of the city's elite. All who were there knew they had seen something they might never see again in their lifetime.

"It would be impossible," Whalen said in a brief speech, "for human tongue to voice an added welcome after that extended by the people of this city today."

Some people tried anyway. Malone told the crowd that he had advanced Trudy money to make her first swim after seeing her in Florida the year before and having her convince him that she could do it. President Coolidge sent regards, and Governor Smith said he was sorry he couldn't be there.

Ederle begged off once again when asked to give a speech. The day was wearing on her, and even her smile was forced by this time.

There was one final engagement after dinner: a performance of the Ziegfeld Follies, a lavish review that featured beautiful chorus girls and top entertainers of the day—a perfect way to end the day. The party set off under motorcycle escort for the Globe Theatre, with police stopping traffic at Broadway to get them through. About ten thousand people had gathered after hearing the news that Trudy was nearby, and police cleared the way through the crowd at Times Square with considerable difficulty so that the Ederles could get to the theater.

Trudy made her way to her seat just as song and dance man Charles King started his act. He stopped, knowing who the true star of this night was, and a spotlight was thrown on her as the audience began to applaud. Trudy bowed right and left, then sat down in the second row, only to have to stand again as the orchestra began playing the national anthem and those on stage joined with the audience in singing it.

The Follies over, the police motorcycles roared to life and sirens echoed throughout the Theater District. The motorcade hurtled down city streets toward home, where crowds were still milling about, despite the late hour. Trudy waved, then headed up the narrow, dark stairway to the second floor, where her bed awaited her. The next day, the first motion pictures of her homecoming would be shown at all leading theaters in the International Newsreel. New Yorkers who hadn't seen her in person could pay fifteen cents to see her on the silver screen.

For this day, though, Trudy was exhausted. She had been cheered and feted more than any man or woman before her, a welcome that Whalen would say, thirty years later, was the greatest he had ever seen for any athlete.

The next morning, even the normally reserved *New York Times* declared the city awestruck. "No President or king, soldier or statesman has ever enjoyed such an enthusiastic and affectionate outburst of acclaim by the metropolis as was offered to the butcher's daughter of Amsterdam Avenue," the paper said.

A great city had proclaimed her greater than anyone. They had embraced her as an American hero unlike any who had come before.

And now the second greatest day of her life was just a memory.

11

The Next One Has to Be a Blonde

In the speakeasies that dotted every New York neighborhood in this sixth year of Prohibition, the chatter grew more excited as the booze flowed. The parade had been over for several hours and mountains of confetti were still being swept up, but it was a Friday night and New Yorkers were still in a mood to celebrate. With Trudy's Channel swim, the home runs being hit in the Bronx by the pennant-bound Yankees, and the hugely anticipated heavyweight-title fight between Dempsey and Tunney a few weeks off, there was plenty happening with America's athletes to keep the conversation flowing as easily as the liquor.

It wasn't hard to find a drink in the city, which now had an estimated thirty thousand illegal speakeasies that served up everything from the nastiest rotgut to the finest of European liquors. And with Henry Ford on the brink of implementing the first five-day workweek for employees in his automobile plants—something other companies would eventually adopt—there was excitement about having another day of leisure and another night in which to drink.

Across the ocean, there was excitement of another sort. The weather was perfect, the tides were favorable, and on this night there would be a rush to get in some of the last attempts at the Channel before September came and the water grew too frigid to make any more crossings this year.

For the townspeople of Cape Gris-Nez, Channel swims had become a familiar sight, but this time there was an added bonus, with three swimmers ready to enter the water shortly before midnight, when the conditions were ripe. Among them were Helmy, who would be making his third and last attempt of the summer, and Frank Perks, the Englishman who was trying for the fourth time to make it across.

And finally, there was Corson, the mother of two, who just a few days earlier had been out scouting routes while watching Cannon in her failed attempt. She was by far the most accomplished swimmer of the three and, like Trudy, her close call three years earlier had merely served to bolster her determination to make it across. She wouldn't be the first woman to do it, but no mother had yet to swim the Channel, and besides, no men had made it in three years.

Helmy started off first shortly before midnight, followed by Perks twenty minutes later and Corson a half hour after that. Helmy had a tug, but even though Corson had the financial backing to hire a tug of her own, she was determined to swim the Channel without one—a clear attempt to separate her swim from the controversy that still raged over Ederle's. A motorboat carried spectators, press, and some friends to cheer Corson on, while her husband rowed beside her in a dory to offer encouragement and nutrition.

For Helmy, it would be another bitter defeat at the hands of the Channel, which he couldn't seem to conquer. The six-foot-three, 253-pounder was swimming against his doctor's advice to begin with and was in the water for just a little more than three hours before collapsing with abdominal pains. Helmy was in such bad straits, he might have drowned had not an alert Wolffe, who by this time was training him, thrown his ample body into the water and swum to his rescue.

Corson and Perks soldiered on, and both were making good progress as night gave way to the gray of dawn over the Channel and the Dover cliffs became faintly visible to those in the boat alongside them. It was now man against woman, a mother at that, a story line that proved irresistible to a press corps looking for something new in Channel swims to get excited about.

Corson was the faster swimmer and passed Perks early in the swim, and though Perks tried mightily to regain his lead, he trailed most of the way. At one point in the morning, he swam past Corson, but then, fatigued by the effort, quickly fell back again. Beating the Englishman would be an added bonus for Corson, though she, like all swimmers, had enough problems just trying to defeat both the natural and man-made hazards of the Channel. In her case, that meant almost going under at one point in the backwash of the Amsterdam steamer *Ulysses* when it passed by a bit too closely in the narrow Channel, which was the most heavily trafficked body of water in the world.

Clemington Corson chatted with his wife and fed her hot chocolate, lumps of sugar, and a few crackers from the rowboat as she swam steadily toward England. On the motorboat, Louis Timson was reprising the role of cheerleader he'd played for Trudy, and his booming bass notes crossed the waves as he sang "Oh, Millie! Oh, Millie! How you can swim!" Other liners and cross-Channel craft added to the encouragement as they went by, hoisting American flags and pounding on their sirens on what was now a sunny Saturday morning.

By now, the people in Dover knew the routine. As word of the strong attempt by Corson and Perks spread, they gathered on the shore by the hundreds, straining to see the pair and their accompanying craft before finally breaking out in excited cheers as the swimmers were spotted about noon.

Corson was about six miles out, while Perks was a mile or so behind. They were both making good progress as they headed straight toward Dover, but then the tide suddenly changed and left them floundering in the water. Both were battling the ebb tide when, just a mile or so offshore, Perks met a heavy swell and swallowed so much seawater that he was forced to quit. Corson was struggling in the same conditions and her eyes were burning from the seawater, but she kept fighting despite her fatigue.

The tide changed again, giving her a boost about the same time she got a second wind, and suddenly the figure barely visible to the crowd onshore grew larger and it became apparent that Corson was going to make it. She sprinted the last three hundred yards to shore before stumbling onto Shakespeare Beach at 3:10 P.M. to the cheers of townspeople and loud whistles from boats that had gathered offshore.

It wasn't quite as dramatic as Trudy's nighttime arrival before roaring bonfires a few weeks earlier, but Corson could now lay claim to becoming not only the second woman to swim the English Channel but the first mother. Unlike Trudy, she had trouble finding her legs and became disoriented, turning to go back in the water toward France before trainer Billy Kellingley grabbed her and covered her in blankets.

"I have to make some money for my kids," an exhausted Corson declared, "but I would not do it again for a million dollars."

Corson's time was fifteen hours and twenty-nine minutes, just fifty minutes longer than it had taken Ederle to make the same swim. But Corson had done it without an accompanying tug and, of course, she was a mother, two points that her supporters would drive home every time they could when comparing the feats of the two women. Corson herself said she would have beaten the record had her eyes not been hurting so much from the seawater, something Ederle had avoided with her one-piece waxed goggles. Still, she had not only beaten a man in a one-on-one across the Channel but also the records of all the five men who had successfully made the swim. She may not have been the first woman to swim the Channel, but she wasn't far behind—and she had some bragging rights of her own.

Lissberger, the tire baron who backed her swim, trumpeted the fact that his swimmer made it without a tug shielding her, and he immediately issued a challenge to "everybody, Miss Ederle not excepted," to swim around the island of Manhattan, a distance of forty-two miles, for $25,000. The money was huge, but the spectacle would be even bigger, and Lissberger could easily afford it after making $100,000 at Lloyd's of London on his $5,000 bet at 20–1 odds on Corson making it across.

"I am particularly interested in a contest between the first two women to swim the English Channel because the English have criticized Miss

Ederle for swimming between two tugs while Mrs. Corson swam the Channel with only a launch," Lissberger said. "I also like a woman with two children showing the world what she can do."

Even bigger was the $100,000-purse offer floated by Alex Mueller, head of the Great American Water Circus, which was now playing at the Philadelphia Sesquicentennial, for a race over a course of twenty miles in Delaware Bay or any other body of water. Mueller didn't say how he would come up with the money for the race, but he did say Ederle's father was considering the offer on her behalf. "We mean business," Mueller said.

In the meantime, the English celebrated with Corson, with newspapers declaring her feat every bit the equal of Ederle's, and splashing photos of her arrival in Dover across their front pages. Maybe, the papers now said, those American women weren't so crazy after all in taking on challenges they weren't supposed to be physically capable of.

The *Daily Graphic* offered its congratulations in a huge headline celebrating Corson's feat. WELL DONE MOTHER, it read.

Trudy was up at 8:00 A.M. the morning after her return home, unable to sleep any more as crowds began to gather once again outside the family home and call her name. Hundreds stood on Amsterdam Avenue, still in a mood to party and eager to catch a glimpse of the neighborhood's most famous citizen. A special detail of thirty-eight police officers patrolled the block, telling the crowds, who were swaying among the vegetable carts at the curb in the hope they could see up the stairway leading to Trudy's apartment, that they had to keep moving.

Still exhausted after a day of celebration that hadn't ended until late in the evening, Trudy sipped a cup of coffee while Meg and Helen answered the phone, which never seemed to stop ringing. Ederle would have been content to stay inside all day, but when Malone came over in a touring car, she went with her parents and a police escort to the Cunard pier at the foot of West Fifteenth Street to look for a piece of baggage that had been lost.

Customs inspector John Borkel, who was an old friend of Malone and had gained a reputation for his minstrel singing at the Rockaway Point Club, entertained them there with a version of "Out of the New-Mown Hay" while Trudy looked for her bag, which she finally spotted among the hundreds of bags left on the pier.

Her happiness at finding the luggage was tempered by a piece of news that had to be disturbing to both Ederle and Malone. Word reached Trudy on the pier that Corson had come ashore near Dover, and now there were two women conquerors of the Channel. The cheers of millions from the day earlier had barely subsided, and suddenly she was forced to come to grips with the reality that swimming the Channel was now an honor that she would have to share the rest of her life.

Ederle nervously asked how long it had taken for Corson to make it across, and she seemed pleased when told it had not been quite fast enough to break her record. She would send a telegram to Corson later in the day, congratulating her on joining the elite club of Channel swimmers, which now numbered five men and two women, but first she had to sort out in her mind just how this was all going to play out.

After consulting with Malone, she settled on an approach that was as good as any that could have been crafted by the day's best public-relations person.

"I am very happy that the Channel has been conquered again, and I have sent my heartiest congratulations to Mrs. Corson," Trudy told reporters. "But I am very proud to have been the first woman to get across and to hold the fastest record that has been made."

Back home that afternoon, she and Malone sat at the family dining table with Pop Ederle for three hours, pouring over the various offers gathered in during the previous weeks. Malone wanted to strike while the iron was hot, and he said he had received theatrical and motion-picture offers totaling $900,000. His eye was on two—one for $100,000 and one for $120,000—but there were also offers for exhibitions, and the William Morris Agency was putting together a proposal for a tour of vaudeville houses.

Malone had always been eager to move fast and get money in hand before the glow of Ederle's accomplishment began to fade, but now there was a real sense of urgency to capitalize on her fame. With Corson's successful swim, the market for Channel swimmers was now as fluid as the Channel itself, and he wanted her performing onstage as soon as possible.

"Miss Ederle is now a free agent," Malone told reporters gathered outside the family home. "She is under no contract with anyone and we are making a careful decision as to the wisest course for her to pursue. No definite decision will be made for several days."

Malone was posturing for his client, hoping to bring in even bigger offers over the next few days than the ones he already had in hand. And indeed, there were hundreds of bids for her services, including one for her to appear the following week at the Sesquicentennial Expo in Philadelphia. If she accepted, it would be her first exhibition swim since her brief dip in the Channel outside Dover the morning after her victory.

But while Malone was a smooth and practiced attorney, highly skilled both in the courtroom and in securing Paris divorces for American princesses, he was not a businessman and had no particular expertise in how the free-agent marketplace worked or what the value of a female athlete really was in the United States at the time. He was so taken with the offers already in hand that he thought even better offers would follow, and he failed to take the best of what he had and get cash deposits before they were either withdrawn or exposed as fake.

There was now competition for the Channel-swimmer dollar, and while Trudy's story was an inspiring one, it had limited legs. There was only so much that could be done, after all, with a shy and nearly deaf twenty-year-old whose aquatic skills might be unsurpassed but whose personality was not exactly suited to making endorsements or selling tickets to movie-house shows.

Gallico would later write, "One can fault Mr. Malone for greed and inexperience, but it must be remembered that the greed was on behalf of his client. How was he to guess that the very sweetness, innocence and guilelessness that characterized Gertrude Ederle was to prove his and her undoing."

To Trudy, the offers seemed as overwhelming as the attention showered on her since swimming the Channel. They were too much for a simple girl who had never finished high school to understand, and they seemed to come from everywhere. It was all too much, with everybody wanting a piece of her. Always shy to begin with, she was terribly unsure how to handle both her new celebrity and the responsibilities that came along with it. The nation had never had a woman sports hero like this before, and there was no way to judge how to do things. Everything was uncharted territory, just as the Channel had once been uncharted territory for the girl who grew up next to her father's butcher shop.

Outside her house was the red roadster given her by the *Daily News.* It had already been damaged in the parade and then later by revelers, who had broken a windshield and gouged the paint during the excitement of the previous day. The car meant more to her than anything, but she couldn't even ride in it because the crowd was still milling in the street below, and motorists driving by for a look were jamming the streets, too.

Trudy couldn't have escaped even if she'd wanted to. She was trapped in her parent's walk-up flat, hostage to a new life she didn't understand. She was frightened and unsure how she would make the money everyone now expected her to make. Most of all, she was simply exhausted. At home that night, she finally collapsed from the toll of it all, and her parents were forced to summon the family doctor. The doctor gave her a hypodermic to offset imminent hysteria and ordered her to bed for twenty-four hours, telling Trudy to relax, even as the sounds of hundreds on the streets waiting for a glimpse of her found their way through her bedroom window.

"Trudy is all tired out," Dr. Robert Bickley said. "She will have to get twenty-four hours' sleep. She has not had a good night's sleep since she swam the Channel."

Ma Ederle fussed about her pale, twitching daughter, uncertain about what to do. What she did know was that there would be some new rules in the neighborhood, if she had any say about it.

"There's been enough of this clamor," she said. "Why, I almost collapsed myself after that first day."

Trudy got some sleep, though it was clear by now that it would take more time for her to recover. She stayed home on Sunday while Malone sifted through offers, but the neighborhood was throwing a block party for her Monday night and there was no way she could let her family's friends, neighbors, and customers down by not showing up for it. And what a party it was, with 25,000 people surging onto West Sixty-fifth Street between Broadway and Amsterdam avenues, filling it from curb to curb. Two platforms were set up on the street, one holding the Firemen's Band and the Police Glee Club, and another holding Whalen, local politicians, friends of the family, and Trudy herself. The massive throng roared as a delegation of 101 neighborhood people who knew her best escorted her to the platform.

James J. Hagen, the assistant commissioner of Public Works, placed a gilded crown on top of Trudy's head, crowning her the queen of the waves, and a cape was draped across her back as she sat on a makeshift throne, her head bowed and her lips trembling, clearly frightened by the outpouring of affection for her. She didn't speak and was soon taken home, her nerves still badly in need of repair. But while Trudy kept quiet, Malone had an announcement to make, much to the delight of the crowd. He said his client would leave in three days for a week of exhibition swimming at the Sesquicentennial, where she would demonstrate to fairgoers the stroke that had gotten her across the Channel, appearing in a stadium that had seating for ten thousand.

It was a good match for both sides. Ederle would get to perform in a regulation pool for her first exhibition, instead of in a tank on a vaudeville stage, while fair organizers hoped her appearance would spark attendance, which had lagged since the exhibition opened at League Island Park on May 31 in celebration of the country's 150th birthday. Some fifty million people had been expected to attend the fair, which would run through November, but the summer traffic was only a fifth of what was expected, so Trudy's signing couldn't have come at a better time.

First, though, there was one more celebration before Trudy could even think of leaving the New York area. This one would take place in

Highlands, where some three thousand dollars had been raised among the town's businesspeople for a homecoming fit for their Channel queen.

This was one welcoming party Trudy was truly looking forward to. With her parents, Meg, and Malone in tow, she motored down to Monmouth County with a police escort, encountering excited crowds at every borough and town along the way. The town of Keyport briefly hijacked the procession to deliver its own bouquets of flowers and a giant key to the city made out of gladioli and asparagus ferns. Ederle was given an escort out of town by firemen in their trucks until she got about seven miles from home, where she was met by the Highlands orchestra, which serenaded her, and about three hundred brightly decorated cars.

The entire procession wound its way to town, where she was greeted by Mayor John L. Opfermann and New Jersey governor A. Harry Moore. A military band from Fort Hancock played, and twenty-four bathing beauties led the parade, followed by delegations from business and civic groups. There were placards on every home and business welcoming her, and it seemed like the entire summer population of twenty thousand had turned out to welcome Trudy to the place where she'd learned to swim.

Once again, Trudy didn't have much to say. Shy among crowds to begin with because her hearing problem made it tough to understand people if they weren't right in front of her, she was becoming increasingly uneasy at the thought of facing large crowds at every stop. She was also beginning to realize that this was the kind of scene she would have to endure almost daily as she sought to capitalize on her swim the way Malone intended.

But she was happy to be home, and even happier later that day when the official receptions were over and she could join her father in an hour-and-a-half swim in the Shrewsbury River. That night, there was a quiet dinner just for family and friends at McGuire's Hotel.

It was good to be home, good to be back in the waters where she'd spent so much of her childhood. But things had changed dramatically for Ederle, and her life would never be the same.

Harpman wrote in the *Daily News* that three months earlier she had sailed with a carefree kid with a booming laugh and a determination to swim the Channel, only to return with a woman no longer so carefree.

"She is now a business—a big business, without the privilege of opening her soft unpainted lips, unless she's told to do so. If she eats some of her own Pop's bologna, she'll probably have to do so secretly for fear her picture will be snapped while she's eating and some concern will use the snapshot as an advertisement."

The new Trudy was different indeed, but no less endearing to Harpman, whose fondness toward her was reflected in her newspaper copy.

"She is the most wholesome, unspoiled and thoroughly natural girl I've ever met. She is affectionate, and honest and utterly unconceited."

Indeed, that was the Trudy who boarded a train in New York a few days later for Philadelphia, accompanied by Aileen Riggin and Helen Wainwright, her former rivals and Olympic teammates. They had signed on to be featured divers and swimmers for $250 a week in the act that would be tested at the Sesquicentennial before going on a twenty-six-week tour to vaudeville houses and theaters around the country.

The New York Express, with Ederle's private car at the end of a long string of cars, was late in arriving at the Philadelphia train station, much to the dismay of the approximately ten thousand people who had crowded around the arriving tracks to greet her. Her arrival was compared to that of President Coolidge, who had come on July 4 to visit the fair. And like Coolidge, she had given up shaking hands. Malone explained that this was because he didn't want her to injure her arm.

Dressed in a neatly tailored blue suit with a light blue hat and silk scarf, Ederle tried to avoid the crowd as she made her way to her limousine, but people surged after her as the car moved toward City Hall. Cameramen were everywhere, snapping away with their big black boxes, and movie men were contorted over their range finders. Once inside the mayor's reception room, she faced a battery of cameras, with flashbulbs popping like machine guns.

"I'd rather swim the Channel than go through this," she whispered to Malone, who looked a bit frightened himself.

Ederle was presented with the key to the city, and then she strained to hear as reporters asked her questions about both her swim and the successful crossing that Corson had made the week before.

"Oh, I'm really delighted that others are swimming the Channel, too," she said when asked for the hundredth time about Corson. "But of course I'm glad that I was the first girl and that the second one was an American woman."

Malone broke up the impromptu press conference and ordered everyone to the line of cars waiting outside. Police shooed people out of the way to give Trudy and the others a path to the vehicles, and the cavalcade headed off in the rain from City Hall to the Alpine House where a banquet was being held in her honor. Still another crowd was gathered outside there to see Trudy, though by now the sight of thousands of people was becoming commonplace to her. The entire week she stayed at the Bellevue-Stratford, people waited in the street outside the hotel to get a look at the swimming maiden, and she was mobbed when she went on a shopping trip downtown.

Trudy, Wainwright, and Riggin soon got down to the business of putting on an act and selling tickets, and they were pictured together in the paper in requisite swimsuits. By now, the women had come up with an outline for the act they would put on around the country for the next six months. Ederle would show off her American crawl, while Wainwright and Riggin would make graceful dives into the water around her. They would then do underwater somersaults together, and then for her grand finale, Trudy would change into the suit she had swum the Channel in. During the actual performance, Trudy's swim was accompanied by the songs that had gotten her across the Channel, like her favorite, "Let Me Call You Sweetheart," and "The Sidewalks of New York." For added effect, a man in a rowboat joined her and fed her from the end of a pole. It all ended with Ederle standing up in the water and saluting the flag as "The Star-Spangled Banner" was played in a triumphant finale.

The performances were well received by large and appreciative crowds, though the rain that dampened the Sesquicentennial all summer played havoc with the schedule. It wasn't all business, though. Trudy and Malone headed down to Atlantic City on September 5 to watch

Dempsey train for his fight with Tunney. The *New York Times* said the spontaneous applause given her upon her arrival "made the applause accorded the heavyweight champion seem like a whisper in comparison."

The week in Philadelphia was a huge success, emboldening the William Morris Agency to fill out the remaining gaps in the tour that would take the swimming stars across the country and back. The appetite for anything Trudy-related seemed insatiable. This was made plain when she stopped in Atlantic City once again after leaving Philadelphia. When Ederle swam in the waters off the seaside resort, large crowds filled the boardwalk, and many people attempted to follow her into the surf. Extra police had to escort her from the hotel to the steel pier, where enthusiasts jostled with lifeguards attempting to keep them away from her.

They needn't have worried, as Ederle outswam everyone, then wowed the crowd even more by taking food from lifeguards in a rowboat to demonstrate how she'd gotten nourishment while swimming the Channel.

The Atlantic City Steel Pier's owner, Frank P. Gravatt, was so impressed that he sent a letter to William Morris in New York, saying the crowds on the boardwalk and beach were the greatest anyone had seen in thirty years. "We believe she is the greatest drawing attraction in America today," he wrote.

Before heading back to New York, Trudy went to see her favorite fighter once again. Like many Americans, she was smitten with Dempsey, the great heavyweight champion, who was coming off a three-year layoff to fight Tunney in Philadelphia in the most anticipated fight ever. She had watched Dempsey a few days earlier, but on this weekend he was sparring at the nearby dog track in his last big public workout before the fight, and she wasn't going to miss it.

Ederle joined five thousand people who paid $1.10 each to watch the workout, and she got a chance to chat with Dempsey before being introduced herself to loud applause. She then watched him spar five rounds with Charles Anderson, a black heavyweight from Chicago, who was helping the champ by emulating the fighting style that the crafty

Tunney employed. The fight would match brawler Dempsey against boxer Tunney, and it was clear who had Ederle's affection.

"He [Dempsey] is so big and strong," Ederle said. "It is so exciting to watch a prize fighter in action."

Ederle told reporters she planned to take a two-week vacation to rest before for her upcoming tour, and that she would take in the fight on September 23. Asked if she was going to stay around for the Miss America Pageant, she demurred, saying her schedule was busy and she had other priorities.

"I am a businesswoman now," she said.

As a businesswoman, she had a lot on her plate. In addition to the tour, there were offers to race from seemingly every city that had a large body of water. One of the most attractive came from gum magnate William Wrigley, Jr., who thought he would try to boost tourism for Catalina Island, the sliver of land he owned off the Southern California coast, by offering $25,000 to the winner of a race from Long Beach to Catalina, a distance similar to that of the Channel swim.

Trudy was intrigued, just as she was by offers from Lissberger to race against Corson and others around Manhattan. But she wondered how she could train properly while touring the country in advance of the planned race in January in California. Besides, she said, danger lurked in the waters off the California coast. "I understand there are a lot of sharks in the Pacific," she said.

After a summer of failures, interrupted only by Ederle's successful swim, things were happening with alarming speed in the English Channel. First, Corson had doubled the exclusive club of women who made it across, and then Germany's Ernst Vierkotter would become not only the first man to make it in three years but the person to break the record set by Trudy just a few weeks earlier.

Vierkotter, who had come close on his first try, only to fall short due to the fog, made his second swim only after wiring Crown Prince Frederick William of Germany and begging him to send some money so he could try again. The crown prince, known as a sporting sort, agreed, and Vierkotter, a war veteran who could see out of only one eye, swam a perfect line on August 30, walking onto the beach near Dover twelve hours and forty-two minutes after he'd begun.

In just a few days' time, Ederle had lost not only her place as the only woman to swim the Channel but her spot as the fastest person to make it across.

"The worm has turned," the *New York Times* said in an editorial. "Man, surpassed as a swimmer by a mere girl and by a mother, and derided as the weaker vessel, has now crossed the Channel in 12 hours and 40 minutes."

Both Ederle and Corson cabled their congratulations to Vierkotter, and Ederle said in the same cable that she hoped to beat him in a Channel race the following summer. Always on the lookout for a way to make a buck, Malone telegraphed the new record holder that there should be a three-way race across the Channel the next year between the German and the two women.

When Ederle was in Atlantic City watching Dempsey train, word came that yet another swimmer had made it across, and in an even more startling time. Georges Michel, a doughty French baker, who had abandoned a try just a few days earlier because of a storm, swam through the night before coming ashore on the wave of favorable tides in just eleven hours and five minutes. For Michel, who was now trained by Burgess, this was a tenth attempt at the Channel, and it had almost cost him his life. During the night, Burgess and those in the accompanying boat had lost sight of the white-capped swimmer for about fifteen minutes, until he'd heard them yelling and had swum back toward the boat.

The Channel-swimming frenzy was becoming old hat by now, as evidenced by a boatman who spotted Michel heading in toward St. Margaret's Bay and yelled out, "Shiver my timbers, if it isn't another one of those Channel swimmers." Two Frenchmen waiting onshore ran into the water to celebrate with their countryman.

"I have beaten the German," Michel declared before promptly slipping through the crowd to a nearby inn, where he ordered a double whiskey.

Rutherford wrote in the *New York Times* that Michel had balanced the scales between men and women for the summer. Two of each sex had made it across the Channel, bringing the total number of Channel conquerors to nine as the season finally came to an end, much to the dismay of inn operators and boat captains on both sides of the water.

Newspapermen were trying to figure out what it all meant, but they had not lost their appreciation for Ederle. She, they reasoned, was still the first woman to have made it across, and she still held the record for her sex. Men were naturally stronger and more powerful, they argued, but what Trudy did would stand the test of time.

Syndicated columnist Heywood Broun agreed that, yes, others had come across. "But Gertie softened it up for them," he wrote

Indeed, America was thrilled with its water goddesses and what they had accomplished. A country filled with people who thought they could do the impossible celebrated not only the brash teenager who had done it first but also the mother who'd soon followed. It mattered little that one was a Danish immigrant and the other a daughter of German immigrants. Both were seen as true American heroes.

And then there was Barrett, who had captured the imagination of many with her shoestring try, which had ended in defeat, with the French coast so close that she'd almost been able to touch it. Barrett had run up bills of about two thousand dollars while trying to become the first woman across, and she was barely able to scrape up enough spare change for third-class accommodations for herself and Leister when they sailed back on the *Leviathan* to New York.

Passengers on the liner heard about her plight and, led by Gen. John J. Pershing, the great war hero, who was also onboard, they raised enough money at a gala Saturday-night concert on the *Leviathan* to pay her debts. The first five hundred dollars was wired from London by humorist Will Rogers, who described the hulking Barrett as "a wonderful specimen of American womanhood."

Rogers had been in England, broadcasting on the BBC. His fee was described as the largest ever paid a radio personality in the country—a fee he donated to a hospital charity. He, like many in England, was caught up in the hysteria over Channel swimming, but, of course, he had a different take on it. Rogers gave England half the credit for Ed-erle's successful swim, saying the country "furnished the beach for Gertrude to land on, otherwise she would be swimming yet." But he chided the British for casting aspersions on the swim, saying that if the six-foot-three Barrett had made it, they never would have believed it. "She is so tall they would have said she waded across it," Rogers said.

Pershing, whose ability to raise an army of some two million men and then get it overseas for the climactic battles of the war had made him a national hero of epic proportions, was particularly taken by the fact Barrett and her companion were resolute in their efforts, even though they were up against teams of swimmers who could afford tugs, motorboats, trainers, and hotel bills.

"I don't know of any man who could have undergone what she went through," Pershing said.

About five hundred admirers, including members of the Rotary Club from Barrett's hometown of New Rochelle, New York, came to see her disembark in New York. They stood at the first-class gate, straining to see her, not realizing that Barrett was getting off at the back along with the rest of the lower-class passengers.

Like Trudy, Barrett got a procession down Broadway, though it wasn't much of a parade. The schoolteacher, who had lost sixteen of her more than two hundred pounds while overseas and wore an obviously faded sports suit and felt hat, rode with Leiszer and waved to spectators from their convertible. From there, it was on to her home in New Rochelle, where, she said, she would consider expected offers to race for startling sums of money in marathons. But she added that she had no plans to quit teaching swimming and physical education at James Monroe High School. "I'm not going to give up my job. Jobs are not too easy to get," she said.

Still, there was some money to be made, and Barrett hurried to do so before Corson got back home and stole her thunder. She quickly signed to do vaudeville, and she made her stage debut only two days after landing, when she appeared in Port Chester, New York. There was no pool, something of a hindrance to a swimmer, but Barrett made up for it by singing "Mighty Lak' a Rose" and "At the End of a Perfect Day" in what the reviewer for the *New York Times* would say was a voice as loud as she was big.

Barrett's manager said he had lined up twelve weeks' worth of appearances for his client at one thousand dollars a week, money that the schoolteacher wasn't going to turn down, even if Pershing and the others had retired her debt.

Corson's return was more eagerly awaited, even coming so soon after the city had seemingly exhausted its reservoir of love for Trudy. Corson had wanted to visit relatives in Denmark and return to the United States in October, but when it was explained to her that she needed to avoid Trudy's mistake and get home and make money, she cut short her trip and sailed in on the *Aquitania*. She was met by the *Macon*, with Whalen on board, when the liner docked at the quarantine station.

As the *Macon* made its way toward the city amid the loud whistles of tugs, Corson's new agent filled her in on the offers that had been pouring in since she'd launched a celebration of all things to do with motherhood by swimming the Channel. There were some two thousand offers, he told her, totaling about $250,000. He had already accepted one, he said. She was to appear just three days later in the vaudeville show at the Loew's State Theater for a fee later reported to be between five and ten thousand dollars a week.

Trudy had captured the hearts and attention of New Yorkers because she was the first woman to swim the Channel and she was so young. But the story of Corson seemed in some ways almost better, because she was a mother at a time when mothers were celebrated as saints who could do no wrong. Of course, Corson played up her motherhood at every opportunity, telling anyone who would listen that she'd made it across because the thought of disappointing her children was just too much to bear.

On a Friday afternoon exactly two weeks after Trudy returned home, Clemington Corson, Jr., age four, dressed in a white sailor suit, and his two-year-old sister, Marjorie, wearing a pink dress, stood at Pier A to greet Mom as she arrived in the *Macon*. Tabloid photographers thought this family scene would surely be the money shot that would appear on the front page of newspapers the next morning. But the photo op turned sour when Marjorie didn't recognize her mother, who had spent most of the summer in England, and started crying, forcing the swimmer to give the child to her husband to pacify.

Things got better as Corson and her husband sat in the back of an open car for a ticker-tape parade up Broadway, which, though it may not have matched Ederle's in size, was impressive nonetheless. Like Ederle, they motored to City Hall, where mounted police, who had learned their lessons in crowd control two weeks earlier, kept the crowds tightly gathered on the sidewalk while the swimmer and her entourage went in for an audience with Mayor Walker.

Walker seldom made it to his offices at City Hall, and when he did, he would sometimes use a room adjacent to his office to shake off the effects of the night before. But like any astute politician, he knew how to get votes, and he wasn't averse to cashing in on the wholesome aspects of a mother accomplishing what she had for mothers everywhere.

"You have brought perhaps the only additional wreath that can be placed on the head of American motherhood," the mayor told Corson. "You make us happy to see you happy, back with your own wonderful little family."

Corson broke down in tears, sobbing as she told the mayor that she didn't deserve all of the attention but that she was so happy, she couldn't believe it.

"When I was fighting the dark and the waves during the many hours of the night, I had these little babies in front of me and I was thinking about how wonderful it would be for a mother, as so many people said, to swim the English Channel."

Like Ederle, all the long, lonely hours training for and then swimming the Channel hadn't prepared Corson for the frenzied crowds that would clamor for her when she got home. And, like Ederle, it didn't take long for Corson to become overwhelmed by it all. She was bundled into a city car with her husband for a trip back down to the water, where she retired to a cabin on Eagle Boat 51 to rest while it took her to the USS *Illinois,* where another celebration awaited.

The crew of the *Illinois* had all chipped in to rent the Corsons a new apartment on West Ninety-seventh Street, and they presented the keys to the place to their former swimming instructor on the ship. There were speeches, cheers, and chants for the wife of one of their officers, and then it was on to the new apartment, which had already been furnished with three thousand dollars' worth of new furniture, courtesy of the Adolph Deutsch store.

Corson barely had a moment to reacquaint herself with her kids and get them to their new home before it was on to a torchlight procession down Broadway to Loew's State Theater to promote her upcoming appearance on Monday. She was cheered by crowds on the street and given a standing ovation in the theater as the band played "The Star-Spangled Banner." She left early, but not before apologizing to the crowd. "I've had only a few moments with my children in six months," she told them. "If you'll excuse me, I do want to go back to them."

Unlike Ederle, Corson seemed to realize that she would have to get her money while the getting was good. Her sponsor, Lissberger, had plenty of it after winning his big bet on her swim, and he pronounced himself ready to back a $100,000 race between his swimmer and Ederle across the Channel the next summer. Lissberger also posted a $25,000 cashier's check for the race he had proposed earlier—the swim around Manhattan—or any other long-distance race to be held before winter.

In a rare display of bravado, Ederle told the William Morris Agency to "take that bet, because I can spot her a mile and win." But with both women booked into vaudeville performances for quick money, and Trudy taking a few weeks off to rest, the race would never take place.

There was plenty to keep sports fans occupied as Ederle rested. The Dempsey-Tunney fight dominated the sports pages, and the Sultan of Swat was carrying the New York Yankees to yet another World Series, this one against the St. Louis Cardinals. Those who weren't reading were doing, and women across the country were jumping into the water, inspired by the two Channel conquerors.

The New York Association for the Blind, located on Fifty-ninth Street, said the swims had given hope to blind girls, who used to be able to do one hundred yards in a pool but could now do a mile and a half because Ederle and Corson had inspired them. Then there were the two twelve-year-old twins who greased up and swam seventeen miles on the Hudson River, going from Yonkers to the Battery in only six hours and fifteen minutes. Phyllis and Bernice Zitenfield both used the same American crawl as Ederle, and the two said they planned to swim the Channel within two years and make some history of their own as the youngest to make it across.

First, though, the shivering girls were whisked home and then to a victory celebration at Pomenrantz's Restaurant at Ninety-fourth and Broadway. There, their stage father said that, weather permitting, they would swim from the Battery to Sandy Hook to try to break the record Trudy had set on her swim the year before.

The boys on the USS *Illinois* seemed spoiling for a fight, even if their star swimming instructor wasn't. In the wake of Corson's swim, they tried to claim her feat as the first by telling reporters they had seen motion pictures of the tug helping Ederle, while their swimmer had no such help. Corson wouldn't be dragged into the fray, saying, "I think Gertrude Ederle made a wonderful swim. She is a great credit to America." But she also left no doubt who she thought was the best swimmer, and said she hoped that Ederle would join her in the Wrigley race in January, if not earlier.

"If I have to swim against Gertrude Ederle, I am going to try to beat her, but I am going to think a whole lot about Gertrude Ederle until I get there," Corson said.

Support for Ederle and her accomplishment came from an unlikely source, the same trainer she had blamed for not allowing her to get across the Channel the year before. Wolffe was back in England when he told reporters he questioned the times set by swimmers in the wake of Trudy's swim. Ederle, he said, had done it under terrible conditions, while Corson had had calm waters, making it even more incredible that Trudy had the quicker time. And he claimed that both Vierkotter and Michel had shaved time off the real clock in breaking Ederle's record, something he blamed on the lack of organized supervision of the Channel crossings.

"Knowing the speed of which these swimmers are capable it all leaves me quite sick," the portly trainer said. "It is like comparing the speed of a racehorse to that of a donkey."

It wasn't long before the conversation took on a racial overtone. Trudy's trip to Germany before coming home still stuck in the craw of some, including Malone, who was not only upset by the timing but by the fact it was Germany she'd gone to. Little wonder that George Trevor wrote in the *Sun*, "As readers well know, she is the 'Norse girl' when she loses and the 'Yankee champion' when she wins."

Ederle wasn't alone among popular athletes of the day when it came to racial insults. The same remarks applied to Berlenbach, who was roasted by boxing fans with anti-German insults, even though his mother was French. The war was still fresh in everyone's mind, and the *Progressive* magazine noted that German-American athletes were paying for it: "They are not given half the credit that is due them, if we scan the roster of stars in popular athletics, but in the past they have been content to wait for others to do the shouting—and others are not always disposed to be so generous."

The members of the German-American Societies of New York were still seething about having the parade they'd organized for Trudy taken over by the city, and they were unhappy with what they considered their diminished role in welcoming her. They took out their displeasure on Malone, who had already raised their ire by making Oberwager cut short his speech on the *Macon* when he began extolling the wonders of German womanhood.

Frederick F. Schrader sent a letter to Malone on their behalf, telling him that he ought to give credit where credit was due.

"I ask you to be candid and say why the American Germans, who alone gave her encouraging welcome when her first brave attempt ended in defeat, should not be allowed to greet her without being insulted when her second attempt met with success and everybody was scrambling to get a seat on the bandwagon?"

The *New Yorker Staats-Zeitung* also took exception to what it perceived was the slight heaped on the entire German-American population by the Irish-American lawyer and diplomat.

"Stressing the race might hurt Miss Ederle, opined the lady's legal adviser. He wished this to be a purely American welcome. With your leave Mr. Malone? Whatever is really great in American life is what originated from the contribution of the various race groups composing our polyglot population. And the country is indebted for not a little of it to German industry and German efficiency. We have every reason to be race proud and just for that reason we are good Americans, who have no cause to allow ourselves to be reduced to a subordinate rank," the paper stated.

Ederle had other things to worry about than her standing in the immigrant community. She was back home in New York, counting the first fruits of her professional career, money earned from the Sesquicentennial and her swim at the Atlantic City Pier. Soon she would be out on a twenty-six-week national tour, for which she would be paid an astonishing $6,500 a week, minus what would turn out to be considerable expenses.

About to set off in a touring vaudeville show in which she would swim in a replica of her two-piece Channel suit in a giant tank that could be folded up and taken to the next stop, Ederle was adamant that she would only go so far to make money and would not compromise her beliefs or values just to get more endorsements. She declared once again that she wasn't going to endorse things she didn't know anything about and would never endorse cigarettes, since she didn't smoke.

Malone made it clear that her rights would be guarded closely, and he backed it up by filing for an injunction against a music-publishing company selling the song "Trudy," even though the renowned Irving Berlin was a member of the firm that backed it. Malone wanted royalties for the song, which was being hummed by New Yorkers all around the city.

Ederle, though, was thrilled with the song and couldn't stop singing it, mostly to herself or her sisters as she traveled around the country. It didn't take long before she knew the lyrics by heart:

Trudy we love our swimming daughter,
Trudy you're like a fish in water,

You swam the Channel that treacherous sea,
But you went through it,
We knew, we knew that you could do it, Trudy
To think a girl like you, dear,
Broke the world's record too,
Trudy now that you've done your duty,
Trudy, Uncle Sam is proud of you.

The first money was coming in, prompting the Ederles to move into better digs. Her father bought a nine-room house on Stadium Avenue, two blocks from Pelham Bay, because, Trudy said, "We thought it was time we were getting some good out of our money."

The money served another good purpose. She and Malone had ringside seats—at $27.50 a pop—when Dempsey met Tunney in Philadelphia, where Ederle was greeted with big applause by the crowd of 120,557, which included celebrities like Charlie Chaplin, Tom Mix, and the Roosevelts, at Sesquicentennial Stadium. The rainy evening would not end well for her hero, who lost a ten-round decision, but Ederle was both fascinated and enthralled with being at the big fight.

Malone didn't let on, but by then it was becoming clear to him that the tour was going to be Ederle's only real moneymaker. Most of the other offers—aside from a movie deal that would pay Ederle eight thousand dollars—had either dried up or were made in the euphoria over her success and withdrawn when it came time for actual negotiations. Malone had his eye set on other riches, but they would not be profiting the swimmer. Though Dempsey was Ederle's favorite fighter, Malone liked Tunney, mainly because he saw him as his next cash cow, but also because he saw some of himself in the dapper and well-read boxer. He would soon be promoting the heavyweight champion of the world, taking over a role that had been filled by Tim Mara, who also owned the New York Giants of the fledgling National Football League. Malone quickly lined the victorious Tunney up for an eight-week vaudeville tour of his own at $7,500 a week.

Mara told Tunney a few weeks after the fight that he was making a mistake. "What could Malone do for you that I couldn't?" he asked Tunney. "Malone didn't make such a success managing Gertrude Ederle."

The vacation over, it was time now for Trudy to really go to work. Her first tour appearance would be the day after the Dempsey fight at Madison Square Garden, part of a three-day swimming carnival. She enjoyed being home for a few days, knowing well that for the next six months she would be out earning a living. The gig at the garden would be the debut of her indoor act as well as a test for the six-thousand-gallon tank that would serve as the centerpiece of the show. For years, Kellerman had made an art form out of swimming in a tank in her vaudeville show, and Ederle's had to be big enough to perform in but not so large that it couldn't be taken apart and hauled to the next city.

The tank was a wonder, glassed in on the sides and illuminated from the bottom. Foliage would hide the diving board and shield the backstage, giving the audience the impression that all they were seeing was an illuminated globe. A carpenter came on tour, because it was almost a full-time job reinforcing the stage, setting up the tank, and then tearing it down for the next stop—and without the tank, there was no show.

Riggin was leery of the tank from the first time she saw it. It made her nervous, and with good cause, because while it was just broad enough to do a swan dive in, she would have to pull her arms in or she would hit the sides. Diving was a nightly adventure, and both Riggin and Wainwright more than earned their $250 a week just by making their plunges in the tank.

Figuring out a show to put on inside the tank was another problem. Trudy couldn't carry the act alone, no matter how captivated they were with the stroke that had carried her across the Channel. She could spend ten or fifteen minutes crisscrossing the narrow tank, but she needed a supporting cast to bring the show home, and that is where Riggin and Wainwright came in.

The act that would tour the country over the next six months evolved quickly into a fast-paced show that could be played several times a day.

Ederle would be introduced, they would show some film of her Channel swim on the screen, and then she would come onstage in a replica of the two-piece suit that she'd worn to make the swim. Trudy would go in for a swim, showing off her impressive stroke, then get out while Riggin and Wainwright did two dives apiece from a board not far above the tank.

After changing her suit, Trudy would go back to give a short speech, and then the divers would do two more dives. Then they would all get in the tank and do some fancy dolphin strokes and pinwheels together underwater, something that usually awed the crowd and was a predecessor of what would later become synchronized swimming.

The tour quickly settled into a routine. At most of the early stops, there would be a welcome committee to meet Trudy, her sister, Helen, and her fellow swimmers at the train station. The mayor would usually be on hand and there would be a procession to City Hall, where inevitably there would be a luncheon with a lot of long-winded speeches. Thousands would turn out just to get a glimpse of Ederle, and thousands more would sit in fascination in the theaters, watching her swim.

People couldn't get enough of it. The tour hit Toronto, Buffalo, Rochester, Chicago, and was so popular, it was held over for as long as three weeks in some cities. Occasionally, they would swim in a pool, as they did in St. Louis for two days at the Coliseum pool, where reviewers marveled at her stroke, but mostly they swam in the tank onstage, traveling from city to city, with no rest in between.

Trudy's appearance in Columbus was billed in the local paper as "America's most famous woman" in person and in action, while in Seattle the reviewer said that while it was Ederle's show, she also made the others look good. "In the tank, Ederle, Riggin and Wainwright do some of the neatest fancy diving and swimming ever witnessed in Seattle." But there were other acts, too, because anyone paying thirty-five cents during the week and fifty cents on Saturday to watch the show expected more. The acts varied, but there was usually a singer, Lady Alice's pet show, and Marjah, the man who answered impossible questions from the audience. There was also an orchestra on hand to add dramatic music, and, of course, the patriotic climax was always "The Star-Spangled Banner."

As winter approached, things got even more dicey with the tank. It arrived late by train one night in Toronto, and by the time the carpenter got it set up, it was too late to heat the freezing cold water taken from under the ice of Lake Erie. The show had to go on, however, and the girl who'd swum the Channel put on a noon show for the press, gamely swimming in the frigid water while Riggin and Wainwright dived in beside her. On another occasion, the tank wasn't properly grounded and Riggin was shocked on the iron stairs. Those playing down below in the orchestra took their own chances of getting wet from either overflow or leakage from the wood-and-glass structure.

The crowds kept coming, though, and it was easy to see why. America loved this innocent girl of simple taste who had a strong attachment to home and modest domestic ideals instilled in her by her mother.

"There is something genuinely appealing in the personality of a girl of nineteen [*sic*] in this age of flappers, cigarette fiends and short skirt lip painters," the *Progressive* magazine said.

Trudy's future marital plans were always a topic of interest wherever she went. The New York *Evening Graphic* magazine devoted a huge layout to what kind of man and life Trudy would want when she was done swimming. In an interview, she said she wanted to live in a little cottage covered with roses with the man of her dreams and three kids.

"We will swim, play golf and tennis, go off on weekend hikes and do all the beautiful things that a man and his wife can do when they are happy together," she said, adding that she knew she didn't want any weaklings, drunk party boys, or nightclubbers to apply.

"What I want is a really good pal, not a petter."

Wainwright wasn't quite as picky. While on tour in Texas, she had a romance and married a saxophone player in the orchestra there, and Riggin seemed to have both friends and boyfriends at every stop. Unlike them, Trudy generally kept to herself, retiring to her room after the shows or socializing with her sister Helen rather than joining her fellow performers for a night on the town.

She told reporters she had plenty of time to get a man and understood her place in a family, something that must have horrified the feminist leaders who were so proud of her in the first place. Ederle might have been famous, but she was still famously unsophisticated, and she reflected the cultural upbringing of her German roots.

"When my husband tells me to do something, I want him strong enough to make me do it," she said. "Women never will be able to do all that men can do. Men are just naturally stronger and we will never be able to compete with them in athletics. Of course, when it comes to endurance, I think a woman has a man beaten almost every time."

As the year came to a close, Trudy was in the middle of her tour and seemingly as popular as ever. The Niagara Knitting Company brought out a line of Trudy swimsuits, and there were also "Little Miss Trudy" suits for children ages two to eight. In Chicago, Mrs. Minna Schmidt, who for fifty-three years had designed and dressed wax figurines of the most famous people in history, added an Ederle doll to her collection, though she made sure to dress it in a one-piece suit instead of the more risqué suit Trudy had worn in the Channel.

Just how big Trudy had become showed when she won the 1926 W. R. Hearst trophy for athletes in a popularity contest voted on by readers of Hearst newspapers across the country. There were 30,000 votes cast and Ederle was the first pick of 6,922, compared to 4,731 for Babe Ruth, who finished third, behind tennis player Helen Wills. Dempsey got 1,188 votes, while Tunney received none, despite having beaten Dempsey in the fight of the century. Cartoonists portrayed Trudy as one of the strongest athletes, male or female, and papers showed photos of her and the heavyweight boxers as the biggest figures of the year in sports.

In December, Ederle and her tour were in Los Angeles, where the Wrigley ocean marathon was going to be held the next month, with a purse of $25,000. She was the guest of William Wrigley, Jr., on a yacht, the party sailing between Catalina and Los Angeles. Ederle said she thought she could swim the distance if she wanted to. What she didn't know was whether she wanted to. There wasn't much to be gained by swimming the waters between Catalina and Los Angeles, other than the big money that would be awarded the winner, and if she happened to lose, it would destroy the aura of invincibility she'd built up by swimming the Channel. Plus, she was already making sure money as the highest-priced athletic attraction on tour in theaters.

"After I have accomplished the biggest swim in the world, why should I try something not so big?" said Trudy.

The money to tour, though, was never as good as it was supposed to be. Westbrook Pegler would later sit down and figure it out, and considering that he was married to Julia Harpman and had bonded with the Ederles during their summer overseas, his figures were presumed fairly accurate.

For the first weeks of the tour, the money seemed huge, with Trudy getting eight thousand a week to take her act on the road, a sum that was reduced to six thousand a week as the novelty started to fade a bit and the tour was booked into smaller cities. The William Morris agency got 10 percent of that, while one thousand dollars a week went to Malone as his agent's cut and still another thousand went to her father.

Trudy also had a payroll of $1,000 a week for Riggin, Wainwright, and the show's other performers, while her manager got $2,000 a week and the union carpenter who set up the tank at every show received another $100. There was also a press agent who was paid $175 a week to go to towns before the show arrived to drum up publicity and sell tickets.

Trudy kept touring, though, partly because she had no choice. She was determined to make money as a professional and show both her father and her critics that she could cash in on her big chance. But Pegler wrote that the showmen of sports felt sorry for her as both the victim of mismanagement and bad timing.

The challenge races, which had seemed so enticing a few months before, weren't going to happen now. Trudy was stuck touring and had no time for any serious training; besides, the frenzy over women long-distance swimmers had calmed down, and even Lissberger quit talking about the $25,000 he'd offered to the winner of the swim around Manhattan. It also became increasingly clear there would be no match the next summer between the men and women who had swum the Channel.

There was always the Wrigley race, but Ederle passed on this without giving it serious consideration. She was not in shape for the endurance

swim, nor could she take the chance of being beaten if she was still going to get thousands of people to pay money to see her every week. Corson, whose own vaudeville career proved to be short-lived, also dropped
out of the Wrigley race, but for different reasons. She had planned to
swim, but then she heard that a few women, including Charlotte Moore
Schoemmell, the first woman to swim around Manhattan, planned to do
as the men and wear nothing but ten pounds of grease when they entered
the water.

"If Mrs. Schoemmell thinks she will be clothed by 10 pounds of it
when she finishes she will learn differently," Trudy said.

Wrigley's $25,000 race drew 102 swimmers, 15 of them women, to
swim the twenty-two miles from Catalina to San Pedro. True to her
word, Schoemmell was clad only in grease, along with two other women,
though they wore robes down to the water's edge to prevent too much
controversy. None of the women finished, and only one man made it
across, a seventeen-year-old Canadian by the name of George Young,
who had traveled to California with a friend on an old motorcycle with
a handcar just for the race.

Ederle's marathon tour, meanwhile, was draining her strength more
than her marathon swim across the Channel had. In every city, she was
pictured in a different car, part of a promotional deal put together by
Malone, and in Dallas that spring she was shown with a knife in hand
and a side of beef in an ad for Piggly Wiggly, which said she endorsed its
meats, and personally selected a roast served at a luncheon given in her
honor at a home for crippled children.

The first tour was nearing its end, and though Ederle was still drawing decent crowds and getting good coverage in the local papers, she
was already trying to figure out what to do with the huge tank she had
traveled with for months.

"I suppose I could put it in the back yard and let the kids in the neighborhood swim in it," she said.

The summer of 1927 was approaching and there would be another
run on the Channel, and another woman, Mercedes Gleitze, who would
conquer it. Ederle's record for a woman's time would hold, though, and
there would never be another summer like the one the previous year,

when aspirants from around the world had gathered at the decrepit hotel by the lighthouse to make history.

Wolffe, meanwhile, was again hoping to find the perfect swimmer for the upcoming season. He thought a good-looking, intelligent blond woman could make a lot of money by beating Ederle's record, and he was on the prowl for just that swimmer.

"She would have to be a blonde, genuinely blonde," Wolffe said. "Brunettes are not stickers. They give in. They are nervous."

12

"Don't Weep for Me"

T he huge crowd surged into Central Park, jostling for space near the grandstand amid reports that Charles Lindbergh was drawing near. June 13, 1927, had been declared a holiday in New York City, and already millions had cheered Lindy as his homecoming parade came through the Canyon of Heroes and was buried in a blizzard of ticker tape.

Ten thousand troops preceded him, and another ten thousand schoolchildren sang "Hail the Conquering Hero Comes." Trudy's parade had been largely a spur-of-the-moment affair, with little coordination, but New York was getting used to honoring heroes, and the man who had flown across the Atlantic by himself was the biggest hero of all. Now, as the biggest parade New York had ever seen reached Central Park, the excitement grew as the crowd of about 200,000 strained for a glimpse of Lindbergh, who would be presented the New York State Medal for Valor by Governor Al Smith.

At first, hardly anyone noticed the young woman under a hat who was trying to get near the grandstand for a better look. A burly police-man blocked her way, but someone in the crowd shouted out her name and soon those around the grandstand began applauding. They recognized the woman who had had her own parade only ten months earlier, but who was now just one of many trying to get a sight of Lindy. Smith himself noticed the commotion, and seeing Ederle, he helped her into the grandstand to watch the proceedings. She later called it a "freak of fate" that she was recognized by the governor, yet as she sat on the grandstand, she couldn't help thinking about her own glorious moment less than a year before, when all the applause and confetti were for her.

Ederle had been on the road with her vaudeville act when Lindbergh made history the month before, and she'd sent him a telegram congratulating him on doing something seemingly even more impossible than swimming the English Channel.

"Heartiest congratulations from one pioneer to another," it read. "Your courageous feat is another brilliant page in history. I, too, was told it could not be done when I attempted the Channel. However, youth will be served."

Some newspaper reports said that Ederle warned Lindbergh to cash in quickly on his success, and portrayed her as being bitter that her own fame seemed so fleeting. She would later deny that, but there was no question that Lindbergh's crossing of the Atlantic would further reduce Ederle's already-ebbing celebrity among Americans, who were getting used to their countrymen doing astonishing things.

Sure, they had been thrilled the summer before when Ederle became the first woman to swim the Channel. But they were awed by what Lindbergh had accomplished, and they attached more significance to it not only because of the danger he'd faced but because he was a man. Ed Sullivan mirrored the tenor of the times when he wrote that Lindbergh's feat was far more worthy than Ederle's because he "jousted with death for the fun of the thing; the sport of it."

America seemed to be getting a new hero every week, but there was no doubt Lindy was the biggest of all. His triumph in spanning the continents by air not only thrilled the country but opened up possibilities that couldn't have been imagined at the time Ederle swam the English

Channel. Ederle's star was already fading, and no one could have guessed then that Lindbergh would live in the country's heart for decades to come.

It wasn't long, though, before the mood of public opinion seemed to be shifting against people who did something just to be the first to do it—especially if they were women.

Later that year, aviator and renowned looker Ruth Elder tried to become the first woman to fly the Atlantic nonstop when she and George Haldeman piloted their *American Girl* plane through bad weather and mechanical difficulties across the ocean. When they realized they would never make it, they scoured the sea for help, finally sighting the Dutch tanker SS *Barendrecht.* Circling low, the pilots dropped a message on the ship's deck: "HOW FAR ARE WE FROM LAND AND WHICH WAY?"

The ship's captain wrote the *Barendrecht*'s coordinates and direction on the deck and the plane went on, making it to within 520 miles of the coast of Portugal before being forced to ditch because of oil-pressure problems. Both pilots were rescued.

Eleanor Roosevelt was still a few years away from becoming First Lady, but she declared the attempt "very foolish," and others were just as critical.

"Even if she had succeeded, what would she have accomplished for the common good?" asked famed sociologist Katherine B. Davis.

Winifred Stoner, a well-known educator and founder of the League for Fostering Genius, chimed in by saying she would rather have a dozen women learn to become fast typists than be the first to fly across the Atlantic. Stoner, who wrote the poem every schoolchild was taught ("In fourteen hundred ninety-two, Columbus sailed the ocean blue") was just as critical of Ederle, intimating that she'd done what she had only to gain fame and fortune.

"I am much opposed to people who do things of this kind solely to bring their names before the public," she said. "Gertrude Ederle is another example. Just as I think it is insane to swim across the Channel when there are ships and airplanes to take you across, I think it is foolhardy to attempt a flight across the Atlantic when nothing whatever will be accomplished by it."

The backlash was not universal. Women's groups still cheered the triumphs and trials of female pioneers, and at a dinner of the National Woman's Party at the Ambassador Hotel, suffrage leader Doris Stevens honored Elder and evoked the accomplishments of both Ederle and Corson as proof that women were not the weaker sex.

"Gertrude Ederle smashed the myth of woman's physical inferiority. Mille Gade Corson smashed the myth that motherhood means invalidism," said Stevens, the former wife of Dudley Malone. "Ruth Elder smashed many myths, the most diverting of which [is] beauty in women need not be unaccompanied by ability and ambition for a career."

Lindbergh's tumultuous homecoming was still fresh in Ederle's mind when she hit the road again the following week, this time with a reduced supporting cast but the same glass and wood tank that went with her everywhere. Her first tour was over, and now she had been booked for a few dates in vaudeville houses in New England before leaving for Hollywood to shoot her first movie with Bebe Daniels.

She had a few endorsements, but they didn't add up to much. Newspapers along her vaudeville route advertised the new Trudy swimsuit for $6.95, and there was also the junior Trudy for younger girls. She was also featured in an ad as the "world's greatest sportswoman," wearing the Benrus Princeton-model watch, which could be bought for a dollar down and a dollar a month for fourteen months.

Trudy, meanwhile, was looking at other athletic endeavors outside the water. She discovered golf, partly to while away the hours on tour as she waited to perform in her act. She was pictured at the Worcester (Massachusetts) Country Club, where a reporter watched as she hit a one-hundred-yard drive down the fairway on the first hole, before hitting it into the water and making a nine. She wasn't much better on the next hole, scoring a ten, but her road manager, Harry E. Keller, told writers that Trudy was going to be quite the player.

Ederle had met Bobby Jones a few months earlier in Atlanta, and the greatest golfer of his time had also predicted success for her on the course, even after watching her for part of a round in which she shot a bloated 116. Golf writer O. B. Keeler, who was Jones's close confidant, devoted an entire column to Trudy, saying that after seeing her in a swimming suit, he had come to the conclusion that she had the "ideal musculature for golf."

Worcester was Ederle's last tour stop before she boarded a train to cross the country to Los Angeles, where she immediately headed for Long Beach, where the movie *Swim, Girl, Swim* was already being shot. The star was Daniels, the top comic actress of the day, and Trudy got a chance to get a feel for the Hollywood lifestyle by staying with the actress at her Santa Monica oceanfront estate during the filming. The two would go swimming in the Pacific together every day.

Ederle's increasing deafness wasn't a problem in the movie, because it wasn't until later that year that *The Jazz Singer*, the first real talking movie, would come out. But she needed lessons in makeup and appearance, and Daniels was pictured showing her the art of applying lipstick and other makeup while sitting in a director's chair during the movie's filming.

Swim, Girl, Swim would come out in September to mixed reviews. The *New York Times* said there was "nothing outstandingly original about this Bebe Daniels farce, but there is no gain saying the fact that its swiftly moving scenes make a good impression." Ederle didn't exactly get rave reviews, but her part in the movie was basically limited to playing herself and giving advice to Daniels on how to swim and dive.

"Miss Ederle may not be an actress, but she is emphatically graceful when it comes to diving and giving an exhibition of her crawl stroke," the newspaper said.

There wasn't a lot of call for swimmers in Hollywood, though, and the movie offers that had once seemed to come in by the handful weren't coming at all anymore. Her moviemaking days over after one picture, Ederle returned to the grind of the vaudeville tour, where she could still sell tickets, though by now it was clear to her that she wasn't going to get rich doing so.

But the nation hadn't completely forgotten her. On November 7, while on tour in Washington, D.C., Ederle was received at the White

House by President Coolidge, whose wife had once imitated her stroke. "I am amazed," Coolidge told Trudy, "that a woman of your small stature should be able to swim the English Channel. It was a remarkable feat."

Trudy was back out again on the vaudeville circuit in 1928, but by now interest was waning in her swimming talents and the towns and venues weren't so big. She had once gotten welcomes from big-city mayors, formal committees, and frenzied crowds, but now she was lucky if one or two people would greet her party at the railroad station to show her the way to the hotel. Still, she was big news in little towns. Uniontown, Pennsylvania, welcomed her with newspaper ads proclaiming her the "greatest scoop in [the] theatrical history of Uniontown." The ad said she was the highest-priced stage attraction ever in the town, but for a dime you could see her at the matinee, while fifty cents was the top price for a good ticket at night.

A few weeks later, Ederle did an interview with a newspaper in Richmond, Virginia, and the paper reported that she "is still a mere child with dark expressive eyes, sleek brown bobbed hair and an engaging personality."

The questions by now were all the same wherever the tour stopped. Local papers wanted her to recount her swim for their readers, then explain to them when she was going to get married and to whom. Her answer was always the same for the first part, but it changed day to day when it came to possible romances in her life.

"I don't want to be an old maid," she told one paper. "Of course I'd like to meet a nice man and get married."

Her show, meanwhile, had been trimmed because she couldn't afford the costs of bringing well-known fellow swimmers, such as Riggin and Wainwright, along with her anymore. She relied more on vaudeville comedians to carry most of the load, and she was now swimming with much cheaper talent, such as sisters Ethel and Marion Baker. In Syracuse, the drama critic of the *Herald* reviewed her show at B. F. Keith's and said she was the star of a show "overburdened with funny men." Chester B. Bahn wrote, however, that he was pleasantly surprised a good portion of the matinee audience was men, because "as a rule, athletes of the feminine persuasion are not endowed with Mme. Elinor Glyn's favorite quality . . . if you know what I mean."

The men reading certainly did know what Bahn meant. Glyn was an author of female erotica, and Trudy was still being sold as a body first and a swimmer second. Men who couldn't tell the difference between a breaststroke and the American crawl put up a quarter or fifty cents to see her take a few laps across the small tank and do somersaults underwater so they could see a female body in a tight-fitting swimsuit, something that was still hard to find in 1928.

Ederle was now twenty-two, a grown woman in every sense of the word. She traveled the country, trying to make a few bucks, and if she was disappointed over how she wasn't the hottest attraction anymore, she tried not to let on. But the Associated Press quoted her as saying the Channel swim had not been worth it, and as America's 1928 Olympic team was chosen, she admitted to feeling a bit lonely and out of place, because as a professional she was banned from the games.

While a new era of swimmers like Albina Osipowich and Martha Norelius were overseas winning gold medals in Amsterdam, where Johnny Weissmuller would add to his collection with two more, Ederle was at the Rumson Farm Kennels in Fair Haven, New Jersey, to watch Tom Heeney spar for the final time before his fight on July 26 with heavyweight champion Gene Tunney.

Dempsey was going to be a cornerman for Heeney, so he was there, as were most of the New York media, to watch Heeney get roughed up by James Braddock, who years later would become heavyweight champion. Ederle sat with Harpman, the first time they had seen each other in nearly two years. She told the reporter that her contract with Malone had expired in May and that she was happy to be on her own.

Gallico wrote, "Trudie is thinner and a little sadder," and he lamented that she had blown her only real chance to cash in on her swim. "She discounted about a quarter of a million dollars worth of ballyhoo for $20,000 and the chance will never come again," he said.

The girl who had swum more than thirty miles in the worst conditions of the English Channel was now an adult reduced to swimming in a tank that allowed her to take only a few overhand strokes and a couple of kicks before hitting the other side. Still, she proudly noted that most of the twenty-nine records she had set—for distances ranging from fifty yards to nearly a mile—were still intact. "The day will come when I can do some more competitive swimming and I am sure I will show my old ability," she said.

That time came in August, when Ederle, coaxed by the fifteen thousand dollars in prize money at stake, decided to enter her first competitive race since swimming the Channel two years earlier. It was in Toronto, where another Wrigley marathon, a swim of ten miles in Lake Ontario, attracted most of the top professionals of the time, including Ederle and Corson. The fact that they were swimming together competitively would, by itself, have gotten huge money had it occurred two years earlier, but times had changed.

It would be the first time Ederle would swim for prize money in a race since she'd beaten the men in Miami two and a half years earlier and promptly forgotten to pick up her winnings. It would also be her last.

Pop Ederle came up for the race, and so did her brother George, who walked around the exhibition grounds the night before offering to bet twelve hundred dollars even on his sister against the entire field of fifty-three women in the female half of the third Wrigley race. On a perfect late August day, fifty-two of them were in swimming attire, while Charlotte D. Gants of Providence, Rhode Island, was racing au natural, covered only by a thick coating of grease.

Like her brother, Trudy seemed confident before the race, laughing, talking, and looking forward to the swim in the relatively warm and calm waters of the lake. Trudy was in her two-piece suit, wearing her signature goggles and red hat, the same outfit that she'd worn in the Channel, while Corson, who by now was not so concerned with what other women wore or didn't wear, had on a one-piece outfit and was covered in white grease applied by her husband.

The women's start drew a huge crowd of men, many of whom waded out into the water, trying to steal a glimpse into the dressing tents that were set up onshore for the female contestants. When the women emerged from the tents, they gathered at the start, leaving behind mascots and blankets and robes, except for Gants, who would discard hers only in the final few steps of a mad dash into the water.

Ederle had trained for a month in the river at the family summer home in Highlands, then spent five days making trial swims in Lake Ontario. It was her first real effort to get into swimming shape since making it across the Channel, yet she was considered by most the favorite in the race simply because of her ability to generate great speed over any distance.

It proved to be a speed race, just as she wanted, but, shockingly, Ederle was never a factor. Little-known Ethel Hertle of the Bronx sped out to an early lead with a first lap of 1:11:34.5, while Trudy was fourth and floundering after the first turn. Hertle would go on to win the race by a big margin, finishing a stunning fifty minutes ahead of Ederle, who finished sixth and out of the money.

The woman who had set the standard for speed was beaten by someone faster, and though Ederle chalked it up to poor conditioning, it was an embarrassing result for someone so famous. The crowd that waited expectantly for her to finish couldn't believe she wasn't even in the money, and neither could Hertle's father.

"The only one we feared was Ederle and she wasn't in it," Charles Hertle said. "I am sorry. We expected real opposition from her. It was a great surprise when Ederle could not keep up with Ethel."

Ederle said she'd known early on she couldn't win because her legs weren't strong enough. But she was determined to finish the last lap, and Hertle showed respect by sticking around to greet her warmly. The only consolation Trudy had, if any, was that Corson finished even farther back in the pack and was never a factor, either.

"Since the Channel I have had little or no competition, except for an occasional exhibition," Ederle said. "I feel I could do as well as ever, but my stage bookings keep me so busy that it is out of the question. I am booked up for stage appearances in America for the next eight months and after that there is a possibility of swinging into Europe for a tour."

There would be no European tour, though, and the vaudeville show that Ederle had been putting on for nearly two years was heading for demise. The crowds weren't coming anymore, Ederle was worn-out, and now she wasn't even the fastest swimmer in the world.

Even she acknowledged that things had not exactly gone according to plan in the time since she had made it across the Channel.

"Things aren't always smooth," she told one reporter. "I was pretty young when I found that out."

The touring came to an end partly because of decreasing demand and the costs of putting on the show, but mostly because of Ederle's failing nerves. Two years on the road had taken a toll on her, and she had become worn by the strain of five shows a day in cramped theaters filled with smoke and leering men. She felt rushed the entire time, running from city to city, always having to perform and attend some function or another to welcome her to whatever town she was in that week.

By now, she was almost completely deaf, a condition she blamed on swimming the Channel and spending the next two years in small tanks with water of questionable quality. A reporter who saw her as the tour ended wrote that her voice was taking on the flat quality of the truly deaf, having little intonation. She went to doctors constantly to try to find a way to regain her hearing, but the treatments of the day never worked.

There were plans for a two-year tour of Europe, beginning in the summer of 1928, but by now Ederle's hands were shaking and she couldn't seem to concentrate. She was suffering from nervous exhaustion, barely able to hold a fork steadily enough to eat, and doctors told her that her heart was being affected by too strenuous an ordeal for such a young person.

Ederle was bedridden after that, and a few weeks later, she lost almost all that was left of her hearing. At the age of twenty-two, just two years after her momentous crossing of the Channel, she was a shell of the brave young woman who had boldly waded into the English Channel and swum all the way to Dover.

"I finally got the shakes," she told an interviewer years later. "I was just a bundle of nerves. I had to quit the tour and I was stone deaf."

After more than two years of being on almost constant display, Ederle retreated from public view, surfacing only occasionally, as she did on March 23, 1929, when she appeared in court on a charge of doing thirty-five miles per hour in her beloved red roadster on Riverside Drive. She was exonerated by a magistrate—"because you did so much for your country," he said—a ruling that prompted about one hundred men and women in the courtroom to stand and applaud.

Ederle, who told the judge she'd been on her way to see her doctor at the time, initially couldn't understand his ruling, but then a court clerk stood and yelled out loudly what was happening so she could hear. Later that year, she was fined fifty dollars on another speeding charge; she was represented in court by a lawyer, who said she was indisposed at home. By now, the stock market had crashed and the Depression had begun. Any thoughts Ederle might have had of making big money racing against Corson and others had largely disappeared. There were no Lissbergers or Wrigleys offering obscene amounts of money, and the market for vaudeville swimming had dried up.

The wild projections by Malone and others about what Ederle would make off her Channel swim turned out to be just that—wild projections. She was now out of show business, but she still wanted to stay involved in swimming, and she took a job at the Playland pool in the town of Rye, New York, in 1930, where she wore a suit with EDERLE printed in large block letters on the back and gave swimming lessons.

When a reporter came by to find out what had happened to the girl who'd taken the country by storm just a few years earlier, she told him that she'd made $150,000 on her tours, but she declined to say how much of that she had kept after all her expenses had been paid. She also said she was spending a lot of money on doctors, who were treating her for both her deafness and her nerves. She would visit her ear specialist every other day for tests and expensive treatments, and while the cost added up, nothing seemed to help much.

She could still hear some with the help of hearing aids, enough to recognize when the orchestra played "Let Me Call You Sweetheart" at the occasional dance. It was the song she had sung to herself when she was swimming the Channel, the song that thousands of New Yorkers had sung to her upon her triumphant return home, and it touched a nostalgic spot in her heart.

"And then it all sort of comes back over me again, and I have to sneak away or somebody will see me cry," she said.

Her ambition was to have her own pool, Ederle told the reporter, but that was too expensive. Now she just wanted a good job at a club with a pool so she could keep swimming.

Speaking of the mismanagement of her career, Pegler wrote that her delay in returning from Europe had cost her valuable money. While Malone "gestured and posed and took all the bows," he said, the first thing they knew was that people had lost their interest.

Pegler said it didn't help that others had swum the Channel right after her, and said she could walk down Broadway or tool along in her red roadster without causing the slightest commotion. "This is sad, but the public can't run around screaming about one person forever," he wrote.

By now, there wasn't much clamor at all about her Channel crossing. Women had made it across, men had regained the record, and as America struggled with the Depression, the thought of being excited about someone swimming between France and England bordered on preposterous. Even Helmy had abandoned his annual summer pursuit (but not before making a successful swim in 1928), leaving him, in Pegler's words, "with absolutely no object in life."

With her show-business career over, Ederle did what she could, taking a job as a manager at the Bronxdale pool, where she worked from 10:00 A.M. to 9:30 P.M. in the summer. She was pictured in the *New York Journal-American* teaching her sister Meg's three-year-old twins, Gertrude and Helen, how to swim. Ederle told the paper that she was doing occasional exhibitions and was thinking about swimming the Channel once again. She grew irritated at rumors that she was both deaf and broke, saying that her hearing wasn't that bad and that, although she should have made more money, she had thrifty German parents who had invested it wisely and kept her financially independent.

Will Rogers lamented that Ederle had not been treated better, saying she and other women athletes were the country's best hope for success.

"We can always depend on a Gertrude or a Helen Wills bringing home the first prize, but when our men compete it's got to be miniature golf or tree sitting or we do nothing," he wrote.

Ederle, meanwhile, was making plans for a comeback of sorts, six years after she'd swum the Channel. She wanted to swim competitively once again in the 1932 Wrigley Marathon in Lake Ontario, where she had finished a disappointing sixth four years earlier. Ederle went to Toronto in late August, where two-time defending champion Margaret Ravior was the favorite, but on the day of the swim, Trudy was one of seven of the thirty-one women who failed to start in the chase for what was now a much-reduced first prize of three thousand dollars.

Ederle would never swim competitively again, but soon she had bigger worries. After she slipped on loose tile and fell down a flight of stairs at a friend's apartment in Hempstead in December 1933, breaking her pelvis and tearing ligaments in her back, doctors told Ederle she might never be able walk again. She was an invalid for a year, sleeping nights on the floor and wearing a cast, as well as a tight leather strap around her back. She saw fifteen different specialists during her recovery. Compounding her woes, she was hospitalized again for an appendix operation in late 1935.

The press visited to find out how she was doing, but now it wasn't the *New York Times* or the *Daily News* knocking on the door. Instead, reporter Warren Cox of the East Bronx *Herald* called on her. He found Ederle hard of hearing but otherwise looking well in a red sweater, a pleated tan sport skirt, and tan oxfords. Ederle said she wanted to thank her supporters for the outpouring of sympathy for her, but she complained about newspaper reports that she was deaf, blind, and a cripple.

Trudy was thirty now and spending much of her time making clothes at home, while also trying to market earplugs for swimmers. Made of a puttylike compound, the earplugs would, she hoped, protect others from the kind of hearing loss she had suffered from being in the water.

Cox covered all the usual topics, including the obligatory question about her future marriage plans.

"Marriage?" she asked pensively, fingering the helm of her skirt.

"Not at present." Trudy then gave a short laugh and said, "Some day perhaps. I have so many things to do. I've got to think of old Father Time. He creeps up on us, you know."

A few months later, the Associated Press visited and found her still upset about people who thought she was a hopeless cripple. She felt the same way about this as she had about newspaper headlines a decade earlier that told of her quitting her first Channel swim. She was working on the outline of a book about her career, she said, and going over the press clippings she meticulously kept in a closet.

Then her anger gave way to a bit of melancholy as she remembered the fantastic day in the channel, when it seemed like there was nothing she couldn't do in her life.

"I doubt if I'll ever have another day as great as the day of the Channel swim. When I read the clippings it seems like something that happened in a dream," she said wistfully. "I hope my book will be more of a financial success than my Channel swim. By the time I got all my representatives and manager paid, there wasn't much left for me."

The tenth anniversary of her swim didn't cause much celebration on either side of the Atlantic. Pegler was in England, writing about political tensions and other world events, but he took a side trip to Cape Gris-Nez, where he visited the Hôtel du Phare for the first time in a decade. The hotel, he said, now had electric lights but still no running water. No one swam the Channel anymore, he reported. They had quit about the same time that Corthes, the tug captain who took so many across, died.

Ederle, meanwhile, was honored on the tenth anniversary at an AAU water carnival at Manhattan Beach, where the crowd of about ten thousand, there for other reasons, applauded her when she was introduced. The day before, Meg had been interviewed while working in the cashier's booth at the Ederle Brothers Meat Market. She said her parents were still alive and well and that the family planned to attend the water carnival.

A few months later, Ederle limped to court for her fifty-thousand-dollar lawsuit against the apartment complex where she had been injured. Testimony in the trial showed she had a contract to do her vaudeville show immediately after swimming the Channel. Her initial pay of $3,750 a week had dropped to $1,750 a week the next year. After that, she made anywhere from $60 to $250 a week as a swim instructor before becoming injured.

Trudy would settle the suit for what her attorney said was a "substantial sum" after the first jury deadlocked. She returned to work at a Manhattan dress store for large women, where she was a saleswoman and fashion consultant. Her life had settled into a rhythm of work and summers teaching at the pool, and any thoughts of being in the spotlight again now appeared as remote as her chances at swimming the Channel in the first place.

The idea of getting Ederle back in the public eye was first floated in an open letter from Ted Worner, sports editor for the *Herald-Statesman* in Yonkers, to Grover Whalen, who was still the official city greeter but now had greater responsibilities as president of the committee for the New York World's Fair. Worner penned it in October 1938, well in advance of the fair's opening date of April 30, 1939.

"You must be a very busy man these days down in that modern Babylon your men are creating in Flushing Meadows," Worner wrote. "Building a huge fair is a Herculean task, probably the greatest you've ever tackled. But could you take time out to spare me just a couple of minutes?"

Worner went on to ask Whalen whether he remembered the young woman he had squired on her victory parade and if he knew what they were now saying about her, things that have "torn at the heartstrings of this girl who's still the same modest and unassuming athlete that she was twelve summers ago." Worner said he didn't know if there were plans for a swimming exhibition at the world's fair, but even if there wasn't to be a pool, he felt there should be a place for the woman who first swam the Channel. Contrary to reports, he said, she was not crippled, not blind, but in relatively good physical condition, except for her deafness.

"She's not looking for publicity to shoo her back into the limelight," he wrote. "But she could use a job, for you and I know that a scrapbook full of flattering things has never and will never pay the rent or the electric bill."

It turned out there was going to be a swimming exhibition at these games, an extravaganza first begun in Cleveland by Billy Rose, who had combined elements of early synchronized swimming and music with a cast of hundreds in his aquatic show. Ever the promoter, Rose figured that Ederle could still sell tickets, even surrounded by mermaids and swimmers nearly half her age. He called Ederle and offered her a spot in the Aquacade show, which would be one of the highlights of the fair.

Worner hadn't exactly been on target when he had described the state of Ederle's health. In fact, she had been wearing a cast for nearly five years and was barely able to put one foot in front of the other. But she was badly in need of an incentive to regain her fitness, and the idea of swimming in the World's Fair proved just the tonic she needed.

Ederle discarded the cast and began practicing how to walk again. It took her a month to be able to make it a block, but soon she was walking two miles. She had once been the greatest female swimmer in the world, but in the pool she had just as much difficulty as she had walking again. At first, others had to move her legs up and down for her as she wept in pain at having to learn to swim all over again. But finally she was able to swim one lap, then two, then twenty.

Finally, Rose stopped by the pool one day to see if she was well enough to appear in his show. He asked her to swim a lap, and she sprinted as fast as she could across the pool.

"Billy said, 'I want you to swim fast, Gert, but not like a bat out of hell,'" Ederle recalled later. "Oh, I could have hugged him. Because from that day on, I began to walk again naturally without falling."

Rose's Aquacade stole the show at the world's fair, drawing 8,500 people the first night and thousands for every performance afterward. Cheap seats were forty-nine cents and the more expensive were ninety-nine cents, and on some days, the show grossed thirty thousand dollars. The stars were Weissmuller, Ederle's former Olympic teammate, who was now even more famous for having starred in a handful of Tarzan movies, and Eleanor Holm, the party-girl swimmer who won a gold in the backstroke in the 1932 Olympics, only to be tossed off the 1936 Olympic team for having had a bit too much fun on the boat over to Germany.

Ederle's part in the Aquacade wasn't big; it consisted mainly of making a short swim across the water while others dived in around her. But it was a return to performing, and on August 6, 1939, the thirteenth anniversary of her swim, she rode in an open-car parade with Whalen, re-creating her homecoming celebration. They were preceded by the fair's mounted Indian guard of honor to the amusement area, where she plunged into the Aquacade pool in her two-piece suit. Just a handful of people watched this parade, compared to the several million who had feted her in 1926, but once again Trudy could sit on the back of a car seat and raise her hand in triumph.

Rose wrote in a guest column for the vacationing Walter Winchell that Ederle was the biggest draw in the show, despite being in the water for only forty-six seconds each performance. And the Aquacade show was a big deal, netting over a million dollars in 1939, the first time a theatrical production had done that during a twenty-six-week period. Ederle wasn't the big draw, of course, but Rose knew how to milk a good story. Mostly, the crowds would give her polite applause after her brief swim, then look eagerly for the next bevy of beauties invariably around the corner. Still, it was the first work she had in a pool since giving swimming instructions in Rye nearly a decade earlier, and she was eager to perform.

Though one writer said he thought Trudy seemed depressed because she could not hear the applause, the opposite seemed true to those around her, who thought she was rejuvenated by the performance. Ederle traveled with the Aquacade production to appear in a sister show in San Francisco, where she was pictured on the cover of the August 1940 edition of the Pacific Greyhound *Grapevine*. The photo showed her in a group of ten women surrounding Weissmuller in front of a Greyhound bus. Part of the deal was that Trudy wear a replica of the two-piece suit she had worn to swim the Channel, something that had to be embarrassing to a woman now in her mid-thirties, especially when the younger beauties were all in one-piece suits.

When the Aquacade show opened in San Francisco, Yancey Smith did a piece on Ederle for the local paper, describing her as a husky woman with a character-lined face, a stark contrast to the fair-haired, sleek-bodied youngsters walking backstage at the Treasure Island performance. He waited outside while she changed into a replica of her outfit, complete with goggles. When she returned, she told him how the same kind of determination that helped her conquer the Channel had helped her overcome her injury.

"I told them they couldn't keep me in a wheelchair all my life," she said. "I made up my mind I'd swim again if I had to crawl to the water on my hands and knees."

Trudy got third billing—behind Weissmuller and Morton Downey, but ahead of Esther Williams—for the San Francisco shows. Tickets were priced at forty cents, and once again those who came saw her swim in a small pool, while at each end others dived in the water and women in costumes paraded around. When the tour ended, so did Ederle's career as a performer. She traveled to Puerto Rico that winter to teach swimming, and penned a piece the next spring that she hoped would finally stop people from feeling sorry for her. It was entitled "Don't Weep for Me," and Ederle said she was happy, had no grudges or resentments, and never brooded about the past. The Channel swim, she said, had brought her enough money for the rest of her life, and she pointed out that she owned two cars, four fur coats, and jewelry.

Indeed, though her father had lost large sums of money from real estate investments that went bad during the Depression and had also lost money he had invested for her, Ederle was never in the bad financial straits that some newspapermen suggested she was.

"I'm all right," she concluded, "really I am!"

The world, though, wasn't. War came and lives changed, and Trudy's was no exception. When her brother Henry joined the U.S. Army as a cadet, she enrolled in an airplane-craftsman course and worked at La Guardia Field. Sitting at a table, she overhauled instruments used on transatlantic flying boats—a job she would keep until several years after the war.

Fame had indeed proven fleeting. The girl who had been picked as the top athlete of 1926 by the Hearst chain was overlooked when the Associated Press polled sports editors in 1944 on the greatest achievements in sports history. Bobby Jones's Grand Slam topped the list, followed by Babe Ruth's sixty home runs and Jesse Owens's performance in the 1936 Olympics. Ederle wasn't mentioned on any of the ballots.

In Highlands, a small park next to the river where she had learned to swim was named after her, and her name also graced the pool at the Flushing fair grounds. But Ederle's life was never going to be the same whirlwind—never could be the same whirlwind—as it had been in 1926, when she accomplished something nobody thought any woman could.

Ederle, who still wanted to have something to do with swimming, applied to become a swimming instructor in the New York school system, but the New York City Board of Education rejected her because of her deafness. Later, though, she joined the staff of the Lexington School for the Deaf in New York as a volunteer swimming coach. She found solace again in the water, this time with children who, like her, couldn't hear. To them, she was a middle-age woman who had once achieved some kind of fame, but she felt like one of them. She had come full circle in her life, and now she cherished golden moments like those.

When writer Gay Talese visited her in 1958 in the Queens home she shared with two longtime friends, he found a hefty woman of fifty-three who voiced no regrets about the turn her life had taken. She told Talese that she could never overcome her shyness and that this had cost her in life. "Because of my hearing I've run away from people, I guess, and always run back to my family where I felt sheltered."

She was working on another project at this time, a screenplay with a television producer, again with the working title *Don't Weep for Me*.

"It doesn't really matter if they've forgotten me," she said of the public. "I haven't forgotten them."

The anniversaries of her swim piled up, going mostly unnoticed until 1976, when, a few months before the fiftieth anniversary of her swim, she was honored with other sports heroes of the past half century. Ederle expressed gratitude that she was still remembered, but she would not talk to a *New York Times* writer who went to her house, only to see her peeking out from behind a curtain inside. Ederle was still mourning the death two months earlier of her roommate and close companion, Julia Lachwit, who'd had a heart attack almost at her feet. Her other roommate, Pura Espada, had lived in the Flushing home for thirty-two years and said all three were like sisters and very close.

Espada went outside and told the reporter that Ederle was a simple woman who was devoted to helping others and good at fixing things around the house. This day was hard for Ederle, Espada explained, because she didn't want to face people but couldn't hear unless looking directly at someone. Still, she said, Ederle's family wanted her to go, and she would attend the awards ceremony.

That night, she seemed aglow, despite her heavy heart, excited that she was being honored along with other notables like Whitey Ford and Sugar Ray Robinson at the Boys' Athletic League dinner.

"I think it's a beautiful thing after 50 years," Ederle said. "The fact that they remember you I'm grateful."

She was grateful for that, and much more.

"If God called me tomorrow, I'd go willingly," she said. "I've led a full life, a beautiful life."

Epilogue

The windows were closed, the curtains drawn, and no one answered a knock at the door. The two men from the International Swimming Hall of Fame had come to the modest home in Queens to see Gertrude Ederle, and now they waited outside her house, hoping for an opportunity. The woman next door said Ederle always came out promptly for her afternoon mail and that would be the best chance to see her.

Ederle had been in the initial class inducted into the Swimming Hall of Fame in 1965, joining Johnny Weissmuller, Buster Crabbe, and others. The two Tarzans had attended the induction ceremony in Fort Lauderdale, as had the other honorees, but Ederle had not. Her revolutionary two-piece swimsuit is on display there, but Ederle had never made the first trip to Florida to see it or the other items in the exhibit honoring the woman who conquered the English Channel. In fact, the two men at her door, ISHOF officials, had never met her. It was the day after her eighty-ninth birthday, and Buck Dawson and Bob Duenkel wanted to correct that.

When the mail came, so did their opportunity to meet Ederle. They yelled out introductions to the gray-haired old woman, who struggled to understand who they were but welcomed them once she found out.

For an hour, they stood on her front porch, writing down questions and handing them to her to read so she could respond. She did so with enthusiasm, talking in a loud voice about her life, her one love, and the events of nearly seventy years before. She remembered them as if they'd happened yesterday, and memories spilled, tumbling over one another, as she talked to Dawson and Duenkel.

She had had unimaginable highs in her life when still very young, but life was never the same again. It couldn't be, because the adoration of millions is almost always fleeting and there's always a time when the cheering stops. When it did, she withdrew, living a quiet life with her friends and family and doting on her nieces and nephews.

The doctors could never do anything about her hearing, other than offer sympathy and sell her the latest hearing aid. She remembered that one doctor had told her that it was a shame she wouldn't be able to hear her sweetheart when he said, "I love you." And, to answer all the questions from the newspapermen, there had once been a sweetheart. He was a man she knew from Highlands. He was close to popping the question to her in 1929, but Ederle suggested to him that it might be difficult being married to a woman who could not hear. To her surprise, he had agreed. There had never been another.

"I figured if he felt that way, all men must feel the same way," Ederle said. "I didn't know. I just thought I'd be a problem to any of them."

She came of age in an era where anything was thought possible, and when women were finally being recognized for doing things other than bearing children and baking pies. She epitomized that era, but it was inevitable that both it and the long-distance swimming craze would end. A decade that celebrated heroes would also end, the Depression would begin, and Americans would be preoccupied with more pressing things, like getting enough to eat or paying the electric bill.

The years hadn't always been kind. Being deaf meant living in a world where fitting in was always difficult, and the pain from the accident on the stairs had never really subsided. When things got too rough, Ederle would always think back to the day in the Channel, when things were even rougher, and yet she still overcame her fears.

"I try to take that courage and carry on with life," she said.

Her life had been a long one, and she lived it with few regrets. She had long ago accepted her fate with men and come to terms with the fact that the cheering stopped way too soon. Still, her failure to win three gold medals in the 1924 Olympics prompted her to cry every time she saw the Olympics on television.

Invariably, everything centered on that fateful day when she conquered the English Channel and won over the world. She had kept meticulous scrapbooks filled with newspaper and magazine clippings from the time she was a teenager through her days with the Aquacade show. If she was having a good day, she would excitedly show visitors to her home the "Channel Room" on the second floor, where the real treasure was.

Her three Olympic medals were there, along with the William Randolph Hearst silver cup for being voted the world's most popular athlete in 1926. (The latter is now housed in the Smithsonian.) There was the scroll Mayor Walker gave her on her return to New York and a large key to the city, and the Joseph P. Day cup she received for swimming from Manhattan Beach to Brighton Beach in the race that first made her a star.

On the wall in this room was a large picture of the ocean, with waves breaking against rocks, as well as a painting of her walking onto the beach at Kingsdown, with bonfires burning on the beach and excited people everywhere. On the desk lay fan mail and photos of herself, which Ederle would autograph and send out to fans.

The mail still came, though by now it was just an occasional letter from young swimmers or someone who had read about her in a history book. Pegler had been right when he wrote that the public can't run around screaming about one person forever, but if Ederle was still bitter about lost fame and fortune, she didn't show it.

She had once held twenty-nine different swimming records, but as time went on and swimmers improved and got faster, these were all surpassed. Her time for a woman crossing the Channel was one of the last to go, lasting twenty-four years, until Florence Chadwick did it in thirteen hours and twenty minutes in 1950. Remarkably, she held one record until after her death—that for the twenty-two-mile swim from the Battery to Sandy Hook, which she undertook as a final tune-up just before leaving for her first challenge of the Channel.

Australian long-distance swimmer Tammy van Wisse broke it on July 21, 2006, in a swim she made to honor Ederle and her achievements. She said she felt the spirit of Ederle along the way.

"Gertrude Ederle was a woman I admired for her 'never say die' attitude and amazing perseverance," van Wisse said. "Her swims meant more than just records. She advanced the acceptance of women in sports, and she did it at a time when women were discouraged from participating."

Ederle was the last surviving charter member of the Golden Age of sport, and while other women athletes would eventually do significant things, hers may have been the greatest single accomplishment in women's sports history. She was America's first female sports hero, a woman who never set out to be a pioneer but became one anyway. The two million people who watched her triumphant parade through the Canyon of Heroes still stands as the greatest turnout for any athlete, male or female.

They once cheered her in New York, danced and sang to her on the beach at Kingsdown, and couldn't keep their hands off her in Germany. But the last half century of her life was lived privately, mostly in a small world where her deafness wasn't as much an issue. She rarely traveled once her vaudeville tour was over, and she never returned to the Channel that made her so famous.

Despite her hearing problems, two songs stuck in her head from long ago. There was "Let Me Call You Sweetheart," the song she hummed on her way across the Channel and the song people sang to her during her celebrated homecoming. And, of course, there was the song written about her by Charles Tobias and Al Sherman in the heady days following her Channel swim.

She didn't need to be prodded to sing it, and on the day she met Dawson and Duenkel, she cheerfully sang the lyrics:

> *Trudy, Trudy, you're our American daughter.*
> *Trudy, Trudy, you're like a fish in water.*
> *You swam the Channel, that treacherous sea,*
> *But you went through it,*
> *We knew, we knew that you could do it, Trudy,*

A few years later, she was singing the same song again, this time in an exuberant voice to a reporter on the seventy-fifth anniversary of her swim. She was living at the Christian Health Care Center in Wyckoff, New Jersey, where she sat in a chair by her bed, her legs wrapped in a red plaid blanket. Her body was frail, but her memory remained sharp as she reminisced about things that had happened so long ago.

Tears welled in her eyes as she finished the song, then talked about her sister Meg, who had died recently.

"Meg, she's the one who actually made me become a swimmer," Ederle said. "I never cared for it, really. I was lazy. I liked to fool around in the water, but I didn't like being serious about it.

"Meg's the one who wanted to make me a champion. I used to get these entry blanks in the mail and tear them up. Meg fished them out and mailed them in."

The people in the nursing home had a faint idea of who she once was, but there was no way they could imagine what she meant to her country and to women everywhere. She had in her room the painting of her coming out of the water in Kingsdown, a book full of pictures of her in her youth, and a *Sports Illustrated* article.

The waterproof goggles she wore went to the Smithsonian, the swimsuit to the International Swimming Hall of Fame. Her niece, Mary Ederle Ward, kept Trudy's meticulous scrapbooks, which would later be the foundation for this book. Ederle had always planned on writing a book herself, but somehow it never got done.

In the Canyon of Heroes on lower Broadway, she is still remembered by plaques in the sidewalk that commemorate both the parade of the 1924 Olympians and her own tumultuous reception two years later. Her final honor came in the last year of her life, when she was inducted into the National Women's Hall of Fame. She was too frail to go, but her niece spoke on her behalf and the crowd gave her aunt a standing ovation. The same year, however, Trudy was able to attend the rededication of the park at Highlands and did an interview for a television series on sports pioneers, even though she fretted she would not be able to hear the questions.

Ederle died at the nursing home in the early-morning hours of November 30, 2003, after being in failing health for about a week. Mary Ward and her husband, Martin, were by her side. She was ninety-eight.

Ward had helped take care of her aunt during much of her later life, and she remembered what Ederle had told her.

"Don't cry for me when I die, because God gave me a wonderful life," she'd said.

For the first time in her life, Mary didn't listen to her beloved aunt.

On the morning of her funeral, a package arrived from the U.S. Olympic Committee. Inside was an Olympic flag, which was draped over the coffin, and escorted by six nieces and nephews to the chapel at Woodlawn Cemetery in the Bronx.

A big storm had hit the East Coast and there was too much snow and wind to go immediately to the grave site. Good-byes would be said in the chapel, and one special good-bye was saved for last.

Friends and family stood around the casket. Together, they began singing Trudy one last song.

> *Let me call you "Sweetheart," I'm in love with you.*
> *Let me hear you whisper that you love me too.*
> *Keep the love-light glowing in your eyes so true.*
> *Let me call you "Sweetheart," I'm in love with you.*

Notes

Gertrude Ederle's Personal Archive

Gertrude Ederle assembled a personal archive that contained innumerable articles, news clippings, and other memorabilia, with a good deal of the material relating specifically to her first Channel attempt in 1925 and eventual successful Channel swim in 1926. Some of the background information in *America's Girl* was taken from newspaper articles in this archive (four hundred pages with more than fifteen hundred articles). Most of the archive material is preserved and intact, but some articles do not have dates or bylines. We have made every attempt to document specific sources, but, in some instances, the citations are incomplete.

Gertrude Ederle's Memoir

Gertrude Ederle planned to write an autobiography, but a busy life interfered and she did not complete *The Highlights of My Life Story*. We would like to thank Robert Ederle, Mary Ederle Ward's brother, for allowing us to use this unpublished material, which was written and compiled in 1951 and covers her life up to her second Channel attempt. Some of the quotations attributed to Trudy in *America's Girl* are taken directly from this unfinished memoir.

Gertrude Ederle's Diary

In addition to the memoir, Robert Ederle provided us with Trudy's personal diary, which was used as a source though not quoted directly. The diary began with her boarding the S.S. *America* for the 1924 Olympics and ended with Ederle on the *Berengaria* in 1926 on her way to France.

1. *"Bring on Your Old Channel"*

The coverage of Trudy's Channel swims was extensive. Often, as a result, the spelling of names (for instance, Trudy versus Trudie, *La Marinie* versus *La Morinie*, Costa versus Corthes, Helmi versus Helmy) as well as some of the facts (Trudy's age, for instance) were inconsistent. The newspaper articles are cited verbatim, but we did correct spellings and inaccuracies in the text and chose consistency whenever possible. The spellings used, we believe, are the most accurate.

Page 1   *Two nights earlier:* From "Sharks Menace Miss Ederle: Channel Infested with Them as Girl Prepares for Swim." This information comes from a short news item that appears in the Archive, without a byline or newspaper name, and also from an Associated Press article, "Miss Ederle Starts Her Swim; Jazz Band to Cheer Her on Way." Ederle mentioned in her memoir that she was tired of listening to all the naysayers' talk about the treacheries of the Channel. The first news item says, "Unless someone becomes conscience-stricken and tells her, the ambitious 19-year-old New Yorker will take to the water in ignorance of the fact that two 6-foot sharks were caught seven miles off Boulogne, near here, on Sunday night." And the AP article says, "Precautions have been taken to keep the news of the sharks' appearance from Miss Ederle." According to subsequent reports, Jabez Wolffe became "conscience-stricken" and told Trudy about the sharks right before her attempted swim in 1925. Elsie Viets, Trudy's WSA chaperone during the first Channel swim, complained bitterly that Wolffe told Trudy about the sharks to scare the young swimmer. Viets called the so-called sharks "porpoises."

Page 3   *"I'm not sure I'll make it":* From "Gertrude Ederle Admits Channel May Best Her." Archive.

Page 3   *Lloyds of London opened betting at 20—1:* From a brief news article. Archive.

Page 4   *The* Evening World *summed up:* From *New York Evening World,* August 4, 1922.

Page 4   *"It is insignificant":* From Jane Dixon, "Swim for It." Archive.

Page 5   *Babe Ruth and Jack Dempsey:* From Frank O'Neill, "Miss Ederle's Marvelous Chest Expansion Gives Her Great Chance in Channel Swim," *New York Evening Journal,* August 17, 1925. Archive.

Page 5   *"Nature has equipped":* Ibid.

Page 5   *Calvin Coolidge was president, and his wife:* From *Time* magazine, August 17,

1925. Additional information was obtained from the Calvin Coolidge Presidential Library and Museum located at the Forbes Library in Northampton, Massachusetts, where Coolidge practiced law and served as mayor. The Coolidge Library technically opened in 1920 when Coolidge began donating various records and memorabilia to the Forbes Library. This collection was further enhanced in 1956 when the government of Massachusetts established the Calvin Coolidge Memorial Room at the behest of Grace Coolidge, who died the following year, in 1957.

Page 6   *Ederle was still a teen:* Most of the articles written in 1926 regarding Trudy's successful swim cite her as being nineteen years old. This, in fact, was not true. She was twenty years old when she completed the swim on August 6, 1926. Trudy never corrected the oversight and seems to have gone along with the general consensus (even in her memoir twenty-five years later). She was encouraged to go along with this oversight. Partly it had to do with the fact that being a teenager made better copy than being twenty years old. Johnny Weissmuller, her contemporary, also misrepresented his age, even, according to David Fury in *Johnny Weissmuller: Twice the Hero* (Minneapolis: Artist's Press, 2000), going to the trouble of forging his brother's birth certificate to qualify for the 1924 Olympics.

Page 6   *Charlotte Epstein, the club's founder:* Without a doubt, Trudy would not have developed into such an extraordinary athlete without the unwavering support of Charlotte Epstein. Not only did she found the WSA, but this no-nonsense, tirelessly committed woman forged a path for all female swimmers. Her name will always be associated with the Olympians who developed at the WSA. We relied heavily on the news articles in the Archive for information about Epstein, but, in addition, we also viewed the short documentary film *Settlement Houses to Olympic Stadiums: Jewish Women in American Sport,* created, produced, and directed by Linda Boorish and Shuli Eshel.

Page 7   *"Margaret, what, are you crazy?":* From family history as related by Trudy to Mary Ederle Ward. Trudy was in Ward's care for the last twelve years of her life.

Page 8   *Trudy liked Wolffe upon meeting him:* In some respects, the portly Wolffe physically resembled Trudy's father, but it didn't take Trudy long to bristle under his domineering tutelage. When Trudy rejected Wolffe's advice about swimming the breaststroke as opposed to the American crawl, and even elicited the advice of an independent coach (a Mr. W. Howcroft, Gertrude Ederle's memoir, page 25) to back her up, Wolffe reacted bitterly. He proceeded to chastise Trudy every chance he got, whether it was for playing the ukulele or swimming too fast. Annette Kellerman, who held the record for the woman who was in the Channel waters the longest ($10^1/_2$ hours during one of her three attempts) until Trudy broke it, was accompanied by Wolffe (along with Thomas Burgess, Montague Holbien, and Horace Pew) on her first Channel swim on August 25, 1905. In *The Original Million Dollar Mermaid: The Annette Kellerman Story* (Crows Nest NSW, Australia: Allen & Unwin, 2005), Emily Gibson with Barbara Firth report that Kellerman described Wolffe as "Pretty fat for athletic work and [he] would hardly make a distinguished showing in another event but acknowledged he was a very good swimmer."

Page 8 *"I need all the encouragement"*: From bylined story by Gertrude Ederle in the *Daily News,* June 2, 1926.

Page 9 *"Miss Ederle doubtless"*: From "Ederle Swim on Tomorrow: American Mermaid Completes Training and Will Make Start for Dover at 7:45 a.m.," August 16, 1925. Archive.

Page 10 *"I don't go in for skipping"*: From "Gertrude Ederle Ready for Try at Channel," *Sunday [Daily] News,* July 26, 1925. References to her training also appear in Marguerite Mooers Marshall, "Fifteen Year-Old Girl, New Swimming Champion, Just a Normal, Home and Fun-Loving American," *New York Evening World,* August 4, 1922.

Page 11 *flexing her muscle and playing leapfrog:* From "American Mermaid Who Plans to Swim Channel," *Midweek Pictorial,* April 30, 1925.

Page 11 *Heywood Broun said some theories of male supremacy:* From Heywood Broun, "It Seems to Me," *New York World.* Ederle penned the date on this article in the Archive as June 18, 1925.

Page 12 *Ederle was not the first to try:* Gertrude Ederle was the sixth person to successfully swim the English Channel, the third to swim from France to England (Burgess, Webb, and Sullivan swam from England to France; Tiraboschi, Toth, and Ederle swam from France to England), and the first woman to complete the swim. The Channel Swimming Association (http://www.channelswimming.net/restext.htm) recognizes Trudy's contribution (the organization has a Gertrude Ederle Award), but she no longer holds the title of Queen of the English Channel. That distinction belongs to Alison Streeter, a British swimmer, who has completed forty-three successful swims (over a twenty-five-year period). Still, along with the women who preceded her, Ederle was a trailblazer. Information regarding Madame Isacescue and Jeanne Sion was taken from numerous articles in the Archive. Information regarding Annette Kellerman was primarily taken from Gibson and Firth's book, *The Original Million Dollar Mermaid.*

Page 12 *until Jeanne Sion:* From "Gertrude Ederle Still Waiting." Archive.

Page 12 *Channel swimming:* From Sparrow Robertson, "Sporting Gossip," *New York Herald Tribune,* June 1925.

Page 13 *In her excitement:* From "Gertrude Ederle Suffers Collapse," *North American Newspaper Alliance,* August 18, 1925. This information also appears in "Seven Ederles Sure 'Trudy' Can Do It," *Evening Graphic,* August 19, 1925. Trudy also refers to this in her memoir, page 35, when she says, "While strolling over from the hotel to the "La Marine" [sic], I noticed I had, in a hurry, donned my skirt wrong side out. They inquired if I wished to go back and change it. I replied, 'I had better not, I feel it might bring me good luck.' "

Page 14   *along with the dashing Ishak Helmy:* Helmy's father, Abdel-Qader Helmy Pasha, was an Egyptian general, which made his son, Ishak, a bek or "notable." Because of Ishak's wealth, he was able to spend summer after summer in France practicing for the Channel swim. He was a fixture in Cape Gris-Nez. Helmy made several attempts to swim the Channel, and did not make it across until August 31, 1928. According to *Al-Ahram*'s special correspondent, "After struggling against the cold waters of the Channel all night, Helmi Bek finally made it to the British coast at Folkestone. He arrived exactly 2:09 p.m. today, after having spent 23 hours and 51 minutes in the water since leaving Gris-Nez on the French coast yesterday." Helmy was nearly disqualified by the Channel Swimming Association because, as a Muslim, he refused to take the association's oath, but eventually Helmy prevailed and received his official certificate (see http://weekly.ahram.org.eg/2001/565/chrncls.htm). Ed Sullivan, in his "Sports Whirl" column, referred to Helmy as the "Egyptian colossus." When Helmy made it across, Trudy told a reporter (in "Gertrude Ederle Drops into Town and Tells Why She Lost Marathon," Archive), "[Helmy] was at Cape Gris-Nez while I was training for the Channel swim. And he finally did get across. As I used to look at him I wondered how he could fail so many times—he looked so big and strong. We used to kid him a great deal and tell him that the only way he would ever get across would be to have a boatload of champagne and pretty girls pace him. But I guess he fooled us. I didn't hear of any such boatloads going across with him." As already mentioned, the spelling of Helmy's name is inconsistent throughout. In the book's text, we used *Helmy*.

Page 14   *"polygamy for aristocrats":* From Gertrude Ederle, "Ederle Enacts Shepherd Role to Pass Time," *Daily News,* June 23, 1926.

Page 14–15   *Helmy . . . dancing on the beach with Sion:* From "Easier than Swimming the Channel," a photograph dated by Trudy August 10, 1925. Archive.

Page 15   *Over the years, the makeup:* From Alec Rutherford, "Every Preparation for Cross Channel Swim Now Complete," August 15, 1925. Capt. Alec Rutherford was a British expert on the cross-Channel swim and eventual *New York Times* correspondent for the second attempt of the Channel by Trudy. Archive.

Page 16   *"I wanted twice to quit":* From John Goldstrom, "Miss Ederle Now Is Channel Hope." Archive.

Page 18   *the musicians got their instruments out:* Three of the four members of the jazz band got seasick. Sparrow Robertson, in his "Sporting Gossip" column, claimed that the only musician still playing as Ederle forged her way through the stormy Channel was the clarinet player, but according to the August 19, 1925, *New York Herald Tribune* story, "The first to succumb was the trombonist. He was quickly followed by the cornetist and the clarinetist. The concertina alone weathered the storm." Archive.

Page 18   *"Just look after all those details":* From "Miss Ederle Tries Great Swim Today," August 17, 1925. Archive.

Page 19   New York Times *hired a Capt. Alec Rutherford:* From "Ready for Long Swim," *The Seattle Times,* August 20, 1925.

Page 19   *"perfect even pace":* From "Ederle on Channel Swim," International News Service, London, August 18, 1925.

Page 22   *"She just hates to go slow":* From "Seven Ederles Send Cheers to 'Trudy' from NJ Coast." Archive.

2. Humbled but Not Beaten

Page 27   *She told Viets that she was determined:* From Gertrude Ederle's memoir, page 42.

Page 28   *didn't want her to make any statements:* From "Gertrude Ederle Sure She Could Have Gone Farther in Channel," dated by Trudy September 18, 1925. Archive.

Page 29   *"I distinctly heard Wolffe cry out":* From "Backs Miss Ederle in Blaming Trainer: Miss Elsie Viets of Women's Swimming Body Disputes Wolffe's Answer," *The New York Times,* dated by Trudy September 21, 1925. Archive.

Page 29   *"And I want the public to know":* From a statement Trudy made at a WOR radio broadcast at 1440 Broadway in Manhattan. In the broadcast she claims that she had "suspicions and facts" that she was going to release to the public within thirty days if the WSA didn't make a public statement saying that Trudy was ordered by Wolffe to be pulled from the water against her will.

Page 30   *Annette Kellerman, the Australian swimmer:* From Gertrude Ederle's memoir, page 44. Kellerman often performed at the Hippodrome, a theater located on Sixth Avenue (between 43rd and 44th streets) that seated more than five thousand people. Trudy said about the welcome home ceremony, "A memorable thrill was given to me when I saw my name for the first time in lights over a theatre marquee. In the huge lobby there stood a sign with large, bright letters: 'Welcome, Trudy.' The Hippodrome in those days was also widely known for its very interesting animal presentations. So my friend was relating that while she was loitering in the lobby awaiting my arrival a passerby seeing the sign said, 'Trudy, what kind of animal is that?' My friend turned and replied, 'A human fish.' "

Page 32   *Two days later, she revealed:* Trudy made the announcement on November 3, 1925. Charlotte Epstein of the WSA said, in response to their decision to turn pro in an article in the *New York Evening World,* November 4, 1925: "Everyone at the WSA naturally regrets the loss to the competitive contingent of such splendid performers as Gertrude and Aileen. But our association is more interested in encouraging swimming generally than in producing stars, and we feel that in the capacity of teachers and coaches these girls will have a far better opportunity to further our aims and ideals."

Page 33   *Burgess wrote back on Nov. 29, 1925:* Letter from Bill Burgess belonging to Mary Ederle Ward.

Page 35   *"In the case of Miss Wills":* From *Tavern Topics,* October 1925.

Page 35   *A week earlier, British bookies":* From *Time* magazine, July 26, 1926.

Page 37   *The Deauville was a palatial hotel:* Gertrude Edele describes in her memoir (page 47) that "The Deauville Beach Club with its attractive circular outdoor pool was a pleasure to swim in and its length ideal to stretch out in for long distance practice, after instructing hours and exhibitions. People marveled at the endurance I displayed when checking the number of times I swam the pool for conditioning." The Deauville was a five-story, 142-room casino and hotel, with the "largest swimming pool in Florida, which opened at Sixty-seventh Street in early 1926. The pool was 165 feet long and 100 feet wide and located on the second floor behind the hotel rooms. Planned as an entertainment capital, the Deauville provided dining rooms, ballroom dancing, entertainers, exhibitions by champion swimmers and divers and state-of-the-art bathing facilities" (http://www.urbanresource.com/community/index.cfm?action=showpage&pageID=5). The Deauville Hotel was destroyed in the Great Hurricane of 1926 (and has been rebuilt several times after subsequent hurricanes).

Page 37   *The rage at the time:* From "Swimming champions in Their Beach Pajamas," *Miami Herald,* February 27, 1926.

Page 38   *Zaring wrote that Ederle:* From *Miami Herald,* February 25, 1926.

Page 38   *"I learned quickly to correct":* From Gertrude Ederle's memoir, page 48.

Page 39   *Dudley Field Malone was an international divorce attorney:* Although Malone often was criticized for his handling of Trudy's affairs, he had a considerable reputation. In "Monster Reception for Gertrude Ederle," in *The Progressive* magazine, September 15, 1926, Malone was described: "Miss Ederle's attorney is Dudley Field Malone. He was the Collector of the Port of Authority of New York under President Wilson and reported to the administration at the time that the *Lusitania* on her last trip was loaded with explosives, contrary to the law governing passenger steamships." In addition, some background information on Malone was taken from letters Malone wrote in 1949 to Harry S. Truman asking the president to appoint him to a government position. The letters (along with his résumé) are from the archives at the Harry S. Truman Library & Museum in Independence, Missouri.

Page 40   *With the money now in hand:* Trudy had sorely missed her sister's support during the first Channel swim. Meg and Pop were back in New York and unable to accompany Trudy. She was determined to have her father and Meg along for the second attempt. She believed that their presence would make all the difference between success and failure.

Page 40   *He finally found the perfect partners:* Capt. Joseph Medill Patterson, the managing editor and publisher of the New York *Daily News,* was a member of the family who owned the *Chicago Tribune*. Along with his cousin, Col. Robert R. McCormick, Patterson founded the New York *Daily News* in 1919. While in England during World War I, Patterson duly noted the success of *The Daily Mirror*, England's first "picture" newspaper. The British tabloid served as a prototype for the *Daily News*.

3. Suited for a Swim

Page 47   *The summer of 1921 got off to a hot start:* From *New York Times*, June 5, 1921.

Page 48   *the right to smoke on most beaches:* Women could be arrested for smoking in public prior to the 1920s. In fact, in 1904, a woman was sentenced to thirty days in jail for smoking in front of her children. And, on January 21, 1908, New York passed the Sullivan Law, which prohibited women from smoking in restaurants and hotels. Two days later, Katie Mulcahey was caught smoking on the street. In the January 23, 1908, *New York Times* article "Arrested for Smoking. First Case Under Sullivan Law Comes from the Bowery $5 Fine," Mulcahey reportedly told the judge, "I've got as much right to smoke as you have. I never heard of this new law, and I don't want to hear about it. No man shall dictate to me."

Page 49   *Rosalie M. Ladova, an expert swimmer:* From *New York Times*, July 28, 1913.

Page 49   *Credit an Australian with both shocking America's mores:* Kellerman was multitalented. In addition to her swimming, vaudeville, and movie career, Kellerman was an avid physical culture advocate. She published two books: *Physical Beauty: How to Keep It* (New York: George H. Doran Company, 1918) and *How to Swim* (London, Heinemann, 1918). In addition, she wrote *My Story*, an unpublished autobiography. In this autobiography, Kellerman said, "The men, who started from different points along the coast, wore no clothes, but I was compelled to put on a tiny bathing suit. Small as it was, it chafed me. When I finished, my flesh under the arms was raw and hurt fearfully." Until recently, *My Story* was held at the State Library of New South Wales, Sydney, but segments of the autobiography can be read on http://www.clinthickman.com/annettekellerman. For more information, see the book by Emily Gibson with Barbara Firth, *The Original Million Dollar Mermaid: The Annette Kellerman Story* (Crows Nest NSW, Australia: Allen & Unwin, 2005).

Page 50   *The Melbourne Exhibition Hall paid her ten pounds a week:* Emily Gibson with Barbara Firth, *The Original Million Dollar Mermaid: The Anne Kellerman Story* (Crows Nest NSW, Australia: Allen & Unwin, 2005).

Page 51   *"This will be the greatest campaign ever launched about a young girl":* Ibid., page 60.

Page 51   *Kellerman appeared in a* black suit: Ibid.

Page 53   *"You don't expect me to go for a":* Ibid., page 61.

Page 53   *"Kellerman's court appearance:* Ibid.

Page 54   *Paul Gallico, the sportswriter, remembered:* From a chapter about Gertrude Ed-erle in Paul Gallico, *The Golden People* (Garden City, New York: Doubleday & Com-pany, 1965).

Page 57   *While the girls weren't prosecuted:* The International Swimming Hall of Fame Web site was invaluable. The information regarding Bleibtry and Boyle's arrest comes from the Web site's article "From Bloomers to Bikinis: How the Sport of Swimming Changed Western Culture in the 20th Century," as well as from remarks made at her induction at the International Swimming Hall of Fame in 1967 (www.ishof.org/ honorees/67/67ebleibtry.html). In addition, we often relied on the expertise of Bob Duenkel, the executive director and curator at the ISHOF in Fort Lauderdale, Florida.

4. Swifter, Higher, Stronger

Page 60   *The mood was confident:* For information regarding the 1924 Paris Olympics, especially in regard to the trip to and from France as well as the accommo-dations at Rocquencourt, we relied on the oral histories of Aileen Riggin, Doris O'Mara Murphy, and William Neufeld, which are archived at the LA84 Foundation. The LA84 Foundation operates the largest sports research library in North America, the Paul Ziffren Sports Resource Center. In addition, the Official Bulletin from the 1924 Paris Olympics, Part 3: 417–94, was also used, as was David Fury's book, *Johnny Weissmuller, Twice the Hero* (Minneapolis: Artist's Press, 2000).

     Aileen Riggin: http://www.la84foundation.org/6oic/OralHistory/OHriggin.indd .pdf

     William Neufeld: http://www.la84foundation.org/6oic/OralHistory/OHNeufeld .pdf

     Doris O'MaraMurphy: http://www.la84foundation.org/6oic/OralHistory/OHO MaraMurphy.pdf

Page 61   *The swimmers did it by putting on:* Swimmers joked that they felt like elephants in a bathtub. From Gertrude Ederle's memoir, page 15.

Page 63   *"The heavier the odds":* From "Olympic Eligibles," dated 1924 by Gertrude Ederle. Archive.

Page 63   *Bleibtrey had turned pro in 1922:* From "Miss Bleibtrey to Turn Profes-sional," *New York Times,* May 10, 1922. Ethelda Bleibtrey was the first female Olympic swimming champion from the United States and the only woman ever to win all the women's swimming events at any Olympic Games. Bleibtrey was America's answer to Annette Kellerman. She was arrested twice: once for removing her stockings on a beach and another time for diving into the reservoir in Central Park to protest the lack of a swimming pool (the *Daily News* paid her $1,000 to do so). Like Kellerman, Bleib-trey began swimming to alleviate a physical condition (Bleibtrey had polio and Keller-man had rickets). From 1920 to 1922, she won every national AAU championship

from fifty yards to long distance in an undefeated amateur career (http://www.ishof
.org/honorees/67/67ebleibtrey.html). Bleibtrey officially resigned from the WSA on
October 19, 1921. (*New York Times,* October 20, 1921).

Page 64   *Bauer beat Stubby Kruger's 440-yard backstroke:* From "History Made at the St.
George's Aquatic Meeting," *The Royal Gazette and Colonist Daily,* October 10, 1922.

Page 64   *"They didn't want to take children to the Olympics":* From "An Olympian's Oral
History: Aileen Riggin" (http://www.la84foundation.org/6oic/OralHistory/OHriggin
.indd.pdf).

Page 65   *Not to be outdone, Weissmuller:* From Neufeld's oral history, "William
Neufeld, 1924 Olympic Games, Track & Field" (http://www.la84foundation.org/
6oic/OralHistory/OHNeufeld.pdf. Neufeld says about that evening, "I might add
that we also saw Johnny Weissmuller when he first became Tarzan of the Apes. The
last night on board ship we had a talent show from our own group, and just as the
show was over, he jumped on the table and he swung on the chandelier, and scratched
his side and let out a yell, like he later did in Tarzan." Even though Weissmuller
would have to take voice lessons before he was given the part of Tarzan, Weissmuller
had perfected his yodeling technique as a young man at the Turn-Verein Society's
summer picnics, where "Johnny listened and learned from the local masters of this
'sport,' which was a custom of Swiss and Tyrolese mountaineers" (David Fury, *Johnny
Weissmuller: Twice the Hero,* Minneapolis: Artist's Press, 2000, page 14).

Page 65   *It was a happy group:* From Gertrude Ederle's memoir, page 16.

Page 65   *Frantz Reichel, the general secretary:* Associated Press, June 25, 1924.

Page 66   *Weissmuller got so worked up:* From David Fury, *Johnny Weissmuller,* page 52.

Page 68   *The man suggested that she join the WSA:* From Gertrude Ederle's memoir,
pages 3 and 4.

Page 69   *"She'll never make a swimmer":* Ibid., page 4.

Page 72   *A highly excitable WSA official:* Ibid., pages 9 and 10.

Page 72   *"Gosh, Gert, what have you got on your feet, propellers?":* Ibid., page 11.

Page 74   *"ambassadors of sports and good will":* From *Ambassadors of Sport Magazine.*
Archive. The article also quoted President Coolidge from a July 18, 1925, event at the
Princeton-Cornell and Oxford-Cambridge Meet in Atlantic City. Also appearing in
the same magazine was a quotation from H.R.H. The Prince of Wales at the British
Olympic Association Dinner, Paris, 1924. This quotation also appeared in Trudy's
memoir on page 12.

Page 74   *"Someone had to hold him":* From Ed Sullivan, "Sports Whirl," *Evening Graphic,*
August 7, 1926. The photograph of Trudy with the bear is in the Archive on page 11.
She posed for the photo, according to the caption, at Ormond Beach, Florida.

Page 76   *"You had to watch out when you were diving"*: From an interview with Aileen Riggin Soule, *Chicago Tribune*, May 9, 1996.

5. Different Time, Same Old Channel

Page 80   *He told Ederle that if Burgess*: Gertrude Ederle said in her memoir that she was very loyal to her teacher and she wanted to prove his theory that the American crawl was as good for long distances as it was for short swims.

Page 80   *William Randolph Hearst had started the* Daily Mirror: Hearst was not particularly fond of the tabloids—the masthead logo of his *New York American* newspaper was "A Paper for *People Who Think*"—so he offered to buy the *Daily News* from Patterson and McCormick several times so he could put the *News* out of business. But Hearst finally relented and published his own tabloid when he realized the *Daily News* wasn't going to go away. Hearst's *New York Daily Mirror* hit the New York market five years after the *Daily News*, but had to fight for circulation with Bernarr Macfadden's *Evening Graphic,* which started three months later in September 1924. Macfadden, a bodybuilder and physical culture advocate, lowered the bar for tabloids and resorted to a bizarre sensationalism. The paper was famous for its "composographs" (but the *Daily News* was the first newspaper to use composographs), which were simulations. When a man was hanged for robbery in 1925, a *Graphic* employee nearly lost his life as he posed hanging from a steampipe with a bag over his head. For information regarding the tabloids, we relied on books by Robert Ernst, *Weakness Is a Crime: The Life of Bernarr Macfadden* (Syracuse, New York: Syracuse University Press, 1991); John Chapman, *Tell It to Sweeney: An Informal History of the New York Daily News* (Garden City, New York: Doubleday, 1961); and Mary Macfadden and Emile Henry Gauvreau, *Dumbbells and Carrot Strips: The Story of Bernarr Macfadden* (New York: Holt & Company, 1953); as well as David Nasaw, *The Chief: The Life of William Randolph Hearst* (Boston and New York: Houghton Mifflin Company, 2000).

Page 82   *While her rivals sailed*: From "Mrs. Corson Self-Trained," *The New York Times,* August 29, 1926. Leibgold laid out a program of diet and exercise for Corson, who sent him cards and letters from England telling him how strictly she was following his instructions.

Page 82   *She wrote that Trudy*: From "Swimmer Confident of Victory to Tell Battle Exclusively to *News,*" Chicago Tribune Newspaper Syndicate. Archive.

Page 82   *"Last year there were 70 people on the tug"*: From "Training Nagging Tabooed This Time Ederle's Edict." Archive.

Page 83   "I don't want to be nagged at my training": Ibid.

Page 84   *"I have never in my life drunk alcoholics"*: From Gertrude Ederle, "Champagne at Dinner but Not for Ederle," Chicago Tribune Newspaper Syndicate, June 3, 1926.

Page 84 *"Five men have succeeded, why not a woman?":* Gertrude Ederle said in her memoir that it would probably take her longer to make the swim because men are stronger, "Yet the possibility exists!"

Page 85 *Her biggest interest onboard was food:* While several newspaper accounts describe Trudy as stout, she was actually perfectly proportioned and only stout in comparison to the 1920s flapper standard. She had a hearty appetite and never dieted, but, for a long-distance swimmer of her caliber, it was not necessary. During the 2008 Olympics, it was reported that Michael Phelps consumed 12,000 calories a day.

Page 85 *There was a brief hang-up in customs:* From Gertrude Ederle's memoir, page 51. Also in Julia Harpman, "Miss Ederle Hugging Medicine Ball Arriving for Second Swim," Tribune Press Services.

Page 86 *Six photographers joined Ederle:* Cape Gris-Nez, which means gray nose in English, is the closest point in France to England. The White Cliffs of Dover are visible on a clear day, but only when the seaside town is not drenched in clouds and fog. In "Gray Dawn Ends in Victory Light," a journalist wrote, "The French, who have an apt thought for nomenclature, do not call this spot 'Gray Noze' without good reason. Even in midsummer wispy shreds of mist clothe forbidding headland for the greater part of the time. Old Cape Gray Nose was true to its best—or worst—traditions today," *New York American,* August 7, 1926.

Page 87 *Writer W. O. McGeehan visited Ederle:* From W. O. McGeehan, "Down the Line with W.O. McGeehan," *New York Tribune,* June 28, 1926.

Page 88 *"A fine start for my swim":* Trudy, in an essay called "Swimmingly Yours," recalled how frustrated she felt when things seemed to be going wrong from the start upon her arrival in France. Archive.

Page 88 *His salary would be ten thousand francs:* From personal letters between Gertrude Ederle and Tom Burgess.

Page 89 *until Harpman stepped in and offered him:* From Julia Harpman, "The Saga of Ederle." Archive.

Page 91 *"I suppose you all are disgusted":* From Julia Harpman, "Ederle Defying Cold, Swims Nearly 8 Miles in 3½ Hours," *Daily News,* June 29, 1926.

Page 91 *"The most terrifying feeling":* From Gertrude Ederle, "Channel Sharks and Jellyfish Trouble Ederle," Tribune News Service. Archive.

Page 94 *"Channel Coo-Coo Club":* From Gertrude Ederle's memoir, page 63.

Page 95 *Wolffe thought as the days went on:* From Julia Harpman, "Where, Oh Where, Wails Wolffe, Is Channel Swimmer?" *Daily News,* July 16, 1926. Also cited in Harry R. Flory, "Wolfe Seeks Revenge on Ederle," International News Service, July 16, 1926.

Archive. As already mentioned, there was a great deal of inconsistency in the spelling of names. In the text, we used *Jabez Wolffe.*

Page 97   *"What am I living for anyway?":* From Julia Harpman, "Channel Queen Unspoiled Kid Despite Fame," August 28, 1926.

Page 98   *the Daily News wasn't going to pass a marketing idea by:* From Paul Gallico, "Hour of Glory," a reflection published in February 1949. Archive.

Page 99   *"I had hoped she would get well":* From Gertrude Ederle, "Ederle Weeps Over Novels to Dodge Channel Croakers," Tribune News Service, July 11, 1926.

6. A Promise from Pop

Page 100–101   *Ederle herself compared it to acid:* Ederle wrote in a bylined story in the *Daily News* that after her first major practice swim, a four-mile effort from Cape Gris-Nez to Wissant, her new specially made goggles leaked terribly. She speculated that she might be able to fix them by sewing a layer of chamois at the edge of the leather that surrounded the goggles.

Page 101   *she was undecided about whether to wear wool:* From Gertrude Ederle, in one of her first bylines for the *Daily News* and the *Chicago Tribune,* June 5, 1926. In this article she also said that her father's meat providers had promised to give her specially rendered lamb fat to rub on her body to protect from the cold, but failed to deliver. She said she had plenty of cold cream and goose grease, though.

Page 102   *"I've got it, I've got it, Meg":* In Trudy's memoir, page 66, in reference to the two-piece bathing suit and the goggles she designed, she wrote, "To those two important swim accessories do I also partially attribute my success in crossing the Channel."

Page 103   *Burgess didn't approve of the beef tea:* From Gertrude Ederle's memoir, page 64.

Page 103   *Helmy's diet, which included both coffee and brandy:* From Bill Burgess, "Trainer Tells of Ederle Diet for Long Swim," *Daily News,* July 15, 1926.

Page 103   *"I do not approve of dope for a swimmer":* Ibid.

Page 103   *Meg cooked a chicken, Burgess got some grapes:* From Gertrude Ederle's memoir, page 64.

Page 104   *She thought she had solved it:* Ibid., page 67.

Page 105   *"I was intoxicated with joy," she recalled later:* In Trudy's memoir, page 68, she said that the wax made her goggles "absolutely water tight!"

Page 105   *The first official attempt, though:* A correspondent for the *London Times* was quite taken with Johnson, whom he described as "medium height, and one of the finest built men it is possible to see. He measures forty-five inches round the chest and can at will inflate it five more." *London Times*, August 25, 1872.

Page 106   *The tide pushed Webb away:* When Webb finally made it to shore after several tense hours battling the tides, those accompanying him feared for his health. They had doctors standing by at the hotel, but Webb drank four glasses of port wine and promptly fell asleep, so they had nothing to do. *London Daily Telegraph*, August 25, 1875.

Page 108   *On July 25, she declared:* From Gertrude Ederle, "Ederle Almost Ready for Swim," Tribune News Service, July 25, 1926.

Page 109   *Pop Ederle had earlier gone to London:* From W. O. McGeehan, "Down the Line the Great Sporting Event," *New York Tribune*, June 28, 1926. Archive.

Page 109   *the* Daily News *went out:* The *News* used its inquiring photographer regularly, mostly on days when there wasn't a bylined story by Ederle, to drum up interest in the swim by asking the man on the street what he thought of it.

Page 110   *Barrett had originally planned:* From Julia Harpman, "Where, Oh Where, Wails Wolff, Is Channel Swimmer?" *Daily News,* July 16, 1926.

Page 111   *"We are not out to make a show":* Alec Rutherford, writing in *New York Times* on August 6, 1926 (the same day that Trudy made her swim), after interviewing Leister on the chances of her companion making a second swim. Leister made a point of comparing the well-financed and well-publicized effort of Trudy's with Barrett's little-funded swim that attracted little attention.

Page 112   *"All you hear is talk of wind":* From Gertrude Ederle, New York *Daily News* bylined article, July 30, 1926. Trudy seemed discouraged, likely from the long wait and tough training conditions. She wrote that boxer Paul Berlenbach told her that in his training camp people were always positive, and that if people around her were as positive as those around the boxer she would have a lot better chance of making it.

Page 114   *"I do not think that you will give up":* From a telegraph Malone wrote to Ederle in Boulogne, August 4, 1926. Malone had more than a rooting interest in Trudy making it; he had advanced her five thousand dollars after asking five friends to kick in one thousand dollars each and being refused by each. *New York Times,* August 12, 1926.

Page 114   *"If the weather continues as is, tomorrow we start!":* From Gertrude Ederle's memoir, page 68.

Page 115   *"I could never face people at home again":* From *The New Yorker,* August 26, 1926. Trudy also told Meg, "I'll swim or sink."

Page 115   *In just a few hours, she would step off the beach:* From W. O. McGeehan, "Ederle's Channel Attempt to Be Greatest World's Sport Story, McGeehan Says: Expert Backs Girl Gamblers Bet on Tides," *New York Herald,* Paris, July 16, 1926.

7. *"Come Out, Gertie." "What for?"*

Page 116 *"I feel as if I can lick Jack Dempsey"*: From Julia Harpman, "Ederle at Epic Zero Hour: Girl Confident as She Awaits Signal to Dip into Channel," *Daily News,* August 6, 1926.

Page 117 *he was as interested in what Trudy*: Dempsey followed Trudy's effort closely, and while he did not watch her swim, she watched Dempsey lose to Tunney in their big heavyweight title fight following her return home. Archive.

Page 118 *"Do we go?"*: From Julia Harpman, "Hour by Hour with Ederle in Epic Swim," *Daily News,* August 7, 1926.

Page 118 *Among them were Pop Ederle*: In Trudy's first attempt at the Channel, an AP account described the scene on *La Morinie* "like that attending the departure of an ocean liner. There were fully 100 persons onboard, including officials, correspondents, cameramen, friends, and well-wishers" ("Miss Ederle, Seeing Skirt Inside Out, Regarded It as an Omen of Good Luck," Associated Press, August 18, 1925). Trudy lamented after the first attempt that she didn't think the crew onboard *La Morinie* were very "encouraging," so she planned to keep the number of spectators on the *Alsace* to a minimum.

Page 118 *The tug was piloted by Corthes*: Ederle used the *Alsace* tug on her second Channel swim, piloted by Joe Corthes (also referred to as Joe Costa in some newspaper accounts as well as by Trudy). Partially it was because she wanted to distance herself from *La Morinie*, the tug she used for her first attempt, and partly because she had become friendly with Joe Corthes, whom she called "a self-appointed overlord of Channel tugs" in her memoir (page 53). She said Joe, the pilot of the *Alsace*, would drop by the hotel "quite regularly at the opportune hour of lunch or dinner time." She liked Joe, but she did not care for his "old cronies," who often tagged along and "let loose with 'Channel woes' frightening enough to shatter iron nerves." During the second attempt, journalists, UPI correspondents, Marconi wireless operators, Lillian Cannon (also vying for a chance to swim the Channel that summer), and an assortment of other "unofficial" spectators piled on *La Morinie* and caught up with the *Alsace* around 10 that morning, about four and a half hours after the *Alsace* started out. The *Alsace* quietly made an early departure on August 6, 1926, with a few close friends and family onboard. Only Helmy, Pop Ederle, Margaret, the boat pilot Joe Corthes, Julia Harpman, and a few other *Daily News* employees were allowed on the *Alsace*. Those on *La Morinie*, which by all accounts was the larger tug, were not pleased.

Page 119 *The job of applying the grease*: Ibid.

Page 120 *A funny little black-and-white dog*: From the *Sunday [Daily] News,* August 15, 1926. The photograph with Trudy being greased by Burgess ran on the front page of the *Daily News* and scooped the competition in the United States by twenty-four hours.

The four-plane relay to get the Channel photographs back to the States involved two land planes and two seaplanes. In "Eats and Honors for Trudy in German Mountain Town," a long caption under a map of the planes' course reads: "Plane No. 2 left Curtiss field, L.I., stopped at Plattsburg and Quebec, then joined Plane No. 1 at Rimouski. Plane 1 got pictures at Seven Islands bay and took them to Rimouski. Half the pictures then were put on Plane 2 and half on Plane 3. Plane 2 went down at St. Eloi [because of fog] and success was up to Plane 3 piloted by George Rumill. Plane 3 stopped at Quebec and going on to Plattsburg met Plane 4. [W. H. McFarlane, a pilot from Curtiss Field], met them and took the pictures and made a last dash in race to West Side Park [now Lincoln Park] in Jersey City." Archive. Earlier pictures ran in the *News*, but they resembled bad photocopies more than photographs. The *News* used a relatively new invention, the Bartlane process, to transmit images via Western Union cable to New York. These earlier photos/facsimiles began appearing on August 7, 1926. A *Daily News* caption reads: "In this marvelous photographic achievement, Gertrude Ederle may be seen entering the water at Cape Gris-Nez, France, starting her epochal swim. . . . This remarkable cable picture was taken at Cape Gris-Nez shore, put aboard a fast tug and sent to Dover, England. From Dover the plate was rushed to London by speedy automobile and there a specially prepared Bartlane process tape was in readiness to receive it. It was cabled to THE NEWS in New York. Just 19 hours elapsed from camera's click until photo appeared in THE NEWS." Archive.

Page 120   *On the side of the tug:* From Alec Rutherford, "Britain and America Thrilled by Great Achievement of New York Girl Swimmer," *New York Times*, August 7, 1926.

Page 121   *The term* play-by-play: Julia Harpman's constant updates and those of other newsmen on the *Morinie* might have been the first use of play-by-play coverage. They relayed updates hourly on the wireless, and some afternoon newspapers in the United States ran them one on top of the others to give readers the feel as if they were seeing it happen in real time.

Page 121   *"It's a Long Way to Tipperary":* No jazz band accompanied the swimmer for her second attempt at the Channel. Trudy said, in an article in the *New York American*, August 7, 1926, "What's the use? The musicians only get seasick." Instead, a Victrola was used, but the crew burst into song to cheer Trudy on when the apparatus broke down. Trudy said, in "Miss Ederle Has Another Swim," England's *Daily Mail*, August 8, 1926, "What spurred me the most was the old-time American songs they sang." Some of those songs were "It's a Long Way to Tipperary," "The Star-Spangled Banner," "Yes Sir, That's My Baby," "Rosie O'Grady," "After the Ball Was Over," "Sidewalks of New York," and, Trudy's favorite, "Let Me Call You Sweetheart."

Page 122   *Don Skene of the* Tribune's *Paris bureau:* From Julia Harpman, "Hour by Hour with Ederle in Epic Swim," *Daily News*, August 7, 1926.

Page 123   *"If I go any slower, I will sink"*: From Julia Harpman, "Hour by Hour with Ederle in Epic Swim," *Daily News*, August 7, 1926. Also cited in "Aquatic Marvel, 19, Is Daughter of Butcher," *New York Herald Tribune*, August 7, 1926.

Page 124   *"Gertie will have to come out"*: From Julia Harpman, "The Saga of Ederle," Archive.

Page 124   *"I won't take the responsibility"*: From Julia Harpman, "Hour by Hour with Ederle in Epic Swim," *Daily News*, August 7, 1926.

Page 125   *"The Sidewalks of New York"*: From "Miss Ederle Swims Channel in Record Time," *New York Herald Tribune*, August 7, 1926.

Page 125   *"You've got two wheels of that roadster now"*: From "Trudy's Chaperon Tells Swim Secrets," *Daily News*, August 28, 1026. Archive, page 137.

Page 125   *On the blackboard she wrote*: From Julia Harpman, "Hour by Hour with Ederle in Epic Swim," *Daily News*, August 7, 1926.

Page 126   *"I won't drown"*: From "Miss Ederle Swims Channel in Record Time," *New York Herald Tribune*, August 7, 1926.

Page 127   *The biggest bet was reported*: From "American Girl Hindered by Heavy Rain on Last Stretch in Channel Try," *The New York Telegram*, August 6, 1926.

Page 128   *Timson had been at his Dover*: From Julia Harpman, "The Saga of Ederle," Archive.

Page 128   *"Hello Lillian," she said*: From Harpman, "Hour by Hour with Ederle in Epic Swim," *Daily News*, August 7, 1926.

Page 129   *"You're wonderful, Trudy, wonderful."*: From Julia Harpman, "The Saga of Ederle," Archive.

Page 131   *"Come out, Gertie. You must come out." "What for?"* This quotation appeared in nearly every major newspaper, national and international. "What for?" became Trudy's signature statement, but, in all likelihood, Julia Harpman of the *Daily News* was probably the first to report this exchange in her account, "Hour by Hour with Ederle in Epic Swim," August 7, 1926.

Page 132   *"Is that England?"*: From " 'Papa, I Did This for Mama' Cries Happy Maid O' the Channel," statement by Gertrude Ederle to Universal Service, August 6, 1926. Archive, page 126.

Page 133   *With the first scrape*: Newspaper accounts of the time said Ederle came ashore at 9:39 P.M., making her swim even faster at fourteen hours and thirty-one minutes. But the Channel Swimming Association, formed in 1927 to govern the sport, lists her official record at fourteen hours and thirty-nine minutes.

Page 133 *Burgess later calculated the swim:* From Bill Burgess, "Trudy's Feat Knocks Out Channel Swim Theories," *Daily News,* August 9, 1926. The *Daily News* also commissioned Bill Burgess to write a first-person account of the Channel training and swim.

Page 133 *"intoxicating feeling of elation":* From Gertrude Ederle, "Cramps Nearly Spoiled Swim, Says Miss Ederle," edited by Morgan Blake, Tribune News Service, August 7, 1926.

Page 135 *"I am the proudest and the happiest mother":* From "Mother Proud of 'Trudie,' but Knew She Could Do It," *The New York Telegram,* August 7, 1926.

Page 135 *"Say, can you tell me:* From Ed Sullivan, "Sports Whirl," *Evening Graphic.* Archive.

8. The Celluloid Web

Page 138 *"She is wonderful,":* From Alec Rutherford, "Return to France Cheered," *New York Times,* August 8, 1926.

Page 138 *Rutherford handicapped the remaining contenders:* From Alec Rutherford, "Miss Ederle Happy, Won't Try It Again," *New York Times,* August 8, 1926.

Page 138 *"The first woman Channel victor?":* Ibid.

Page 139 *Ederle told them she would never swim:* Ibid.

Page 140 *"I know very well if we had been wrong":* From Bill Burgess, "Burgess Acclaims Trudy as Miracle Girl," *Daily News,* August 9, 1926.

Page 140 *"Our starvation plan was the best treatment":* Ibid.

Page 140 *"I congratulate you":* From Julia Harpman, "Ederle, Completely Recovered, Is Feted by Officials and Admirers," Tribune Press Service, August 6, 1926.

Page 142 *Trudy had "stamped herself":* From Ed Sullivan, "Gertrude Ederle Stamps Herself Far Greater Than Lenglen or Collett," *Evening Graphic,* August 7, 1926.

Page 142 The New York Times *had its own photo spread:* The *Times,* like other newspapers, couldn't match the *Daily News*'s scoop on the pictures, so resorted to using a combination of photos that to the casual observer might seem as if they came from the actual swim, when they really didn't. Archive.

Page 144 *The paper* Nachtausgabe *called her feat:* Quotes from German newspapers are from "Gertrude Ederle Beats Channel and All Past Records for the Swim," *New York Times,* August 7, 1926.

Page 145 *"patronizing and condescending":* St. Paul's Pioneer Press. Archive.

Page 145 *"I suppose the men":* From "Men Must Try Again Asserts Miss Collett," *New York Herald Tribune,* August 7, 1927.

Page 145 *Lenglen, the great French tennis player:* From "Rapture Thrills Lenglen at Feat of 'Superwoman,'" *New York American*, August 8, 1926. Archive, page 112.

Page 145 *The longtime coach of the Northwestern University:* From "Channel Victory Hailed as Proof of 'Weaker Sex's' Athletic Emancipation," Associated Press, August 7, 1926.

Page 146 *"It's a far cry from swimming the Channel":* From "Feminist World Rejoices Over Ederle Victory," *New York Herald Tribune*, August 7, 1926.

Page 146 *Mrs. Raymond Brown, the managing director:* Ibid.

Page 146 *"I hardly thought it possible":* From "Praise for Her Wonder Feat Showered on Trudie by Officials and Swimming Champions," *Sunday [Daily] News*, August 8, 1926.

Page 147 *"The slim type of girl will go out of fashion":* From "The Inquiring Photographer," *Daily News*, August 9, 1926.

Page 147 *"Hooray for Prohibition":* From "Trudie, Feeling Fine, Takes Swim," *Daily News*, August 8, 1926.

Page 148 *"Miss Ederle had everything against her":* From "Wolffe-Ederle Hatchet Buried at 'Pop's' Party," special to the *New York Herald Tribune*, August 8, 1926.

Page 148 *"My dearest loving mother":* From a letter that Trudy wrote to her mother, dated August 8, 1926. It was excerpted in the *Daily News* under the headline "Trudy Sings Song of Love in Victory Note to Mother," August 8, 1926.

Page 148 *"I guess we will sell the business now":* From "Offers Galore Given Ederle," United Press, August 9, 1926.

Page 149 *"I wish we could go home immediately":* From Gertrude Ederle, "Trudy Eager for Journey to Germany," *Daily News*, August 9, 1926.

Page 150 *"a general impression here":* Julia Harpman, "Trudy Breaks Camp with Villagers' Farewells," *Daily News*, August 12, 1926.

Page 151 *"If I'm making a mistake":* From Gertrude Ederle, "Walker's Bid Tickles Trudy; City Welcome Pulling Heart Strings," *Daily News*, August 11, 1926.

9. Channelitis Strikes Cape Gris-Nez

Page 153 *"One thing I want you boys to get straight right now":* From Julia Harpman, "Goes to Germany to Visit Kin and Then Will Hurry Home," *Daily News*, August 11, 1926.

Page 153 *Gallico was a better sportswriter:* From Paul Gallico, "Hours of Glory," unidentified magazine, February 1949.

Page 154 *"I never dreamed the name of Ederle":* Grandma Ederle to German reporters in "German Village Honors Miss Ederle," Associated Press, August 13, 1926.

Page 154   *Earlier, Ederle had received a telegram:* From Alec Rutherford, "Britain and America Thrilled by Great Achievement of New York Girl Swimmer," *New York Times,* August 7, 1926.

Page 155   *"I thought I was going to get some rest here":* From "Singing German School Children Greet Trudie at Grandmother's Home," Tribune News Service, August 14, 1926.

Page 156   *"What became of all the Red Grange offers?":* From Paul Gallico, "Cashing In Isn't Easy," *Daily News,* August 11, 1926.

Page 157   *Gallico knew the two liners:* The story of how the *Daily News* got the photo scoop is from "Liner and Planes in 3000-mile Dash to Effect 'Scoop.' " Archive.

Page 159   *"Here you are, old chap":* From Paul Gallico, "Hours of Glory," February 1949.

Page 159   *"If I had any brains":* Ibid.

Page 160   *"I liked him tremendously":* From *New York Times,* August 24, 1926. A few days later Dempsey was in Atlantic City to train for his fight with Tunney and said Valentino had promised him (before he was stricken) he would be at the fight.

Page 161   *"One paper accused Ederle":* From "English Press Knocks Ederle: Claim Help from Tug Boat Minimizes Feat," Tribune Press Service, August 16, 1926.

Page 161   *"did no more for Miss Ederle":* From "The Girl Who Thrilled the World," *The Progressive,* September 1, 1926.

Page 161   *"had something to say if unfair aid":* From "Miss Ederle Issues Challenge on Swim as Miss Cannon Fails," Associated Press, August 17, 1926.

Page 162   *On August 20, Gallico wrote:* From Paul Gallico, "Laugh, Trudy, Laugh!" *Daily News,* August 8, 1926.

Page 162   MOVIES PROVE TRUDY'S CRITICS ABSURD: Refers to a series of six photographs that appeared in the *Daily News,* August 19, 1926, of Trudy "in distress" between the two tugs, *Alsace* and *La Morinie.*

Page 163   *"What's the use?":* From "Suffrage Leaders Enjoy Feat of Woman Swimmer," Associated Press, August 7, 1926. Mrs. Nathan Barrett did not want her daughter to attempt the Channel again. When Mrs. Barrett sent congratulations to Trudy, she told reporters, "But, of course, she did not have as much to combat as my daughter did." "Mother Proud of 'Trudie,' but Knew She Could Do It," *New York Telegram,* August 7, 1926.

Page 163   *"Miss Ederle got over":* From "Swim Trainer Defends Feat of Ederle."

Page 168   *"Well, what am I living for now?":* From Julia Harpman, "Channel Queen Unspoiled Kid Despite Fame," *Daily News,* August 28, 1926.

Page 168   *The Black Orchid* was written by the British writer George Goodchild, who wrote more than 135 novels, many of them mysteries. Goodchild's writing career spanned fifty-five years. Although Trudy was an avid mystery buff, one of the bestselling nonfiction books of the twentieth century—published in 1925 and on the bestseller list in 1925 and 1926—was *The Man Nobody Knows.* Written by Bruce Fairchild Barton, the book depicts Jesus as "the founder of modern business." Michael Korda writes in *Making the List: A Cultural History of the American Bestseller, 1900–1999* (New York: Barnes & Noble Books, 2001): "The notion of portraying Christ as a successful business executive—and, by reversing the analogy, portraying the modern American business executive as performing a Christian act by doing business—was one that was already starting to make people giggle three years later, when America's top business executives had plunged the country into the Great Depression and were no longer seen as Christ-like, but it was typical of the two sides of the twenties: on the one hand, a profound need for the new and startling, so that even religion had to be presented in a different way to succeed, and on the other, an amazing confidence that money and success were God-given and for the soul, that it was now easy (and right) for a rich man to pass through the eye of a needle and enter the kingdom of heaven, and that prosperity was not just its own reward, but virtuous as well."

Page 169   *"A queen's welcome wouldn't be too good for her":* From "Roving Photographer," *Daily News.*

10. A Hero's Welcome

Page 171   *"That's what I've prayed to see for over a year":* From "Ederle Leaves for Home Today," Tribune Press Service, August 8, 1926. Archive, page 115. Also cited in Julia Harpman, "Trudy, Sailing Home, Gets Thrill of Life," *Daily News.*

Page 172   *"Strawberry marshmallow frappe":* From "Home Street Dressed Up to Greet Trudy Ederle, That Fine, Jolly Girl," *New York Graphic.*

Page 172   *"I am delighted that my return home":* From Gertrude Ederle, "Walker's Bid Tickles Trudy," *Daily News,* August 11, 1926.

Page 173   *"She told me many times that she would succeed":* From "Mother Weeps When Told Reception Plan," *Daily News,* August 11, 1926.

Page 174   *"I'll fool them all at home":* From "Ederle Leaves for Home Today," Tribune Press Service, August 8, 1926.

Page 176   *"There she was, hanging half out of the port":* From Paul Gallico, "When Trudy Came Home," *Daily News.* Archive.

Page 177   *"And then, just as Trudy stepped onto the Macon":* Ibid.

Page 177   *"Every line of her face showed the struggle"*: Ibid. Gallico seemed overcome by the homecoming, though he might be excused, having invested most of his summer making sure the *Daily News* got its money's worth from Trudy's swim.

Page 178   *"I'm in no hurry," Ederle replied*: From "City Throngs Give Greatest Welcome to Gertrude Ederle," *New York Times*, August 28, 1926.

Page 178   *"Ordinarily Trudy is not"*: From "Bay Bedlam While Sirens Greet Champ," *New York American*, August 28, 1926.

Page 178   *"I tied a rope around her"*: From "Greatest Welcome to Gertrude Ederle," *New York Times*, August 28, 1926. Archive, page 155. While Trudy's mother takes the credit for teaching her how to swim in this article, other newspaper accounts often give credit to Pop Ederle for Trudy's swimming instruction. In fact, Trudy's mother, in another *New York Times* article, "Mrs. Ederle Taught 'Gertie' Endurance," said, "Her father would lower her into the water with a rope around her little waist and she would paddle about and laugh up at him, entirely unafraid."

Page 178   *"When you failed in your attempt"*: From "Harbor Welcome Rivals the Land's," *New York Times*, August 28, 1926.

Page 179   *"Cut it out"*: From Edward Doherty, "New York Roars Welcome to Trudy," *Daily Mirror*, August 28, 1926. This interchange between Malone and Oberwager appeared in other newspaper accounts as well.

Page 179   *"Yes, I did."*: *New York American*, August 28, 1926.

Page 181   *Canyon of Heroes*: Mrs. Clemington Corson (Mille Gade) was awarded a plaque for swimming the Channel, too. It reads, "The first mother to swim the English Channel," and it is just a half-block from Trudy's plaque, which reads, "The first woman to swim the English Channel." The plaques are on Broadway near Beaver Street, across from the Alexander Hamilton U.S. Custom House.

Page 183   *"There was an old woman about 85 years old"*: From "Greatest Welcome to Gertrude Ederle," *New York Times*, August 28, 1926.

Page 184   *"there was that human touch that struck the populace"*: From "Harbor Welcome Rivals the Land's," *New York Times*, August 28, 1926.

Page 184   *"When history records the great crossings"*: From "Greatest Welcome to Gertrude Ederle," *New York Times*, August 28, 1926.

Page 184   *"I do not know much about this controversy"*: From a speech that Mayor Jimmy Walker gave at Trudy's welcome home ceremony, "Miss Ederle Hailed by Smith and President," *New York Herald Tribune*, August 28, 1926.

Page 187   *"Easy men," a stout sergeant*: From "Greatest Welcome to Gertrude Ederle," *New York Times*, August 28, 1926.

Page 189   *"It's so wonderful, so wonderful"*: From "Miss Ederle Hailed by Smith and President," *New York Herald Tribune*, August 28, 1926.

Page 189   *"It proves that all distinctions"*: From "Harbor Welcome Rivals the Land's," *New York Times*, August 28, 1926.

Page 190   *"It would be impossible"*: From "Greatest Welcome to Gertrude Ederle," *New York Times*, August 28, 1926.

11. The Next One Has to Be a Blonde

Page 194   *A motorboat carried some spectators*: From Associated Press, August 29, 1926.

Page 196   *"I have to make some money for my kids"*: From *New York Times*, August 29, 1926.

Page 196   *issued a challenge to "everybody"*: From "Trudy Waits $25,000 Defi [sic] of Mrs. Corson," *New York American*.

Page 197   *Customs inspector John Borkel*: From *New York Times*, August 29, 1926.

Page 198   *"I am very happy"*: From "Trudy Challenged by Corson Backer," *New York American*. Archive.

Page 198   *theatrical and motion-picture offers*: From "Apologies for Tug Yarn Story Won by Miss Ederle," *New York Herald Tribune*, August 28, 1926.

Page 199   *"One can fault Mr. Malone"*: From Paul Gallico, *The Golden People* (Garden City, New York: Doubleday & Co., Inc., 1965), page 62.

Page 200   *"Trudy is all tired out"*: From "Trudy All In," *New York Evening World*. Archive.

Page 200   *"There's been enough of this clamor"*: From Imogen Stanley, "Nerve-Torn Trudy Collapses," *Daily News*, August 30, 1926.

Page 203   *"She is the most wholesome"*: From Julia Harpman, "Channel Queen Unspoiled Despite Fame," *Daily News*. Archive.

Page 203   *"I'd rather swim the Channel"*: From "Trudy Ederle Captures City; Here for Sesqui," *Philadelphia Inquirer*, September 3, 1926.

Page 204   *"Oh, I'm really delighted"*: Ibid.

Page 205   *"We believe she is the greatest drawing attraction"*: From a letter that Frank P. Gravatt wrote to the William Morris Agency. The letter is part of the collection in the Archive.

Page 206   *"He [Dempsey] is so big and strong"*: From John R. Thorbahn, "Miss Ederle Among Crowd at Dog Park." Archive.

Page 206   *"I understand there are a lot of sharks"*: From "Trudy Ederle Silent on Plans for Future," *New York American*.

Page 207   *"The worm has turned"*: From an editorial in *New York Times*, August 31, 1926.

Page 207   *"Shiver my timbers"*: From *New York Times*, September 11, 1926. By now the Channel swimmers seemed to be coming by every day, but all had their own inspirations. For Trudy it was a red roadster and her mother. For Michel, it seemed to be a double whiskey.

Page 208   *"But Gertie softened it up for them"*: From Heywood Broun, "It Seems to Me," *New York Telegram* (date unknown). Archive.

Page 208   *Gen. John J. Pershing*: From *New York Times*, September 7, 1926.

Page 208   *"a wonderful specimen of American womanhood" [Will Rogers]*: Ibid.

Page 209   *"She is so tall" [Will Rogers]*: From Associated Press. Archive.

Page 209   *"I don't know of any man"*: From Pershing in *New York Times*, September 7, 1926.

Page 209   *"I'm not going to give up my job."*: Ibid.

Page 210   *Of course, Corson played up*: From *New York Times*, September 11, 1926.

Page 211   *"You have brought"*: Ibid.

Page 211   *"When I was fighting the dark"*: Ibid.

Page 212   *"I've had only a few moments"*: Ibid.

Page 212   *"take that bet"*: From "Trudy Claims She Can 'Spot Mille a Mile,'" unidentified newspaper. Archive.

Page 213   *"I think Gertrude Ederle"* From *New York Times*, September 11, 1926.

Page 214   *"Knowing the speed"*: From "Jabez Wolffe Questions Channel Swimmers Claims," *Daily News*, October 20, 1926.

Page 214   *"she is the 'Norse girl'"*: From "Monster Reception to Gertrude Ederle," *The Progressive*, September 15, 1926.

Page 214   "They are not given half the credit": Ibid.

Page 214   *"I ask you to be"*: Ibid.

Page 215   *"Stressing the race"*: Ibid.

Page 216   *"We thought it was time"*: From "Ederle Family Packs for Move to Bronx" (unidentified news brief). Archive.

Page 217   *Riggin was leery of the tank:* From Aileen Riggin's oral history at http://www .la84foundation.org/6oic/OralHistory/OHriggin.indd.pdf.

Page 219   *"We will swim, play golf"*: From Gertrude Ederle, "When Trudy Ederle Picks Husband," *New York Evening Graphic* Magazine Section, October 20, 1926.

Page 221   *"After I have accomplished"*: From " 'There's Room for Modesty in Swimming,' says Trudy," unidentified newspaper in Los Angeles, December 6, 1926. Archive.

Page 221   *Westbrook Pegler later would sit down:* The actual figures of what Trudy made are from Westbrook Pegler, "What For?" *Liberty* magazine, April 9, 1927,

Page 222   *"If Mrs. Schoemmell thinks"*: From " 'There's Room for Modesty: in Swimming,' Says Trudy," unidentified newspaper in Los Angeles, December 6, 1926. Archive.

Page 222   *"I suppose I could put it in the back yard"*: From Violet Short, "Gertrude Ederle Is Afraid to Dive!" *The Dallas Morning News,* April 24, 1927. Trudy spent six thousand dollars for the tank; and when asked what she would do with it after the vaudeville tour, she looked "puzzled." It was a good question. The tank was fifteen feet long, twenty feet wide, and seven feet high, and weighed twenty-two tons when filled with water.

Page 223   *"She would have to be a blonde"*: From "Wanted: One Blonde to Swim Channel," unidentified news brief from London. Archive.

12. *"Don't Weep for Me"*

Page 225   *"freak of fate"*: From "Get the Money, Trudy Ederle Advises Lindy," unidentified newspaper in Worcester, Massachusetts. Archive.

Page 225   *"Heartiest congratulations"*: From "Gertrude Ederle Cables Lindbergh Congratulations," and "Conqueror of Channel Cables Congratulations to Captain Lindbergh," several unidentified news briefs. Archive.

Page 225   *"jousted with death"*: From Ed Sullivan, "Sports Whirl," *Evening Graphic,* May 27, 1927.

Page 226   *"very foolish"*: From *New York Times,* October 14, 1927.

Page 226   *"Even if she had succeeded"*: Ibid.

Page 226   *"I am much opposed"*: Ibid.

Page 228   *"ideal musculature for golf"*: From O. B. Keeler, "O.O.s by O.B. : Miss Ederle Takes Up Golf" (unidentified newspaper in Atlanta, Georgia). Archive.

Page 229   *"I am amazed"*: From *Time* magazine, November 1927.

Page 229   *"I don't want to be an old maid"*: From "Gertrude Ederle Visits the Press," *Pittsburgh Press*, October 23, 1927.

Page 229   In *Syracuse, the drama critic:* From Chester B. Bahn, " 'Trudy' Real Keith Hit, Critic Finds," *Syracuse Herald.*

Page 230   *"as a rule, athletes of the feminine"*: Ibid.

Page 232   *"The only one we feared was Ederle"*: From *New York Times*, August 29, 1928.

Page 233   *"Things aren't always smooth"*: From R. E. Knowles, " 'Trudy' Finds Marathon Swim Not Big Money Making Game," unidentified Toronto newspaper, dated August 13, 1928, by Gertrude Ederle.

Page 233   *"I finally got the shakes"*: From Richard Severo's obituary, "Gertrude Ederle, the First Woman to Swim Across the English Channel, Dies at 98," *New York Times*, December 1, 2003.

Page 234   *She was exonerated by a magistrate:* From "Gertrude Ederle Again Shows Speed, This Time in Auto, But Law Relents," unidentified newspaper article. Archive.

Page 235   *"And then it all sort of comes back over me again"*: From "Gertrude Ederle Pays with Hearing for Channel Swim," Associated Press, July 28, 1929.

Page 236   *"We can always depend on a Gertrude"*: From "Will Rogers Remarks," unidentified newspaper. Archive.

Page 241   *"I told them they couldn't keep me in a wheelchair"*: From "Twelve Years Later, After Licking Paralysis, Trudy Ederle Swims Again at World's Fair," unidentified newspaper. Archive.

Page 241   *"Don't Weep for Me!"* A March 1941 article that Gertrude Ederle wrote to dispel the notion that she was full of regret and ailing. She wrote, "I am perfectly happy, have no grudges and no resentments whatever, and I never brood. . . . No, there is nothing to these stories about poor old Trudy Ederle who took a dive from the heights of fame to the depths of despair." Archive.

Page 242   *"I haven't forgotten them"* From Henery M'Lemore, " 'What If They Have Forgotten Me?' " Also cited in " ' I Haven't Forgotten Them,' " United Press, 1933.

Epilogue

Page 245   *"I figured if he felt that way"*: From oral interview with Gertrude Ederle by Bob Duenkel and Buck Dawson, 1994.

Page 246   *"I try to take that courage and carry on with life"*: Ibid.

Page 247   *"Gertrude Ederle was a woman I admired"*: From *The Star Ledger* (Newark, New Jersey), July 22, 2006.

Page 249   *"Let Me Call You Sweetheart"*: Trudy's favorite song was written by Leo Friedman (music) and Beth Slater Whitson (lyrics). The song was published in 1910 and first recorded by The Peerless Quartet.

Bibliography

Books

Chapman, John. *Tell It to Sweeney: An Informal History of the New York* Daily News. Garden City, New York: Doubleday, 1961.

Conrad, Earl. *Billy Rose: Manhattan Primitive.* Cleveland and New York: World Publishing, 1968.

Crosby, Alfred W. *America's Forgotten Pandemic: The Influenza of 1918.* Second edition. Cambridge, Massachusetts: Cambridge University Press, 2003.

Devaney, John. *Great Olympic Champions.* New York: G. P. Putnam & Sons, 1967.

Engelmann, Larry. *The Goddess and the American Girl: The Story of Suzanne Lenglen and Helen Wills.* New York and Oxford: Oxford University Press, 1988.

Ernst, Robert. *Weakness Is a Crime: The Life of Bernarr Macfadden.* Syracuse, New York: Syracuse University Press, 1991.

Fury, David. *Johnny Weissmuller: Twice the Hero.* Minneapolis, Minnesota: Artist's Press, 2000.

Gallico, Paul. *The Golden People.* Garden City, New York: Doubleday & Company, 1965.

Gibson, Emily with Barbara Firth. *The Original Million Dollar Mermaid: The Annette Kellerman Story.* Crows Nest NSW, Australia: Allen & Unwin, 2005.

Gottlieb, Polly Rose. *The Nine Lives of Billy Rose*. New York: Crown Publishers, 1968.

Greenberg, David. *Calvin Coolidge: The American Presidents Series*. New York: Henry Holt and Company, 2007.

Johnson, Anne Janette. *Defining Moment Series: The Scopes "Monkey Trial."* Detroit, Michigan: Omnigraphics, 2006.

Kellerman, Annette. *Physical Beauty: How to Keep It*. New York: George H. Doran Company, 1918 (microfilm).

Korda, Michael. *Making the List: A Cultural History of the American Bestseller, 1900–1999*. New York: Barnes & Noble Books, 2001.

Macfadden, Mary, and Emile Henry Gauvreau. *Dumbbells and Carrot Strips: The Story of Bernarr Macfadden*. New York: Henry Holt and Company, 1953.

Martin, Richard, and Harold Koda. *Splash! A History of Swimwear*. New York: Rizzoli, 1990.

Nasaw, David. *The Chief: The Life of William Randolph Hearst*. Boston and New York: Houghton Mifflin Company, 2000.

Probert, Christina. *Swimwear in Vogue Since 1910*. New York: Abbeville Press, 1981.

S.D., Trav. *No Applause—Just Throw Money*. New York: Faber and Faber, Inc., 2005.

Smith, Richard Norton. *The Colonel: The Life and Legend of Robert R. McCormick: Indomitable Editor of the* Chicago Tribune. Boston and New York: Houghton Mifflin Company, 1997.

Snyder, Robert W. *The Voice of the City: Vaudeville and Popular Culture in New York*. Chicago, Illinois: Ivan R. Dee, 1989.

Tumulty, Joseph P. *Woodrow Wilson as I Know Him*. Garden City, New York: Doubleday, Page & Company, 1923.

Vickers, Lu, and Sara Dionne. *Weeki Wachee, City of Mermaids: A History of One of Florida's Oldest Roadside Attractions*. Gainesville, Florida: University Press of Florida, 2007.

Weaver, Janice. *From Head to Toe: Bound Feet, Bathing Suits, and Other Bizarre and Beautiful Things*. Toronto: Tundra, 2003.

Whitelaw, Nancy. *William Randolph Hearst and the American Century*. Greensboro, North Carolina: Morgan Reynolds Publishing, 2004.

Articles

Gertrude Ederle's Personal Archive

Gertrude Ederle assembled a personal archive that contained thousands of articles, news clippings, and other memorabilia—with a good deal of the material relating specifically to her first Channel attempt in 1925 and eventual successful Channel swim in 1926. It is a massive resource. Most of the archive material is preserved and intact, but some articles/letters/telegrams do not have names, dates, and/or bylines. We have made every attempt to document specific sources in the notes section, but, in some instances, the citations are incomplete. In addition to the Archive, we relied on the following articles for secondary information:

"Dudley Field Malone Divorced in Paris: Decree Obtained by Wife Just Revealed," *New York Times*, December 2, 1921.

Dyreson, Mark L. "Scripting the American Olympic Story-Telling Formula: The 1924 Paris Olympic Games and the American Media," *OLYMPIKA: The International Journal of Olympic Studies*, vol. V (1996): 45–80.

"Ethelda Bleibtrey Resigns from W.S.A.," *New York Times*, October 20, 1921.

Gary, H. "Eleanor's Show," *Time* magazine, August 21, 1939.

Gray, Christopher. "Streetscapes/New York Marine Amphitheater; At Old Aquacade, Things Aren't Going Swimmingly," *New York Times*, March 28, 1995.

Litsky, Frank. "Aileen Riggin Soule, Olympic Diver and Swimmer, Dies at 96," *New York Times*, October 21, 2002.

"Malone Nominated as Port Collector," *New York Times*, November 11, 1913.

"Miss Bleibtry to Turn Professional," *New York Times*, May 10, 1922.

Unpublished Memoir

Gertrude Ederle's Memoir

Gertrude Ederle planned to write an autobiography, but a busy life interfered and she did not complete *The Highlights of My Life Story*. The 8½×14, double-spaced manuscript was written in Flushing, New York, and is dated September 6, 1951. *The Highlights of My Life Story* by Gertrude "Trudy" Ederle is sixty-six pages. Some of the quotations attributed to Trudy in *America's Girl* are taken directly from this unfinished memoir, which covers her life up to her second plunge into the Channel in 1926.

Web Sites

Bathing suits:

http://www.ocf.berkeley.edu/~roseying/ids110/WHIS.htm. Last accessed October 22, 2007.

http:www.swimsuit-style.com/swimsuit.html. Last accessed February 9, 2009.

http:niwde.blogspot.com/2007/03/history-of-mens-swimwear.html. Last accessed October 20, 2007.

"On Exhibit at the International Swimming Hall of Fame: From Bloomers to Bikinis; How the Sport of Swimming Changed Western Culture in the 20th Century," www.ishof.org/pdf/history_swimwear.pdf.

Bikini Science: Annette Kellerman, the Australian Mermaid: http://www.bikiniscience.com/models/AK19_SS/AK19.html. Last accessed October 10, 2007.

Channel Swimming Association: www.channelswimmingassociation.com. Last accessed August 2, 2007. In addition, e-mail correspondence with Alison Reid, swim secretary, regarding the Channel swim of Annette Kellerman with Henry Mew and M. Holbein was also conducted.

Individual swimmers:

    Mullen, P. H. "Duke Kahanamoku: Passing the Crown," http://findarticles.com/
        p/articles/mi_qa3883/is_200208/ai_n9103761. Last accessed November 30,
        2007.

"Ishaq Helmi: Egypt's First Crocodile." Yunan Labib Rizk. *Al-Ahram Weekly*. http://
    weekly.ahram.org.eg/2001/565/chrncls.htm.

International Swimming Hall of Fame Inductees. Each last accessed December 12,
    2007:

    http://www.ishof.org/exhibits/pdf/aileen.riggin.pdf

    http://www.ishof.org/honorees/67/67ebleibtrey.html

    http://www.ishof.org/honorees/69/69elackie.html

    http://www.ishof.org/honorees/67/67/mnorelius.html

Influenza pandemic:

    http://virus.stanford.edu/uda. Last accessed November 1, 2007.

    http://www.pbs.org/wgbh/amex/influenze/peopleevents/pandAMEX86.html. Last
    accessed November 1, 2007.

Olympics:

Official Bulletin of the 1924 Olympics, Part 3: 417–494, http://www.la84foundation
    .org/6oic/Official Reports/1924/1924part3.pdf. Last accessed November 11,
    2007.

"Jews in Sport," http://www.jewsinsports.org/Olympics.asp?sport=Olympics&ID=
    10. Last accessed December 2, 2007.

"An Olympian's Oral History: Aileen Riggin," Amateur Athletic Foundation of Los
    Angeles, http://www.la84foundation.org/6oic/OralHistory/OHriggin.indd
    .pdf. Last accessed December 1, 2007

"Clarita Hunsberger Neher, 1924 & 1928 Olympic Games Diving," Amateur Athletic
    Foundation of Los Angeles, http://www.la84foundation.org/6oic/OralHistory/
    OHHunsbergerNeher.pdf. Last accessed December 11, 2007.

"Doris O'Mara Murphy, 1924 & 1928 Olympic Games Swimming," Amateur Ath-
    letic Foundation of Los Angeles, http://www.la84foundation.org/6oic/
    OralHistory/OHOMaraMurphy.pdf.

"William Neufeld, 1924 Olympic Games, Track & Field," Amateur Athletic Foundation
    of Los Angeles, http://www.la84foundation.org/6oic/OralHistory/OHNeufeld
    .pdf. Last accessed December 8, 2007.

Prohibition: http://query.nytimes.com/gst/abstract.html?res=9E00E0DC173EE433-
    A25757C2A9609C946996D6CF. Last accessed February 20, 2008.

Swimming coach: Bill Bachrach (USA): 1966 Honor Coach, http://www.ishof.org/
    honorees/66/66bbachrach.html.

Swimming pools: "Plunging into Pools' Contentious Past," http://www.npr.org/
    templates/story/story.php?storyId=10407533. Last accessed October 10, 2007.

Swimming technique: "Feel for Water—Shaving Down," Charles Prawson. http://
    www.usms.org/swimgold/esth/feelwat.htm. Last accessed December 2, 2007.

Letters

Dudley Field Malone: Harry S. Truman Library & Museum in Independence, Missouri. Malone education: letter from Dudley Field Malone to President Harry S. Truman, December 9, 1949. Malone appointments: Letter from Dudley Field Malone to Harry Truman, December 8, 1949. Malone qualifications: "Possible Qualifications of Dudley Field Malone for a Presidential Appointment Within the United States." Papers of Harry S. Truman Official File, Harry S. Truman Library.

Speech of Dudley Field Malone on Labor Day, 1948, to the Mass Meeting of the Allied Labor Locals at Encanto Park, Phoenix, Arizona. Included in a letter to President Truman. From the Harry S. Truman Library. Papers of Harry S. Truman, President's Personal File.

Film

Charlotte Epstein: *Settlement Houses to Olympic Stadiums: Jewish Women in American Sport.* Boorish, Linda, and Shuli Eshel.

Index